...rctic Expedition

Notes from Nowhere: Iceland's Polite Dystopia

The Volcano Erupts: Iceland in Upheaval

Journey to the Center
(on Elín Hansdóttir's Labyrinth *Path*)

SVALBARD

ICELAND

Detroit Arcadia: Exploring the
Post-American Landscape

...volutionary
...ots: On Urban
...rdening

...dison

Concord

Detroit

Wall Street
(New York City)

On the Dirtiness of Laundry and the
Strength of Sisters, or, Mysteries of
Henry David Thoreau, Unsolved

Letter to a Dead Man on the
Occupation of Hope

...w Orleans

...P spill
*Gulf of
Mexico*

HAITI

We Won't Bow Down: Carnival and
Resistance in New Orleans (and Elsewhere)

Reconstructing the Story of the Storm: New
Orleans Five Years After

In Haiti, Words Can Kill

Oil and Water: The BP Spill in the Gulf

Icebergs and Shadows: Further Adventures
in the Landscape of Hope

Lacandón
Jungle,
Chiapas

Revolution of the Snails: Encounters
with the Zapatistas

BOLIVIA

TUNISIA
Mediterranean Sea

IRAQ

EGYPT

The Butterfly and the Boiling
Point (Reflections on the Arab
Spring and After)

INDIAN

OCEAN

ATLANTIC OCEAN

Buenos Aires

ARGENTINA

Praise for *The Encyclopedia of Trouble and Spaciousness*

"Globally wide-ranging and topically urgent . . . will surely solidify her reputation as one of our most independent and necessary freelance intellectuals."
— *Los Angeles Review of Books*

"Her writing takes wing . . . carrying us on a flight that crosses a landscape of sadness, of happiness, through consciousness, desire—what can only be described as a healing enlargement of one's soul—and toward beauty."
— *Mother Jones*

"The important thing to remember about this book is that it was written by Rebecca Solnit, one of the best nonfiction writers working today."
— *Chicago Tribune*

"Insights that are acute and meaningful. . . . [The book] leads to a different, more layered understanding of the world around us."
— *Utne Reader*

"Refreshingly coherent, profoundly smart."
— *BBC*

"Lives up to the promise of its ambitious title."
— KQED, San Francisco

"Thoughtful, eloquent, and often inspiring essays."
— *Kirkus Reviews*

"One mesmerizing volume . . . these lyrical essays stress the importance of collective action and community."
— *Publishers Weekly*

"Beautifully written and fiercely argued . . . showcases the work of an impressive intellect and a brilliant writer."
— *Shelf Awareness*

"Solnit's essays showcase the range and power not only of nonfiction but of words themselves."
— the *Rumpus*

"One of our most provocative, thoughtful essayists."
— *Austin American-Statesman*

A GEOGRAPHICAL INDEX

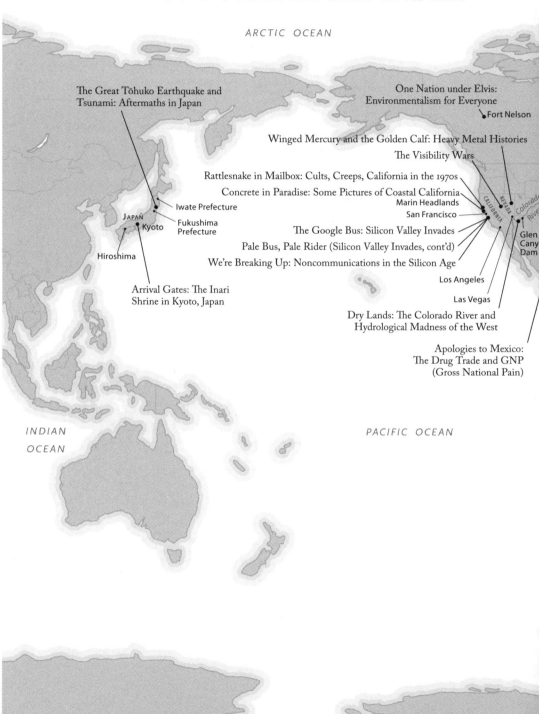

ARCTIC OCEAN

The Great Tōhuko Earthquake and
Tsunami: Aftermaths in Japan

One Nation under Elvis:
Environmentalism for Everyone

Fort Nelson

Winged Mercury and the Golden Calf: Heavy Metal Histories

The Visibility Wars

Rattlesnake in Mailbox: Cults, Creeps, California in the 1970s

Concrete in Paradise: Some Pictures of Coastal California

Marin Headlands

Iwate Prefecture

San Francisco

JAPAN

Kyoto

Fukushima
Prefecture

The Google Bus: Silicon Valley Invades

Glen
Cany
Dam

Pale Bus, Pale Rider (Silicon Valley Invades, cont'd)

Hiroshima

We're Breaking Up: Noncommunications in the Silicon Age

Los Angeles

Arrival Gates: The Inari
Shrine in Kyoto, Japan

Las Vegas

Dry Lands: The Colorado River and
Hydrological Madness of the West

CALIFORNIA

NEVADA

Colorado

River

Apologies to Mexico:
The Drug Trade and GNP
(Gross National Pain)

INDIAN
OCEAN

PACIFIC OCEAN

THE ENCYCLOPEDIA
of
TROUBLE
and
SPACIOUSNESS

THE ENCYCLOPEDIA

of
TROUBLE
and
SPACIOUSNESS

REBECCA SOLNIT

TRINITY UNIVERSITY PRESS ✧ *San Antonio, Texas*

Published by Trinity University Press
San Antonio, Texas 78212

Cover design by Anne Richmond Boston
Book design by BookMatters, Berkeley, California

World map created by Ben Pease/Pease Press using
indiemapper.com

Trinity University Press strives to produce its books using
methods and materials in an environmentally sensitive manner.
We favor working with manufacturers that practice sustainable
management of all natural resources, produce paper using
recycled stock, and manage forests with the best possible
practices for people, biodiversity, and sustainability. The press
is a member of the Green Press Initiative, a nonprofit program
dedicated to supporting publishers in their efforts to reduce
their impacts on endangered forests, climate change, and
forest-dependent communities.

The paper used in this publication meets the minimum
requirements of the American National Standard for
Information Sciences—Permanence of Paper for Printed
Library Materials, ANSI 39.48–1992.

Cataloging-in-Publication data on file at the Library of
Congress.

ISBN 978-1-59534-753-4 paperback
ISBN 978-1-59534-199-0 ebook

18 17 16 15 | 5 4 3 2 1

CONTENTS

INTRODUCTION

Icebergs and Laundry

That thing we call a place is the intersection of many changing forces passing through, whirling around, mixing, dissolving, and exploding in a fixed location. To write about a place is to acknowledge that phenomena often treated separately—ecology, democracy, culture, storytelling, urban design, individual life histories and collective endeavors—coexist. They coexist geographically, spatially, in place, and to understand a place is to engage with braided narratives and sui generis explorations.

This is a book about places, which is to say it's about those many forces in combination. About Shinto landscape in Japan, about yearnings for and intermittent realizations of justice and democracy in northern Africa and Iceland and the United States, about the way Yankee drug consumption is devastating Mexico (in an essay that I first pictured as a map showing pain being outsourced the way labor and toxic waste are outsourced to poorer countries), about why we are obsessed with gardening right now, about what environmentalists got wrong about country music and nearly everyone got wrong about Henry David Thoreau's laundry, about technology and amnesia in San Francisco. And it's about the places themselves: the orange of those Shinto gates, the blue of icebergs, about dancing in the streets of New Orleans, and occupying in the streets of New York.

I think of myself as a San Franciscan, a Californian, and a Westerner, three concentric rings that have enclosed many of my earlier projects. But when I put together the essays in *The Encyclopedia of Trouble and Spaciousness*, I was surprised to survey the breadth of my travels: I'd been reporting from the Arctic to Mexico, from Japan to Detroit to Occupy Wall Street. A few things led me out of my region.

One was that in the Bush era, every American seemed saddled with the weight of the world; our country was in Afghanistan and Iraq (and had, as it did before and does now, about 1,000 military bases around the world and a disproportionate role not only in climate change but also in sabotaging international agreements to do something about it). I was compelled to become a public citizen and to think about broad issues—hope, civil society, revolution, climate—and the questions these subjects raised had answers and ideas cached across the globe.

But it wasn't only responsibility that took me afar; it was invitations and curiosity. I had always wanted to go to the far north, and invitations to go to Iceland in 2008 and Svalbard in the farthest north in 2011 were taken up with alacrity. The latter place fulfilled my wildest desires for northernness, but Iceland turned out to be a complicated political powder keg that would explode not long after I wrote about it. (My first piece on Iceland included in this anthology appeared about two weeks before the country's economy collapsed and its population rebelled. During those two weeks I was told that I'd been harsh on a country that had managed to craft a very pretty image of itself; afterward I never heard that again. I only regret that I wasn't able to cover Iceland's next five years of glorious political experimentation—which faded in spring of 2013, when Icelanders reelected the neoliberals who destroyed the economy in the first place, like a wife going back to her abusive husband.)

I wondered about Detroit for a long time before my Detroit-born friend Sam Green and I decided to go visit in 2005, and when I got there, I realized that the widespread idea that Detroit was about ruins was out of date; I needed to inquire into what comes after ruin, as I did in the 2007 essay "Detroit Arcadia," one of the earliest pieces in the book. In that period I was much preoccupied with disaster—it began locally, with a project in preparation for the centennial of the 1906 San Francisco earthquake, which reawakened my interest in how people behave in disaster. The conclusions were astonishing, and that became an extension of my project on hope—which is a project on how we tell stories about our history, our powers, and our possibilities. Disaster revealed to me that much of what we've been taught about human nature is not true, and so I began the research that became my 2009 book *A Paradise Built in Hell*.

Early in the research, Hurricane Katrina struck New Orleans. The colossal social disaster that resulted got me involved with that city, which I have visited about two dozen times since and written about in two books and various essays (including two here). I didn't go to Haiti; I didn't have to in order to see the media make the same horrific mistakes there they made in New Orleans in 2005 and San Francisco in 1906. Disaster was also what took me to Japan, and I wrote about the triple disaster of the earthquake, tsunami, and nuclear accident in Japan and then later wrote about the lagniappe of the expedition, my day in the Inari Shrine outside Kyoto.

My definition of disaster became broader and broader, and I now see much of our everyday life—for its alienation and its destruction of souls and memory, as well as natural and social places—as a kind of disaster we escape temporarily in those golden moments of uprisings and carnivals. Or reclaiming the story. I see disaster everywhere; I also—as the essay "Icebergs and Shadows" in particular discusses—see generosity and resistance everywhere.

We talk about people coming together, but we sometimes forget that that's a spatial, geographical business: we are civil society when we go out into the streets to be together, when showing up and standing up becomes free speech, when we live in the plazas and squares, from Tahrir Square in Egypt to Mexico City's Zócalo to Liberty Plaza near Wall Street in New York. This is civil society in political engagement, the Apollonian form of being in the streets. New Orleans showed me some of the possibilities of the Dionysian version, as the essay "We Won't Bow Down" points out. There isn't a virtual equivalent of it, which is why (with essays such as "We're Breaking Up: Noncommunication in the Silicon Age") I worry about the withdrawal from public space and public life. Democracy was always a bodily experience, claimed and fought for and celebrated in actual places. You must be present to win.

Wherever I went, I remained preoccupied with democracy and justice and popular power, with how change can be wrought in the streets and by retelling the story, with the power of stories to get things wrong as well as right, with the pleasures and possibilities each place holds, and with the beauties of light, space, and solidarity.

From all this wandering I came home every time, but home began to leave me as San Francisco became Silicon Valley's bedroom community, the subject of three of the essays in this book. My own dear city had long been the far edge of the country, not merely in geography, but in possibility, the left coast that presented alternatives and refuges from the mainstream; when Silicon Valley became a—and in some ways *the*—global power center, it became something else.

Centers are supposed to be good things, but I prefer edges. That's in part because wealth and power are also often disasters, with casualties and wreckage. Maybe what often gets called *wealth* in booms should mostly be imagined as impoverishment of the majority who don't become wealthy and often become displaced or priced out locally, served up with the collateral damage from the concentration of power, resources, and the control of place.

I have been in recent years the author of a bestiary and director of some atlas projects; I've written criticism, editorials, reports from a few front lines, letters, a great many political essays for Tomdispatch.com in particular, more personal stuff, essays for artists' books, and more. As nonfiction—that leftover term apotheosizing fiction—gets defined down as only memoir and essay, I've wanted to open it back up again, to claim it as virtually everything else.

Nonfiction is the whole realm from investigative journalism to prose poems, from manifestos to love letters, from dictionaries to packing lists. This territory to which I am, officially, consigned couldn't be more spacious, and I couldn't be more pleased to be free to roam its expanses. And maybe the variety of forms here is part of the book's breadth along with its geographical range.

Calling this anthology an encyclopedia was a way to call attention to its range and maybe imagine these almost thirty essays as entries in an extremely incomplete encyclopedia. Essays explore; they also define; every essay is an entry in the author's personal encyclopedia. Here is the latest volume of mine.

CYCLOPEDIA OF AN ARCTIC EXPEDITION
for Mike D.

Anchor Chain. The hideous, booming clatter that awoke me our first morning out was, I thought at first, the warning bell that announced we should all assemble on the foredeck and perhaps prepare to zip ourselves into survival suits—those bulky, lurid orange jumpsuits in which you could, they say, float and survive in an arctic sea for up to six hours. Happily, it was the anchor chain going out, meaning that we were at our first destination and that I did not yet have to try out that orange jumpsuit or those arctic waters. The chains were huge beasts in the stern of the boat that rattled like the end of the world on their way up and their way down.

Animals. There was no wait. The morning of the day of departure, a white arctic fox with a limp and a young gray fox cub came begging at the kitchen of the funky hostel-like hotel in Svalbard's small capital, Longyearbyen, and all the animals showed up earlier than expected, *all* being a term that encompasses the fox, the walrus, the seal, the reindeer, and the polar bear—that being all the wingless beasts to be found onshore in this landscape that feels like creation on day two, not day seven or year 4 billion. Except for some tiny gnat-like creatures, and spiders.

Antlers. A skull with antlers was onshore by a rock at the first landing in Magdalenafjord, the antlers whipped back with the particular line that reindeer have and deer lack, a beautiful artifact that seemed to have been placed there as an accent. The skull was bleached white but a bit damp-looking, not like the dry white bones of the desert, and it looked as though it had been planted, an accent piece, a focus for the foreground. Further up the rocks was the lower jaw of an arctic fox. Over the ridge was a school of seals basking, arcing themselves into curved forms, occasionally swimming in the shallow bay, otherwise napping. Later there were more antlers, and occasionally reindeer. (*See also* Reindeer) Around the bend were three polar bears. *See* Sleep (Bear)

A crowd of reindeer together in the seasons when their antlers are fully grown—this must be the forest of this Arctic place far north of treeline.

Arctic Terns. Their Latin name is *Sterna paradisaea*; they are somehow birds of paradise or so named in 1763 by Erich Pontoppidan, the Pietist Danish prelate and contemporary of Linnaeus who wrote a natural history of Norway and an atlas of Denmark in the eighteenth century. He could not have known that of all living things on earth the arctic terns live in the most light and least darkness, but they work for it, flying 70,000 kilometers a year as they migrate from near the north pole to near the south, and when they are not nesting, live almost constantly in flight, like albatrosses. Theirs is a paradise of endless light and endless labor like angels (though they cross the band of day and night on their migration, and the tracking devices set up to plot their migratory course did so by measuring light and darkness). And their scimitar-sharp wings, their fierce cries, their hummingbird hoverings, their swallow-like tails, their gull-like dives.

Cold. Very. Well, pretty.

Color. When the sky is not blue, when moss and grass have not accumulated on the land (which is only 10 percent vegetated, 30 percent being rock and 60 percent glaciated), the world here is shades of gray verging toward brown, blue, and black, and it's white: ice, snow, glacier, cloud. It often looks as though it's heading into being a black-and-white photograph of itself or rather a Chinese ink painting on watered silk. And then come the tufts of moss like landscapes in miniature, various shades of vivid green and brown-green, here in this landscape where grass less than a foot high is the tallest plant around, and only a few things flower. Indigo evening, water and sky. White morning. Gray world out the porthole. Black land with white ice. Glowing gray nights. The water, liquid pewter and iron, with gentle ripples rather than white-crested waves.

And the smeared red of a polar bear's meal on blue-white ice. The cream of a polar bear against the white of ice—our chief guide says at one point that the tiny blob on the hillside is not a polar bear because it's the wrong shade of white. Shades of white: snow, clouds, glaciers, bones, polar bears, quartz rocks.

Expedition. Sets out to accomplish, discover, claim, explore. Sets out with an agenda. Sets out often in these regions in earlier times to fail, to get lost, to suffer frozen blisters, frostbite, cannibalism, forms of poisoning and starvation, discord, blame, remorse, death, being frozen for decades until another exploratory party comes across the remains, undamaged by decay but sometimes snacked upon by bears, as was the case of the small Andrée ballooning party—failed in 1897, discovered in 1930—one man in his grave and two who'd died in the tent become gnawed bones in disarray. The Andrée party's photographs and journals survived intact, and some of the embroidered linens made it to a museum. They planned, but did they anticipate?

Far. That first morning, out the porthole of my cabin there was a little blue iceberg. We were in Magdalenafjord, the bay at the end of the earth, the northwest corner of Svalbard in the high Arctic, more than a dozen degrees north of the Arctic Circle. Beyond it were stony gray hills with glaciers curving down the valleys in between most of them. The idea of being so far north was exciting enough, and then there were all those things I always wanted to see: icebergs, reindeer, polar bears, along with all the things I'm always happy to see: water, sky, spaciousness, landforms, light, scale. More than anyplace I've ever been, this one imposed a dependency: there was no way out except by this boat, and no way to communicate with the outside world except by this boat. Which was also an independency, from the rest of the world. Times when the view went all the way to the horizon and no land was visible on that side of the boat, when the sea was a delicate blue-gray and the sky was the same color, the sea smooth with billowing ripples that did not break into waves, the sky smooth, and only seabirds coasting along the surface of the sea, coming close to their own reflections, bending but not breaking the smoothness and vastness.

The far edge of the world, at the back of the North Wind, east of the sun and west of the moon, as far as *far*, at the back of beyond, out of reach, out of touch, out of the ordinary, beyond the Arctic Circle, beyond so many things. Far.

Fear. See Polar Bear; Cold

Footing. Made difficult by the rubber boots worn for landings in the Zodiac and by the rule that you should step on stone not on moss. Sometimes given a choice between one's own and the mosses' survival, the moss loses. Sometimes it wins. In a Japanese garden the irregularly placed stepping stones are meant to make you conscious of every step. Same here, but the scale varies and in Japanese gardens you never break your leg or fall down a mountain into an icy sea. Though maybe they imply these things.

Frankenstein. The cold of the Arctic rhymes with the cold in the hearts of the polar explorer, Walton, who wants to press on though it may mean death for his men and himself. And the cold in the heart of Victor Frankenstein, who pressed on with his experiment and disavowed responsibility for the results. But what does deep cold mean in an era of melting, thawing, heating? What is the virtue of cold, the refuge, the other ways to describe emotion? Cold as calm, as restraint, as stillness, as inaction?

Glaciers. Pelle the glaciologist speaks to us of glaciers, and the colored lines of his graphs slope down, toward melt and runoff and diminishment and disappearance. The shape of modern gloom is a slant downward from left to right. And of modern despair, the opposite slant—of rising temperatures, seas, carbon.

Graves. The dead—the main thing left behind by many expeditions and whaling parties, left in graves on which rocks are piled or wooden crosses erected, which have sometimes been raided for souvenirs, wooden tomb-stones, clothes, and even bones, says Lisa the guide, deploring it. Some-times it was the wood of coffins they were after in this place where wood is a valuable import. Some of the whalers were buried with pillows under their heads and a clump of their native soil. Hats and other pieces of cloth-ing survived in the cold environment. In the museum in Longyearbyen are seventeenth-century wool hats, including some striped knitted ones.

Guide. I had gotten an email from the Swedish photographer and Arctic historian Tyrone Martinsson the preceding January that said at the be-ginning, "I am writing to you to propose for you to join an expedition tour to Svalbard in September? I have a project here that is getting together 12 artists and scientists on a ship for 7–10 days sailing around Svalbard in the Arctic." Who would say no to that? Not me. Most of the twelve seemed to be photographers, and masses of black boxes and laptops to download them into would clutter the ship's tabletops. Every landing involved peo-ple peeling off one by one to gaze into their instruments and ignore the rest of us, which is not at all according to guidelines. The guidelines for travel in this part of the world are mostly about polar bears and about sticking close to the guide with the signal gun to frighten a bear off and the rifle with the massive bullets to shoot to kill if necessary. And looking around.

The chief guide was named Lisa Ström, and before we got there I'd pictured a no-nonsense outdoorswoman in the conventional mode, but this one was a young vegetarian despite the fact that the northernmost vege-table crop must be harvested hundreds of miles south of here. At first she seemed gentler than the Nordic Lisa I'd pictured, but gradually in conver-sation it emerged that she had tried to repeat Rasmussen's journey across the Northwest Passage by dogsled until the breaking up of the ice stopped her. She was planning to be the guide, along with her younger brother, on a two-month ski expedition to the south pole in November. She was sturdy but not burly, curiously humble and endlessly diligent, with chestnut hair and clear brown skin and a delightful voice and (Swedish) accent. Like older sisters generally, she was consciously and conscientiously affected by gravity; like younger brothers everywhere, hers—who was along as Guide #2—was not. To prove it, he did wild things with his paraglider and told us about them in detail, including the one where he had a rubber dinghy strapped to his back so he could land in the ocean.

And then one evening he began to tell stories at her expense about the misfit sled dogs she rescued and then lodged with her parents, since she travels so much. She joined in and they regaled a dinner table with stories of difficult personalities of the arctic canine and the calamities and hilarities that resulted, complete with impersonations of canine antics and facial expressions. A tall young man in a paneled room on a ship enthusiastically imitating a female dog that comes bounding into your tent.

Gulf Stream. All the way from Mexico and Louisiana. *See also* Wood

Icebergs. The color blue that is cold, pure, fierce, and somehow the blue that you always wanted and had to come to the end of the world to get, the blue you can't have since these sapphires are too big to take and too prone to melt. It's odd seeing an iceberg after so many pictures of them for so long, and odder to make pictures and turn them back into the familiar and maybe safe after seeing these great chunks calved by glaciers actually afloat in an icy sea. Their reflection in the sea doubles them, makes them into great faceted jewels that no one can wear and that won't last forever, and it only doubles their visible self when beneath the reflection is so much more. And the wake of the boat makes them rock on the water so that you can also see that the old adage "the tip of the iceberg" is accurate, for far more of them lies underwater. *See also* Reality and Representation

Infinity. Eternity. Mojave. Sorrow Fjord. At a place named Sorrow Fjord there is a ledge up from the best beach for landing and then a plateau with a couple of wooden houses—the wood gray from time and weather, pulled down into splinters and matchsticks—and then beyond, a great expanse of nearly flat land paved solidly in stones, pink, orange, white, gray, brown. And there is a kind of ecstasy of looking from the tiny detail of the rocks to the distance stretching away toward the sea and the horizon. There were reindeer droppings and small clusters of moss but no actual animals, not even birds, during the hour or two I was allowed to drift across this space whose footing reminded me of the pink quartz and other stones that cobble the area near the Nevada Test Site, and so I also strolled on that other hot inland shore where I spent time twenty years ago and found myself as a writer and a traveler. The sun was out and it was almost warm.

Journey. The pleasure of the boat chugging along and sometimes rocking and swaying when we were on open water, the sense of a continuity of movement and a continuity of landscape flowing by on one side, or the other, or sometimes both, the minor wistfulness that not everything could be seen, not even the landscape on both sides of the boat, the constant measuring comfort against going out on the deck for an unobstructed view, the mystery of what went by in the night when I was dreaming of home in the form of many strange landscapes representing my city with trees, with mounds, with familiar companions amid those nonexistent places, the punctuation of the flow of time in a boat, the clashing boom of the anchor chain going down, the silent business of the crane dropping the Zodiac overboard with a guide inside it, the clambering down the ladder to be transported to another shore, the moment pausing on one of those Arctic shores when I recalled Virgil's *Aeneid*: "Ah, Palinarus, too trusting of the tranquil sea and sky / You will lie naked on an unknown shore." Though we approached ours in layers of down and wool and silk and synthetic fibers and rubber boots and insulated gloves.

Light. This far north the twenty-four-hour cycle of day and night we have further south stretches out into the one-day-and-night-per-year the poles have, as though they were located somewhere other than the earth, which we have been told since our earliest days has 365 days a year. Says one source: "At 74° north, the midnight sun lasts 99 days and polar night 84 days, while the respective figures at 81° are 141 and 128 days. In Longyearbyen, midnight sun lasts from 20 April until 23 August, and polar night lasts from 26 Oc- tober to 15 February." If the town of Longyearbyen has a 99-day-long day in summer and an 84-day-long night in winter, then it has 184 days a year, not 365. And two of those days are many times the twenty-four-hour cycle. I was there near the equinox, so that the daylight hours were getting shorter at a gallop, about seventeen minutes shorter each day. Over the course of ten days the length of a day decreased by nearly three hours. During the course of September the day would have grown shorter by eight hours.

The sky was cloudy, misty, and gray all the days I was in Svalbard but the last, so that there were no shadows, was no sun, until that day when everything looked unrecognizable in the crisp golden light.

Plastic. In the form of bright blue barrels on the north-facing beach, beyond which is nothing but water and ice until the north pole. In the form of a bright yellow ring on the beach by the pile of male walruses. In the form of tattered plastic sheeting that mixes with the seaweed on the beach, near the reindeer. In the form of a Lux dishwashing liquid bottle, well abraded, on the next beach, before the dead bear. And the one after, as marigold and green nylon fishing rope and a blue-green stretch of net with scraps of clear plastic higher up. On every beach.

Polar Bear. What does it mean to delete a photograph of an endangered species? And why is it that everything about polar bears looks familiar except their rather defeated-looking rumps with the tails flattened into them? *See also* Sleep; Reality and Representation

We saw six living polar bears, two in places that prevented us from landing, but we were always, when not at sea, conscious of polar bears, imagining them, organizing all our movements around them. When we landed in the Zodiac, Oskar went ahead with his rifle unsheathed and the big red-tipped bullets ready to be slipped into the chamber, and everywhere we went we were supposed to walk behind these armed guards, to not branch out or venture forward first. So I began to scan all landscapes for bears, looking to see if this distant patch of snow might be a bear, if one might be coming from behind that rise or across that distance. There were bears in the landscape and in my imagination. Safety on Svalbard is an exercise in populating the landscape with even more than the 3,000 or so polar bears it is thought to contain, or maybe it's a process of knowing that you don't know where those 3,000 might appear.

Polar bear #4 on an iceberg on 9/11 having her meal that disrupts the harmony of colors—a red side of seal. Like the icebergs, something strange to see in actuality after so many images and imaginings that are only representations. And a horde of cameras pointing at her, turning her back into the familiar that is the photograph. This one swam away with its seal in its mouth, a v-wake behind her.

Polar bear #5 on a rocky little peninsula where we had intended to land on 9/12. Long, low snaky neck from the knob of the backbone between the shoulders and the shambling long-legged gait, black nose, black eyes, black mouth on creamy ivory. It looked back at us, raising its head to taste the diesel smell on the air, or ours. Lisa tells us they can put radio collars on the females, but the males' necks are thicker than their heads, so they slip the collars off.

Polar bear #6 on 9/13 on another rocky hillside above the German huts, which were the last part of the German military to surrender during World War II, in September of 1945. Spotted from the Zodiac, so we don't dock.

Polar bear #7 was on the rocky path to a glacier, alongside the roaring brown stream that issued forth from it. Most of it had been eaten so thoroughly its hide was smooth and white on the underside, and its massive spine—attached to a dainty pelvis—was tossed away a few feet, separate. Its black nose was intact, its eyes closed, and what seemed like almost a faint smile on its mouth, through which a few bloody fangs protruded. Lisa said it was the first dead polar bear she'd ever seen in Svalbard's wildernesses. Perhaps it died and was then devoured by foxes or bears; perhaps a bear killed it. Further on, there were bear prints in the sand, the four toes distinct, the tracks either of this bear or of its killer or devourer or both. If another bear ate it, that cannibalism may be a sign of environmental stress and hunger.

Polar bear (stuffed). In the middle of the baggage carousel in Longyearbyen, as though laid siege to by luggage, as perhaps polar bears are. In the Polar Hotel in the town, stuffed in prankish positions, including one small bear whose hindquarters are in the dining room but whose front end pokes through the corridor, with boxing gloves on its hands. Lifelike but not so exciting in the museum in Longyearbyen. Ragged and raided in the sad museum of the Russian outpost at Pyramiden. Also in skins, photographs, souvenirs, stamps for postcards, etc. Aids to imagining polar bears.

Reality and Representation. We see polar bears, photograph them, see icebergs, photograph them, and then I want to look at those things in my photographs. I have seen them so often in pictures and never in actuality, and now the actuality too readily turns into a representation. On the fourth day we go out to see a group of walruses on the beach, which obligingly flash their tusks and undulate and otherwise ignore us, but it has begun to snow and the wind is fierce and I'm underdressed (*see* A Warm West) and it's hard to care about anything but the snow blowing sideways and my icy fingers and cold feet and cooling back and chilly face. I go back to the ship at the first chance and decide to read the 1937 compendium *The Arctic Whalers*, by Basil Lubbock, put together at the last moment when the men who worked in the heyday of that industry were still alive or had been within memory of the author. Instead of being out in the fierce cold, I read accounts of those who had been out for far longer at these latitudes and enjoyed the stories almost as much as I do at home at latitude 37°41′ N.

A Captain Ross, former commander of the *Isabella*, was lost for four years, survived with his men by some desperate means near "Navy Board Inlet," and was rescued on August 26, 1833, when he and his three boats of men set off to signal a ship. "The leader of the three boats, a gaunt, grim, bearded man, 'dirty and dressed in the rags of wild beasts,' said, "I am Captain Ross." The mate of the *Isabella* refused to believe him and told him Ross had been dead two years or more.

A few pages before came the account of the loss of the *Shannon*, when on April 26, 1832, at 58°20′ N, she ran into an iceberg during a gale. The ship fell apart under them and partially sank. The captain and what crew members who had not been washed overboard survived on salvaged provisions under a shelter rigged up from a sail. "A Shetlander suggested to the surgeon of the *Shannon* 'that he should bleed him, that he might drink his own blood to quench his intolerable thirst.' The surgeon had his lancet in his pocket; he opened one of the man's veins and collected the blood in an old shoe. The man drank his own blood with delight." The surgeon then bled a dying man to offer him the same meal, but he died, and the shoeful of blood was offered around to the seventeen survivors "and it had an astonishing effect in reviving them. One by one, Captain Davey and the 16 men were then bled in succession, the doctor even bled himself. Some mixed the blood with flour, others drank straight from the shoe, but one and all found themselves wonderfully refreshed." They were rescued by "two Danish brigs bound for Davis Straits with passengers," the *Hvalfisken* and the *Navigation*, the latter headed by a Captain Bang, six days and seven nights after the wreck.

I read these stories and ate a small, fragrant, fresh-baked cinnamon snail (*see* Swedish baking) and some chocolate, along with a shot of calvados and some tea in the warm saloon, looking out occasionally at the snow blowing sideways up here at the Seven Islands north of Latitude 80 on September 12, 2011.

Some of the castaways in these grim accounts sickened horribly from scurvy. On page 319: "All of us that partook of the [polar bear] liver were seized with a dreadful headache. We were nearly all dead with it in a few days; the skin came off our bodies from the crown of the head to the sole of the feet. Around that time our provisions were further reduced to 1½ lbs. of bread per week; we had only 20 cwts. of bread on board, and very little meat. What could we do? We were like walking ghosts."

Lack of vitamin C in the first case. (Here the guide shows us scurvy grass that the Svalbard trappers learned to add to their diet.) And toxic levels of vitamin A in the second. On page 305 a drunk man whose clothes had frozen solid was rescued just before he himself had died of cold.

Would it have been odder to read my biography of Karl Marx and his family or my book on mirror neurons or my Icelandic fairytales than to read accounts of experiences so much more intense and arduous than mine in the same place?

The click of cameras was a constant whenever there were animals or something particularly spectacular, and the lineup of cameras on deck when we went by the prettiest scenery was inevitable. And on every walk, although we were supposed to stick close because of polar bears, the photographers among us would drop off one by one, lose themselves in the making of an image, and stretch our line out to a series of broken dots. The guides were too polite to herd us well. What will become of all those photographs? I took them too; it is a reflexive response to something exciting to look at, and sometimes to something not so exciting to look at but full of potential to mutate into a photograph worth looking at. There are problems with this, and pleasures too.

Reindeer. Antlers on a skull. Then droppings looking charmingly familiar in the unfamiliar landscape. Then tiny figures in the distance, enlarged through borrowed binoculars: definitely the short-legged reindeer of Svalbard. Reindeer, made so engaging by all the images of Sami and Siberian nomads riding and herding them, by the great herds of caribou in northern Alaska, by something about their air of both meekness and ruggedness, by the lovely way their antlers sweep back like the antlers of that famous Scythian brooch. My Mexican reindeer made out of brightly colored wool scraps with their antlers wound in colored yarn and colored tassels everywhere are evidence that their charm carries far, right down to the edge of the subtropical jungle of Chiapas, where I bought the first three. *Reinos* said the receipt when I bought three more of them in Guanajuato, the reinos who watch over me, the household guardians who here evolved into short-legged, solid, furry creatures to conserve body heat, since they don't need to flee predators, the reindeer who Oskar tells me often starve or freeze to death and whose winter grazing only serves to eke out their fat stores a little longer. I keep accidentally calling them caribou: I learned that the two were essentially the same species twenty years ago when a friend repeated the comment of Gwich'in activist Sarah James that she didn't have much use for Christmas but she liked the song about the red-nosed caribou.

Round Portholes. The ship had every charm the word *ship* could possibly convey. The *Stockholm* is from 1953 and looks like the picture of a ship as I would imagine it in ideal form. It weighs 361 tons and is 40 meters long, with round portholes and rigging and various decks and wooden boats for ornament and a Zodiac for landings and coils of thick blue rope in baskets and Swedish colors—dark blue and pale yellow—outside. Inside it has a saloon full of rich wood and comfortable furniture and a dining room studded with old colored engravings of animals from some zoological book and a map of an earlier Arctic sea journey that shows the landmasses radiating from the pole at the center, so that you see that continents don't really describe the organization of space up here. And small cabins with bunks and round portholes and a bridge in which they kept all the old brass instrumentation even though the captain and first mate seem to steer by computer information instead.

I once read that we crave, contradictorily, both security and adventure, comfort and challenge. Thus the child toddles forth to investigate but wants to be able to retreat to its mother's knee. Lying in a rocking top bunk in a cozy little room while the Arctic goes by through a porthole might be the highest possible fulfillment of those two desires in combination. When the rocking of the boat brought up the horizon, I could see the mountains in the distance across the water. When it rocked down or didn't rock at all, I mostly saw the sea and straits and fjords with birds going by. Once I saw a pod of dolphins, black fins arcing out of the water, through the porthole of my cabin.

Russian Ruins. The population of the once-thriving mining town of Pyramiden is now two in the winter and about a dozen in the summer; and though the hotel that looks like a Soviet barracks is technically still open, when we visited, the door that said STAFF ONLY would shut, leaving behind empty corridors and a smell of boiling potatoes. The dingy creatures in the little museum were falling apart, and the teeth and claws of the stuffed polar bear had been stolen. There was a gap in the floor where the heating was being worked on and a handful of Russian souvenirs for sale: nesting dolls and Soviet badges. Next door was a yellowish brick building, much like the hotel, that was fully populated by kittiwakes. They had built nests in the rows of deep window frames, two or three messy nests per ledge, and they screamed like seabirds and sometimes cried like children. | *17* More of them perched atop the swing sets and slide. Everything else was silent.

The delicate blue of the former canteen and cultural center was intact, but inside it the big plants had been allowed to die, so that their leaves were translucent light brown against the light of the windows, and in the big kitchen, paint was peeling everywhere and piling up on the floor. It must have once been the northernmost movie theater in the world. And across what the humorous Russian guide Dmitri called Red Square—a long, greenish rectangle planted with imported grass on imported soil—was the newer cultural center that, he told us, contained the northernmost grand piano in the world, though all the books had been stolen out of the library. In front of the center was a statue of Vladimir Lenin. "A man I never met," declared Dmitri. It was there to be frozen and snowed upon and ignored for the foreseeable future, except in summer, when groups like ours came by and took pictures. The northernmost statue of Lenin in the world, he added.

Perpendicular to the newer center was the swimming pool, a half-size Olympic pool tiled in pastel colors with the lane dividers still stretched across the dusty expanse. Undoubtedly the northernmost swimming pool in the world, in which no one any longer swims.

Sleep.

Bear: One of the three polar bears the captain spotted on the far side of Magdalenafjord our first day was napping. These bears seemed to be performing illustrations of their capacities for us. The first we saw was walking with that long-legged, ambling, shambling gait that seems so different than that of black and brown bears, just as their long streamlined profiles seem different from the dish-faced, domed-forehead faces of grizzlies. Walking alongside a hill of scree, its white that makes it invisible on the ice makes it distinct on the gray slope. The second one was up higher, tearing at something it was feeding on, with gestures of its neck. The third was recumbent upon a bed of green moss, the moss that grows in domelike hummocks, its head and tail just slightly curled in, and it periodically re-arranged itself or looked up at us. It was shocking to have so quickly penetrated to the realm of polar bears' naps and shocking to see the creature so vulnerable and so confident in its own habitat. If it was in that habitat—so far from the sea ice where I think it is supposed to be hunting—maybe it was in crisis. It was hard to tell, but a white bear on green tufts is not exactly camouflaged.

Me: Being here was restful. It seemed both odd to be so comfortable in such a remote place and perfectly sensible to have come to the end of the world for the peace and quiet in which to nap. Which I did deeply and often, and at night I dreamed—of a forest that doesn't actually exist at the end of my childhood street, a house on the corner of a street near Baker Beach in my city that also doesn't exist, and then the childhood swimming pool piled higher than its deep end in wishing coins and debris thrown by neighbor children, and a visit with the infant son of an acquaintance in a house I have not actually been in for twenty or thirty years. It was so peaceful in this quiet place at the end of the world where I could only be reached by the radiotelephone that only my brothers had the number for.

Swedish Baking. Sometimes what looked like rye bread was cake, sometimes what looked like fruit bread was rye with nuts, sometimes a great brown sourdough loaf was baked, sometimes the coffee cake that was put out on the round table in the saloon was extraordinarily moist and delicate, particularly considering that it was made by thin tattooed young women named Hannah and Erica, sometimes one wished that there was not quite so abundant a choice of sweets and starches. Spiral cinnamon rolls, cookies of various kinds with nuts, another moist coffee cake topped with toasted almond slivers and cardamom, chocolate cake, raspberry pie with whipped cream, and more. *See* Sleep (Me)

Underwater Forests with Pink Lanterns. Sometimes when the Zodiac came into the shallows for a landing, you could look down and see whole forests of ruffled seaweed, long pale sheets of it in rows, and branching seaweeds, a kind of lushness that did not exist on shore, though great slimy mounds of kelp did. I said to Lisa, the guide, the forests here are all underwater, right? She beamed in approval that I had recognized this obvious fact. And there were also various kinds of jellyfish, notably, small ones like pink lanterns, like the ghosts of small cucumbers and sea urchins, like tiny zeppelins, floating by in the dark clear water, festively, so delicate, so enchanting, so unlike the massive warm-blooded animals you hear about here. There were urchin shells, tall spiraling seashells, occasional mussel shells on shore where the seabirds flew. These when alive were also wildlife.

Walrus. The first walrus more wrinkled and pink and comic than I had imagined with its eyes invisible and its whiskery lip rising and falling like a gigantic cyclopian eyelid. A fanged eye. Its vast chest wrinkled and creased into chasms or crevasses of dry hide. Its tusks looking mildly dignified when its head is upright but also pointing sideways, and sometimes it scratched itself with its flipper and looked more agile and more like a cat or a dog. More walruses turning their heads in various directions so that their tusks looked like semaphore torches or runes, as though they were sending us messages we were inadequate to receive.

Their Latin name is *Odobenus rosmarus: Odobenus* means "one that walks on teeth," and *rosmarus* comes from Old Norse, meaning "horse of the sea." So the walrus is a sea horse that walks with its teeth. "For me the walrus is a prehistoric animal. I feel like I am traveling back in time when I see them—or even smell them," says Lisa Ström, and she tells us they can use the tusks to get up on the ice and the front flippers to walk on. They have lice, walrus lice, so they are always scratching themselves. The male averages 1,200 kilos; females, 800. Pink wart-like growths stud the male neck and breast. ("Maybe it's attractive!" Lisa speculates.) "The females have straighter teeth and they don't generate the big pink warted neck. Those with the biggest teeth can lie in the middle of the group, in the warmest, nicest spot, protected from predators. Tusks start to grow at age two, and the animals live up to forty years. Killer whales and polar bears prey on walrus but pursue only the females on Svalbard. Diet is sometimes fish, sometimes swimming birds and other seals, but mostly mussels—fifty to sixty kilos of mussels, or 4,000–6,000 *per day*," she explains, guiding us to know walruses.

A Warm West. This is what Tyrone, the expedition leader, told me to bring, grossly understating the degree of cold we would encounter. I liked the instruction, though, since I am always wearing the West in some sense. But this was the far north, and I wish I had brought my faux-fur-lined vest I wore all through my times in Montana and Wyoming in winter and much of Iceland in summer. And not lost my insulated jacket in the Frankfurt airport. A cold north.

Water the Color of Gunmetal. See Color

Wonder. You are north of everything on a ship out of a story, sailing onward, with glaciers, crags, peaks, mists looming up on either side, and the moment requires so many practical reactions it is not until you are sitting in an armchair forty-three degrees south of this experience that the full wonder of it sets in.

Wood. So many long logs on the shores of this place where not even a bush grows, evidence of the great forces that drop trees into water and send them on tides far beyond the scenes of their growth. More wood in the fox traps, the graves, the houses, and other structures that are lightly scattered across the land. The bare wood houses that weather to gray, like driftwood. The house we saw on the last day that was sturdier and more expansive than the rest we'd seen, more like a farmhouse than a survival hut, with fresh wood showing that it was maintained, and inside it, penciled names from the nineteenth century onward written on the bare wood walls, and one massive table with an X, and another structure like a stool for oxen, massive and lone in the sunlight that streamed through the windows we had just removed the protective boards from.

Zodiac. Black rubber raft used for all landings in the wild, expertly captained by Lisa, clambered down onto with a ladder on the side of the boat, and afterward heaved up onto the *Stockholm*'s deck by a crane and pulley. Its name suggests another zodiac, a rubber ring as black as night bearing the arctic zodiac in which the constellations are different and one is born under the sign of fox, walrus, ring seal, whale, polar bear, reindeer, pink jellyfish, ivory gull, spiral snail, scurvy grass, cod, and mosquito.

2013

THE BUTTERFLY AND THE BOILING POINT

Reflections on the Arab Spring and After

Revolution is as unpredictable as an earthquake and as beautiful as spring. Its coming is always a surprise, but its nature should not be.

Revolution is a phase, a mood—like spring, and just as spring has its buds and showers, so revolution has its ebullience, its bravery, its hope, and its solidarity. Some of these things pass. The women of Cairo do not move as freely in public as they did during those few precious weeks when the old rules were suspended and everything was different. But the old Egypt is gone and Egyptians' sense of themselves—and our sense of them—is forever changed.

No revolution vanishes without effect. The Prague Spring of 1968 was brutally crushed, but twenty-one years later when a second wave of revolution liberated Czechoslovakia, Alexander Dubček, who had been the reformist Secretary of the Czechoslovakian Communist Party, returned to give heart to the people from a balcony overlooking Wenceslas Square: "The government is telling us that the street is not the place for things to be solved, but I say the street was and is the place. The voice of the street must be heard."

The voice of the street became a bugle cry in 2011. You heard it. Everyone did, but the rulers who thought their power was the only power that mattered heard it last and with dismay. Many of them are nervous now, releasing political prisoners, lowering the price of food, and otherwise trying to tamp down uprisings.

There were three kinds of surprises about the unfinished revolutions in Tunisia, Egypt, and Libya, and the rumblings elsewhere that have frightened the mighty from Saudi Arabia to China, Algeria to Bahrain. The West was surprised that the Arab world, which we have regularly been told is medieval, hierarchical, and undemocratic, was full of young men and women using their cell phones, their Internet access, and their bodies in streets and squares to foment change and temporarily live a miracle of direct democracy and people power. And then there is the surprise that the seemingly unshakeable regimes of the strongmen were shaken into pieces.

And finally, there is always the surprise of why now? Why did the crowd decide to storm the Bastille on July 14, 1789, and not any other day? The bread famine going on in France that year and the rising cost of food had something to do with it, as hunger and poverty do with many of the Middle Eastern uprisings today, but part of the explanation remains mysterious. Why this day and not a month earlier or a decade later? Or never instead of now?

Oscar Wilde once remarked, "To expect the unexpected shows a thoroughly modern intellect." This profound uncertainty has been the grounds for my own hope.

Hindsight is 20/20, they say, and you can tell stories where it all makes sense. A young Tunisian college graduate, Mohammed Bouazizi, who could find no better work than selling produce from a cart on the street, was so upset by his treatment at the hands of a policewoman that he set himself afire on December 17, 2010. His death two weeks later became the match that lit the country afire—but why *that* death? Or why the death of Khaled Said, an Egyptian youth who exposed police corruption and was beaten to death for it? A Facebook page claims, "We are all Khaled Said," and his death, too, was a factor in the uprisings to come.

But when exactly do the abuses that have been tolerated for so long become intolerable? When does the fear evaporate and the rage generate action that produces joy? After all, Tunisia and Egypt were not short on intolerable situations and tragedies before Bouazizi's self-immolation and Said's murder.

Thich Quang Duc burned himself to death at an intersection in Saigon on June 11, 1963, to protest the treatment of Buddhists by the U.S.-backed government of South Vietnam. His stoic composure while in flames was widely seen and may have helped produce a military coup against the regime six months later—a change, but not necessarily a liberation. In between that year and this one, many people have fasted, prayed, protested, gone to prison, and died to call attention to cruel regimes, with little or no measurable consequence.

GUNS AND BUTTERFLIES

The boiling point of water is straightforward, but the boiling point of societies is mysterious. Bouazizi's death became a catalyst, and at his funeral, the 5,000 mourners chanted, "Farewell, Mohammed, we will avenge you. We weep for you today, we will make those who caused your death weep."

But his was not the first Tunisian gesture of denunciation. An even younger man, the rap artist who calls himself El General, uploaded a song about the horror of poverty and injustice in the country and, as the *Guardian* put it, "Within hours, the song had lit up the bleak and fearful horizon like an incendiary bomb." Or a new dawn. The artist was arrested and interrogated for three very long days, and then released, thanks to widespread protest. And surely before him we could find another milestone. And another young man being subjected to inhuman conditions. And behind the uprising in Egypt are a panoply of union and human rights organizers as well as charismatic individuals.

It was a great year for the power of the powerless and for the courage and determination of the young. A short, fair-haired, mild man even younger than Bouazizi has been held under extreme conditions in solitary confinement in a Marine brig in Quantico, Virginia, for the last several months. He is charged with giving hundreds of thousands of secret U.S. documents to WikiLeaks, thus unveiling some of the more compromised and unsavory operations of the American military and U.S. diplomacy. Bradley Manning (now Chelsea Manning) was a twenty-two-year-old soldier stationed in Iraq when he was arrested the spring of 2010. The acts he's charged with have changed the global political landscape and fed the outrage in the Middle East.

As *Foreign Policy* put it in a headline, "In one fell swoop, the candor of the cables released by WikiLeaks did more for Arab democracy than decades of backstage U.S. diplomacy." The cables suggested, among other things, that the United States was not going to back Tunisian dictator

24 |

Ben Ali to the bitter end and that the regime's corruption was common knowledge.

Martin Luther King and the Montgomery Story, a 1958 comic book about the civil rights struggle in the American South and the power of nonviolence was translated and distributed in the Arab world by the American Islamic Council in 2008 and has been credited with influencing the insurgencies of 2011. So the American Islamic Council played a role, too—a role definitely not being investigated by anti-Muslim Congressman Peter King in his hearings on the "radicalization of Muslims in America." Behind the other King are the lessons he, in turn, learned from Mohandas Gandhi, whose movement liberated India from colonial rule sixty-six years ago, and so the story comes back to the East.

Causes are Russian dolls. You can keep opening each one up and find another one inside it. WikiLeaks and Facebook and Twitter and the new media helped in 2011, but new media had been around for years. Asmaa Mahfouz was a young Egyptian woman who had served time in prison for using the Internet to organize a protest on April 6, 2008, to support striking workers. With astonishing courage, she posted a video of herself on Facebook on January 18, 2011, in which she looked into the camera and said, with a voice of intense conviction:

> Four Egyptians have set themselves on fire to protest humiliation and
> hunger and poverty and degradation they had to live with for thirty years.
> Four Egyptians have set themselves on fire thinking maybe we can have
> a revolution like Tunisia, maybe we can have freedom, justice, honor,
> and human dignity. Today, one of these four has died, and I saw people
> commenting and saying, "May God forgive him. He committed a sin and
> killed himself for nothing." People, have some shame.

She described an earlier demonstration at which few had shown up: "I posted that I, a girl, am going down to Tahrir Square, and I will stand alone. And I'll hold up a banner. Perhaps people will show some honor. No one came except three guys—three guys and three armored cars of riot police. And tens of hired thugs and officers came to terrorize us."

Mahfouz called for the gathering in Tahrir Square on January 25 that became the Egyptian revolution. The second time around she didn't stand alone. Eighty-five thousand Egyptians pledged to attend, and soon enough, millions stood with her.

The revolution was called by a young woman with nothing more than a Facebook account and passionate conviction. They were enough. Often, revolution has had such modest starts. On October 5, 1789, a girl took a drum to the central markets of Paris. The storming of the Bastille a few months before had started, but hardly completed, a revolution. That drummer girl helped gather a mostly female crowd of thousands who marched to Versailles and seized the royal family. It was the end of the Bourbon monarchy.

Women often find great roles in revolution, simply because the rules fall apart and everyone has agency, anyone can act. As they did in Egypt, where liberty leading the masses was an earnest young woman in a black hijab.

That the flapping of a butterfly's wings in Brazil can shape the weather in Texas is a summation of chaos theory that is now an oft-repeated cliché. But there are billions of butterflies on earth, all flapping their wings. Why does one gesture matter more than another? Why *this* Facebook post, *this* girl with a drum?

Even to try to answer this you'd have to say that the butterfly is borne aloft by a particular breeze that was shaped by the flap of the wing of, say, a sparrow; and so behind causes are causes, behind small agents are other small agents, inspirations, and role models, as well as outrages to react against. The point is not that causation is unpredictable and erratic. The point is that butterflies and sparrows and young women in veils and an unknown twenty-year-old rapping in Arabic and you yourself, if you wanted it, sometimes have tremendous power, enough to bring down a dictator, enough to change the world.

OTHER SELVES, OTHER LIVES

Early 2011 was a remarkable time in which a particular kind of humanity appeared again and again in very different places, and we saw a great deal more of it in Japan before its triple catastrophe was over. Perhaps its first appearance was at the shooting of Congresswoman Gabrielle Giffords in

Tucson on January 8, where the lone gunman was countered by several citizens who took remarkable action, none more so than Giffords's new intern, twenty-year-old Daniel Martinez, who later said, "It was probably not the best idea to run toward the gunshots. But people needed help."

Martinez reached the congresswoman's side and probably saved her life by administering first aid, while sixty-one-year-old Patricia Maisch grabbed the magazine so the shooter couldn't reload, and seventy-four-year-old Bill Badger helped wrestle him to the ground, though he'd been grazed by a bullet. One elderly man died because he shielded his wife rather than protect himself.

Everything suddenly changed and those people rose to the occasion heroically not in the hours, days, or weeks a revolution gives, but within seconds. More sustained acts of bravery and solidarity would make the revolutions to come. People would risk their lives and die for their beliefs and for each other. And in killing them, regimes would lose their last shreds of legitimacy.

Violence always seems to me the worst form of tyranny. It deprives people of their rights, including the right to live. The rest of the year was dominated by battles against the tyrannies that sometimes cost lives and sometimes just ground down those lives into poverty and indignity, from Bahrain to Madison, Wisconsin.

I have often wondered if the United States could catch fire the way other countries sometimes do. The public space and spirit of Argentina or Egypt often seem missing here, for what changes in revolution is largely spirit, emotion, belief—intangible things, as delicate as butterfly wings, but our world is made of such things. They matter. The governors govern by the consent of the governed. When they lose that consent, they resort to violence, which can stop some people directly, but aims to stop most of us through the power of fear.

And then sometimes a young man becomes fearless enough to post a song attacking the dictator who has ruled all his young life. Or people sign a declaration like Charter 77, the 1977 Czech document that was a milestone on the way to the revolutions of 1989, as well as a denunciation of the harassment of an underground rock band called the Plastic People of the Universe. Or a group of them found a labor union on the waterfront in Gdansk, Poland, in 1980, and the first cracks appear in the Soviet Empire.

Those who are not afraid are ungovernable, at least by fear, that favorite tool of the bygone era of George W. Bush. Jonathan Schell, with his usual beautiful insight, saw this when he wrote of the uprising in Tahrir Square:

> The murder of the 300 people, it may be, was the event that sealed Mubarak's doom. When people are afraid, murders make them take flight. But when they have thrown off fear, murders have the opposite effect and make them bold. Instead of fear, they feel solidarity. Then they "stay"—and advance. And there is no solidarity like solidarity with the dead. That is the stuff of which revolution is made.

When a revolution is made, people suddenly find themselves in a changed state—of mind and of nation. The ordinary rules are suspended, and people become engaged with each other in new ways and develop a new sense of power and possibility. People behave with generosity and altruism; they find they can govern themselves; and, in many ways, the government simply ceases to exist. A few days into the Egyptian revolution, Ben Wedeman, CNN's senior correspondent in Cairo, was asked why things had settled down in the Egyptian capital. He responded: "[T]hings have calmed down because there is no government here," pointing out that security forces had simply disappeared from the streets.

This stateless state often arises in disasters as well, when the government is overwhelmed, shut down, or irrelevant for people intent on survival and then on putting society back together. Even if it rarely lasts, the process does change individuals and societies, leaving a legacy. To my mind, the best regime is one that most resembles this moment when civil society reigns in a spirit of hope, inclusiveness, and improvisational genius.

In Egypt, there were moments of violence when people pushed back against the government's goons, and for a week it seemed like the news was filled with pictures of bloody heads. Still, no armies marched, no superior weaponry decided the fate of the country, nobody was pushed from power by armed might. People gathered in public and discovered themselves as the public, as civil society. They found that the repression and exploitation they had long tolerated was intolerable and that they could do something about it, even if that something was only gathering, standing together, insisting on their rights as the public, as the true nation that the government can never be.

It is remarkable how, in other countries, people will one day simply stop believing in the regime that had, until then, ruled them, as African Americans did in the South here fifty years ago. To stop believing means no longer regarding those who rule you as legitimate, and so no longer fearing them. Or respecting them. And then, miraculously, the regimes begin to crumble.

In the Philippines in 1986, millions of people gathered in response to a call from Catholic-run Radio Veritas, the only station the dictatorship didn't control or shut down. Then the army defected, and dictator Fernando Marcos was ousted from power after twenty-one years.

In Argentina in 2001, in the wake of a brutal economic collapse, such a sudden shift in consciousness toppled the neoliberal regime of Fernando de la Rúa and ushered in a revolutionary era of economic desperation, but also of brilliant, generous innovation. A shift in consciousness brought an outpouring of citizens into the streets of Buenos Aires, suddenly no longer afraid after the long nightmare of a military regime and its aftermath. In Iceland in early 2009, in the wake of a global economic meltdown of special fierceness on that small island nation, a once-docile population almost literally drummed out of power the ruling party that had managed the country into bankruptcy.

CAN'T HAPPEN HERE?

The United States often seems to lack the attunement between governed and governors and the symbolically charged public spaces in which civil society can be born. This is a big country whose national capital is not much of a center and whose majority seems to live in places that are themselves decentered.

At its best, revolution is an urban phenomenon. Suburbia is counterrevolutionary by design. For revolution, you need to converge, to live in public, to become the public, and that's a geographical as well as a political phenomenon. The history of revolution is the history of great public spaces: La Place de la Concorde during the French Revolution; La Rambla in Barcelona during the Spanish Civil War; Beijing's Tiananmen Square in 1989 (a splendid rebellion that was crushed); the great surge that turned the divide of the Berlin Wall into a gathering place in that same year; the insurrectionary occupation of the Zócalo of Mexico City after corrupt presidential elections; and the space in Buenos Aires that gave the Dirty War's most open opposition its name: Las Madres de la Plaza de Mayo (the Mothers of the Plaza of May).

It's all very well to organize on Facebook and update on Twitter, but these are only preludes. You also need to rise up, to pour out into the streets. You need to be together in body, for only then are you truly the public with the full power that a public can possess. And then it needs to matter. The United States is good at trivializing and ignoring insurrections at home.

The authorities were shaken by the uprising in Seattle that shut down the World Trade Organization meeting on November 30, 1999, but the actual nonviolent resistance there was quickly fictionalized into a tale of a violent rabble. Novelist and then–*New Yorker* correspondent Mavis Gallant wrote in 1968:

> The difference between rebellion at Columbia [University] and rebellion at the Sorbonne is that life in Manhattan went on as before, while in Paris every section of society was set on fire, in the space of a few days. The collective hallucination was that life can change, quite suddenly and for the better. It still strikes me as a noble desire.

Revolution is also the action of people pushed to the brink. Rather than fall over, they push back. When he decided to push public employees hard and strip them of their collective bargaining rights, Wisconsin governor Scott Walker took a gamble. In response, union members, public employees, and then the public of Wisconsin began to gather on February 11. By February 15, they had taken over the state's capitol building as the revolution in Egypt was still at full boil. In February 2011, the biggest demonstration in Madison's history was held, led by a "tractorcade" of farmers. The Wisconsin firefighters revolted too. And the librarians.

Oppression often works—for a while. And then it backfires. Sometimes immediately, sometimes after several decades. Walker has been nicknamed the Mubarak of the Midwest. Much of the insurrection and the rage in the Middle East isn't just about tyranny; it's about economic injustice, about young people who can't find work, can't afford to get married or leave their parents' homes, can't start their lives. This is increasingly the story for young Americans as well, and here it's clearly a response to the misallocation of resources, not absolute scarcity. It could just be tragic, or it could get interesting when the young realize they are being shafted, and that life could be different. Even that it could change, quite suddenly, and for the better.

There was a splendid surliness in the wake of the economic collapse of 2008: rage at the executives who had managed the economy into the ground and gone home with outsized bonuses, rage at the system, rage at the sheer gratuitousness of the suffering of those who were being foreclosed upon and laid off. In this country, economic inequality has reached a level not seen since before the stock market crash of 1929.

Hard times are in store for most people on earth, and those may be times of boldness. Or not. The butterflies are out there, but when their flight stirs the winds of insurrection, no one knows beforehand.

So remember to expect the unexpected, but not just to wait for it. Sometimes you have to become the unexpected, as the young heroes and heroines of 2011 have. I am sure they themselves are as surprised as anyone. Since she very nearly had the first word, let Asmaa Mahfouz have the last word: "As long as you say there is no hope, then there will be no hope, but if you go down and take a stance, then there will be hope."

March 2011

RATTLESNAKE IN MAILBOX

Cults, Creeps, California in the 1970s

It's true what you heard about macramé. Partly some mutant version of a craft tradition and partly something for the fidgety hands and wandering minds of the drugged, macramé was also the means to create harnesses from which a million planters were hung from a million ceilings to create gratuitous clutter. You can think of macramé as some vernacular extension of 1960s soft sculptures by Bruce Conner, Eva Hesse, Robert Morris, and Claes Oldenburg, but its aesthetics had grown monstrously. There was something quintessentially 1970s about these pendulous burdens—obscuring views and dripping foliage—something that tied them to the fern bars of the era and to the overall aesthetics of horror vacui. This era of shag rugs and feather-bedecked roach-clip hair ties rivaled the Victorians when it came to clutter, ornament, jewelry, print, pattern, texture, flourish, tassels, fringes, tendrils, frizz, dangly bits, lace, laces, buttons, and other distractions for the eye.

Dangling, creeping plants were at the heart of 1978's definitive film, Phil Kaufman's horror movie *Invasion of the Body Snatchers*, filmed in San Francisco. Donald Sutherland as the restaurant-inspector-turned-alien-detective walks into Brooke Adams's house and finds a clone of her growing in a lush, damp sort of greenhouse alcove full of plants; later Jeff Goldblum is cloned in a bathhouse, also full of houseplants. San Francisco's hills, trees, fog, and intricate Victorian gingerbread houses suit the film's sensibility. In one scene, a teacher out with some small children in a park near the Haight-Ashbury ominously encourages them to pick the pretty flowers and take them home. Eleven years earlier Los Angeles's Mamas and the Papas had sung "San Francisco (Be Sure to Wear Some Flowers in Your Hair)," promising the city would be full of gentle people, a "love-in."

Now the flowers were monstrous and the emotions were null. Technically the threat in *Invasion of the Body Snatchers* is colonizing plants from a destroyed planet, but the film makes an allegory of the fuzzy thinking, fuzzy surfaces, spreading tendrils, and labyrinthine passages that were both the culture and the landscape of San Francisco during the late 1970s. In other words, the city—and by extension, the world—is being eaten by the counterculture; and being taken over by the pods turns people into affectless ambulatory vegetables.

Blank is the word that comes to mind for this condition, though *blank* also sounds like a refreshingly uncluttered surface in that context. Blankness calls up Richard Hell and the Voidoids's anti-anthem of the year before, "Blank Generation." Punk rock arrived like a machete in the jungle, hacking at all that stadium rock, chopping the tendrils, paring away everything unnecessary and slicing down to the rage, the indignation, the energy, and the essence. The jungle was the meandering, woolly, over-decorated excesses rock-and-roll had sunk into during the 1970s—the fourteen-minute tracks, the long instrumental solos, the excess of studio polish, the pointlessness of songs about bored decadence and sybaritic luxury, the stale formulas. The Eagles's 1977 hit "Hotel California" was a flawless piece of craftsmanship, but it was about upscale fatalism and gilded cages, about the hotel you can check into but never leave. It sounded as though Joan Didion had started writing lyrics. As Don Henley sang, "They stab it with their steely knives, / But they just can't kill the beast."

Punk rock could, and the beast was rock-and-roll itself. I was fifteen in 1977, the year punk hit California. When it arrived, most rock-and-roll sounded as though it was made to be listened to in a hot tub; the music had slowed down and sprawled out. The operative word was *mellow*. In *Invasion of the Body Snatchers*, the aliens clone you when you're sleeping and then turn you into ashes; relaxation is perilous. Punk came along as a fierce corrective to the excesses and errors of the 1960s, at least in the United States. British punks were perhaps more farseeing; their protest was against a mainstream that would grow more grotesque in the Thatcherist 1980s, while songs like the Dead Kennedys's "California Über Alles" (1979/80) seemed to imagine progressive and occasionally loopy Governor Jerry Brown as an enduring oppression—insidious, like those tendrils and pods. By the time that song was released in June of 1979, former California governor Ronald Reagan was on his way to the presidency, and decades of Republican governors were on their way to Sacramento. (California wouldn't have a strong Democratic governor again until 2011, when a seventy-something Brown was reelected.)

"California Über Alles" seems to imagine that the counterculture won. Few foresaw that the right—which seemed in abeyance since Nixon had slithered back to San Clemente—was on the brink of resurgence. Nevertheless, punk rock would have plenty to say about Reagan and the right when the time came: San Francisco's MDC (Millions of Dead Cops, an important, less-remembered political punk band that eventually changed its name to Multi-Death Corporations) would release "John Wayne Was a Nazi" in 1981, and a host of hardcore bands like L.A.'s Wasted Youth would launch more vitriolic attacks. Even the generally apolitical Ramones would record "Bonzo Goes to Bitberg" in 1985, about Reagan's infamous laying of a wreath in a cemetery full of Nazi graves. It was possible to hate both possibilities—and dystopic punk was never very good at envisioning solutions and alternatives. It arose from an adolescent's sensibility of outrage and dissent—the antithesis of *visionary*—hostile to the Emperor and his embroidered new clothes.

The 1970s is a decade people would apparently rather not talk about and hardly seem to remember. Perhaps the best thing that can be said about the 1970s is that its experiments—the failed ones that people learned from and the successful that continued—laid the groundwork for movements to come during the 1980s and after. But in 1978, mostly the mistakes and excesses were on display.

1978: THE YEAR OF FORENSIC EVIDENCE

For San Francisco in particular and for California in general, 1978 was a terrible year in which the fiddler had to be paid for all the tunes to which the counterculture had danced. The sexual revolution had deteriorated into a sort of free-market, free-trade ideology, in which all should have access to sex and none should deny access. I grew up north of San Francisco in an atmosphere where, once you were twelve or so, hippie dudes in their thirties started to offer you drugs and neck rubs that were clearly only the beginning—and it was immensely hard to refuse them. There were no grounds. Sex was good; everyone should have it all the time; anything could be construed as consent; and almost nothing meant no, including "no." Those who remember feminists as being angrily anti-sex during the 1980s don't recall the huge task they undertook—and undertook successfully—of pointing out that, like everything else, sex involves power; power is distributed unequally; and unequal power not uncommonly deteriorates into exploitation.

It was the culture. Rock stars were open about their liaisons with underage groupies, and forty-something Woody Allen had cast underage Mariel Hemingway as his love interest in his film *Manhattan* (1977). In 1978, Louis Malle released *Pretty Baby*, in which a then-eleven-year-old and sometimes unclothed Brooke Shields played a prostitute. (Two years earlier, Playboy Press had published nude photographs by the aptly named Gary Gross of a painted, vamping Shields at the age of ten in a book titled *Sugar and Spice*. In 1978, British photographer David Hamilton published *Young Girl*, a collection of prettily prurient photographs of half-undressed pubescent girls; as Hamilton's stock-in-trade for years, these images were everywhere as posters and books. On February 1, 1978, forty-four-year-old film director Roman Polanski decided to skip bail and headed for France after being charged with raping a thirteen-year-old girl he had plied with champagne and Quaaludes. (His implied excuse was that everyone was doing it.) Some defended him on the grounds that the girl looked fourteen.

In 1978, former beauty queen and right-wing demagogue Anita Bryant was crusading against basic rights for gay men by portraying them as child molesters, among other things. In California, Bryant's campaign led to the Briggs Initiative on the state ballot on November 6, 1978, which would have banned queer people from working as teachers. Thanks to a groundswell of gay men coming out to their friends, family, and co-workers and great organizing work, the Briggs Initiative lost, a final victory for San Francisco supervisor and statewide organizer Harvey Milk in a year when people of color, women, and gay men pressed hard for their rights. The first annual Take Back the Night march of feminists against pornography—pro- and anti-porn feminism was one of the debates of the times—took place the same month.

It was a violent time, and there were so many kinds of violence to choose from. On October 11, members of the Bay Area's Synanon cult nearly killed a lawyer helping some former members by putting a rattlesnake in his mailbox. On November 18, the mass murder–suicide in Jonestown, Guyana, of 918 members of the San Francisco cult, the Peoples Temple, constituted the largest single violent loss of American civilian lives before 9/11. And on November 27, a disgruntled and deranged former policeman assassinated San Francisco mayor George Moscone and Milk in the same City Hall where the cloned vegetal menaces of *Invasion of the Body Snatchers* loaded trucks with proliferating alien pods. The horror movie would be released on December 20 that year.

Another 1978 ballot included a much more famous proposition, known then as the Jarvis-Gann Act, now as Proposition 13 (the initiative that froze property taxes and required a supermajority to vote in tax increases; the measure began to starve California's educational system, libraries, and other county and city services). That one won on June 6, bringing on the beginning of the taxpayer revolts of the past three decades and the beginning of the end of a half-century of economic leveling. Proposition 13 was the narrow wedge of the economic violence that would weaken public institutions, undermine social safety nets, and bring back dire poverty on a grand scale over the next few decades. During the 1970s, the long movement toward economic democratization went into reverse so that, by 2010, the United States would return to the level of economic disparity of 1928: 23 percent of the nation's wealth would be concentrated in the hands of 1 percent of its population.

The same ruthlessness of capital brought about, after several years of resistance, the August 4, 1977, eviction of the elderly Asian residents of the International Hotel in downtown San Francisco, amid huge throngs, violence, ladders, mounted police, and dismay. The eviction was carried out by the police at the behest of a developer intent upon building something more lucrative on the site, a project that never came to fruition. The low-income residential I-Hotel had housed a gallery and some activist organizations, as well as those vulnerable seniors. It had been a key location for the Asian-American rights movements of the decade, which paralleled the indigenous rights movement launched at Alcatraz in 1969; the Chicano movement tied to Cesar Chavez's organization of farmworkers from the early 1960s onward; and, of course, the African-American insurgency that was the Black Panther Party, founded in Oakland in 1966. Financial district expansion had already devoured the rest of Manilatown, and urban renewal had gutted the neighborhoods of two other low-income communities just before—the African-American Western Addition/Fillmore in the 1960s and the South of Market area, full of retired waterfront workers during the 1970s. The space in which to be decently poor was drying up, and a few years hence, in the age of Reagan, the armies of the homeless would begin to march through the city streets.

Maybe 1978 was when the 1960s ended and the 1980s began. Maybe there were no 1970s. Even punk rock, arguably the decade's most original offering, died a little when the Sex Pistols broke up in January of 1978, after the Winterland hatefest that was their final concert. Winterland was around the corner from the Peoples Temple, the site of Jim Jones's cult before he led his devotees on a paranoid flight to Guyana that culminated, ten months later, in drinking all that cyanide-laced Kool-Aid. One of San Francisco's leading punk venues, the Mabuhay Gardens, was just around the corner from the International Hotel. It was all pretty tied together, like some kind of macramé of conspiracy, paranoia, and decline. Mostly it was a bleak landscape in which the dying experiments were easier to spot than the embryonic new forms that would matter immensely during the 1980s and after.

AVENGERS

Working all night as an extra, I carried a big green gherkin-like papier-mâché pod in the City Hall scene of *Invasion of the Body Snatchers*, though if I made it into the movie, it was only for a flickering second. Around the same time, I started hanging out at the Mabuhay Gardens—or Mab, as it was sometimes called—though I didn't find out what the Tagalog word *mabuhay* meant until much later. I went to shows at the Peoples Temple when it turned into a punk venue after all its former parishioners were dead or scattered. I didn't get it about the International Hotel until long afterward, though I remember the hotel, the protests, and then the hole in the ground where it had been. I saw the Sex Pistols's last show on a rainy night when country music fans had been whipped up into a fury against punks and came to spit and hurl projectiles, back in that divisive, intolerant era when punks hated disco and country right back—but I didn't know what a historic and final moment it would be.

Punk wasn't defined yet. Or rather it was defined in opposition. It was anti-rock, for starters. It was exceedingly anti-hippie and anti-disco too. It wasn't yet cool. In 1977 no one knew what it meant to be a punk yet, though the short dyed hair, chains, safety pins, and shredded clothing were catching on. It was a moment that belonged to outsiders; but by the early 1980s when California punk had become hardcore, and hardcore was dominated by macho L.A. bands like Agent Orange and Black Flag, it was all about insiders, mostly male insiders. What began as the slam dancing of geeks and girls turned into the mosh pit that only the most rugged could safely venture into. "Different like everybody else," was my epithet for a lot of it, and I moved on. But there was a glorious moment when no one knew what was going on, and what was happening seemed utterly new. A revolution opens up possibilities and dismantles existing authority and is usually followed up by the assembling of new authority. Punk rock followed this mode. Maybe the 1960s did too, with the wave of authoritarian cults that followed.

Punk was in some ways a retro movement. We wore clothes from the 1950s—tight clothes, narrow-legged jeans, motorcycle jackets, slicked-back hair, eyeliner, spike heels (in contrast to the platform shoes that were everywhere then)—and went for an aesthetic of the lean, the sharp, the spare, the straight, the antithesis of all the fuzzy floral flowing abundance around us, as though we wanted to go back twenty years and then take the other fork in the road, the one that didn't lead to hippies and long drum solos and stadium rock and all the fuzzy, fake, feel-good sentiment of the

1970s. We wore a lot of black back when no one else did, unless you were an old Catholic widow or a Swedish film director. Death was everywhere: in high art, like Linda Montano's 1977 piece, *Mitchell's Death*, for her late husband; in pop culture, like Bruce Conner's photographs of De Detroit of UXA wrapped up like a mummy at the Mab, mourning the drug-overdose death of her boyfriend; and in the news of assassinations, murders, and massacres.

It was an era when cities themselves were dying (a famous *New York Post* headline of 1975 read, "Ford to NY: Drop Dead"), or rather, the old industrial cities and their blue-collar jobs were vanishing, crime was spiking, and a new kind of bland white-collar metropolis was being born in the ruins. Deindustrialization and the ruinous, partly abandoned cities were the landscape of punk.

Punks tried out wearing trash bags tailored with safety pins. And the hair—the aesthetic was with Huysmans and against nature. It was amusing in later years to see young punks try hard to be nonchalant while sporting twelve-inch-high mohawks in five different colors. They had dyed, shaved, and put powerful fixatives in their hair—some used actual glue—and then pretended they couldn't be bothered with their appearance. Against nature—nature had become the moral standard of the previous generation, which went back to the earth, went braless, went for all that Indian cotton and faded embroidered organic-looking stuff. We liked plastic. Or rather, plastic expressed us, and we didn't necessarily like it or ourselves. If the hippies had had insincere naturalness—all those neck rubs and ethnic appropriations—we had earnest artifice. Think of it as clippers shearing away all the luxuriant fringes and foliage, the occluding moss and dangling tendrils of the post-hippie aesthetic. Style was a statement of ideology as well as aesthetics; punk was profoundly reactive, and the failures and excesses of the post-hippie era gave us plenty to react against.

If the 1960s and early 1970s had been about the removal of barriers—around segregated institutions, around activities like sex, and around emotions—the late 1970s were the reckoning. What had been let loose was not all peace, love, and happiness (which, incidentally, became the charming name of a 1980s Bay Area punk band, better known as PLH).

A cascade of angst, fury, and violence had been let loose. "Ask not what you can do for your country," shouted Penelope Houston of the Avengers, one of San Francisco's first punk bands, "but what your country's been doing to you." Looking back thirty years later, I see how much punk was of its time as well as against it. After all, violence and negativity were all around us, and the task was to name it and then maybe tame it. And it did get tamed, one way and another. Some punk turned into hardcore; some punks turned into the activists that made the overlooked 1980s a radical decade to rival the 1960s (and improve upon it, a lot, when it came to internal politics).

DEVOLUTION

Punk rock was born in the ruins, the ruins of industrial America, but also the ruins of the utopian hubris of the 1960s, which was self-destructing pretty spectacularly then. Synanon, for example, had started in Southern California in the late 1950s as a drug rehabilitation program. Rather than cycle people through, however, it acquired members and kept them. Members played "the game," in which people confronted each other about their weaknesses and told each other harsh truths or just nasty opinions. Perhaps that was the origin of the counterculture notion that all truth was a gift, that to say even the ugliest thing was to be honest, a virtue aligned with naturalness and authenticity. (I just want to share with you that your body is really repulsive to me; I hope you're grateful I'm so honest.) By the 1970s, Synanon had become a cult.

In 1976, cult leader Chuck Dederich decided that all men in Synanon should have vasectomies; female members were, according to some reports, coerced to have abortions. In 1977 the vasectomies became mandatory for all men, except for Dederich, and hundreds underwent the procedure. Violence was already institutionalized there. For example, the minors the state sent them to reform were placed in "punk squads" and beaten for infractions. (The word *punk* originally meant either a sort of jailhouse concubine or a juvenile delinquent; Synanon was not reflecting the contemporary music scene.) An arsenal built up. Perhaps Synanon's most durable legacy is all the brutal boot camps for reforming or subduing teenagers around the country, along with Dederich's slogan: "Today is the first day of the rest of your life." The leader of what had begun as a drug rehab program began drinking, and things got crazier.

Richard Nixon's paranoia was legendary, but it was everywhere in the 1970s. Dederich said:

> Our religious posture is: Don't mess with us—you can get killed dead, literally dead. We will make the rules. I see nothing frightening about it. . . . I am quite willing to break some lawyer's legs and next break his wife's legs and threaten to cut their child's arm off. That is the end of that lawyer. That is a very satisfactory, humane way of transmitting information. . . . I really do want an ear in a glass of alcohol on my desk.

People who left the cult were sometimes beaten up. One came home to find his dog had been hung. Lawyer Paul Morantz had helped some members leave and get their children out, a task he knew was so dangerous he asked the state attorney general for protection. When he came home from that meeting, he reached into the mailbox attached to his front door and was bitten by a rattlesnake that had had its rattles removed. It took eighteen vials of antivenom to save his life.

That rattlesnake in the mailbox—is that what the 1960s had become? What had begun as one of a host of idealistic and innovative projects during the previous era had gone off the deep end. Nature, which was supposed to be the great touchstone ideal, had been turned into a particularly malicious weapon against a threat to the absolutist power of this tiny kingdom. Authoritarian leaders and strange cults proliferated. "Only the dregs of the counterculture movement—the hangers-on, the junkies, the derelicts, the freaks, and the weirdos—were anywhere in evidence," Patty Hearst said of Berkeley in the early 1970s, when she was a college student there, just before she was kidnapped by the Symbionese Liberation Army.

The violent extremism and conspiracy theories that have been the property of the American right since the 1990s belonged to the left in that long-ago era.

Mark Rudd, in his memoir of being a member of the Weathermen and then a fugitive from 1970 to 1977, writes,

Seeking to emulate the revolutionaries we admired in Cuba, China, and especially Vietnam, we convinced ourselves that violence would be successful in this country. We saw the black-power movement, led by the Panthers, already fighting a revolutionary war from within the United States. In our heroic fantasy, eventually the military would disintegrate internally and the revolutionary army—led by us, of course—would be built from its defectors. But as I postured and gave speeches on the necessity for violence, I was terrified.

Synanon had the Game; the Weathermen adapted the Chinese Communist criticism/self-criticism model into collective attacks on individuals for being bourgeois or counterrevolutionary or a host of other sins: it was revolution as sibling rivalry and peer pressure. The Peoples Temple also included public interrogations and confessions that often ended, by the mid-1970s, with beatings and humiliation. Some of the Weather Underground supported the Symbionese Liberation Army; Rudd considered the SLA "true terrorists without any limits or any sense. They claimed they were acting for the liberation of black people, but actions such as the assassination of Marcus Foster, the first black Oakland school superintendent, or their spraying with bullets a bank lobby filled with customers could only be interpreted as terroristic." These small groups were to real revolutions what air guitar is to music; they imitated some of the form and never got near the content. They had weapons, titles, rhetoric, and delusions, but not much else.

When the SLA kidnapped newspaper heiress Hearst, she was first of all an audience for their delusions of grandiosity—the flipside of paranoia. Donald DeFreeze, aka "General Field Marshal Cinque Mtume," the ex-convict African-American leader of the cult, described to his captive a powerful nationwide army he headed. It was only months later that Hearst was told that the SLA was made up merely of the handful of delusionaries camped out with her in the same small fetid apartment. The SLA's hostage gave them colossal media coverage, and they gloried in it. "I was their passport to fame and popularity," Hearst noted in her memoir.

"Death to the fascist insect that preys upon the life of the people" was the tagline in the SLA's communiqués. The SLA used a communal toothbrush, because private property was bourgeois. While Hearst lived blindfolded in a closet, they fed her on mung beans and rice—the food of the poor, she was told—and peppermint tea, which was most certainly the drink of hippies. Once she joined, she was told that to meet each others' sexual needs was "comradely," and so a bunch of young women who thought of themselves as feminist made themselves available on demand to the men in the group. Hearst didn't get much sympathy afterward.

On the A side of her first recording in 1974, underwritten by Robert Mapplethorpe's patron/lover Sam Wagstaff, protopunk New Yorker Patti Smith remade the old standard "Hey Joe"—the one that goes "Hey Joe, where you goin' with that gun in your hand." In a spoken-word piece tagged on, she said, "Patty Hearst, you're standing there in front of the Symbionese Liberation Army flag with your legs spread I was wondering will you get it every night from a black revolutionary man and his women."

THE ARC OF JUSTICE

Even failure has interesting consequences. The first ransom demand the SLA had made was that the Hearsts feed the poor. Their original demands would have cost $400 million, which was out of reach, even for a major newspaper magnate. The Black Panthers—despised by the SLA in that golden age of infighting—had run little-remembered, extremely effective programs to feed Oakland kids for a few years. The food program set up by the coerced Randolph Hearst was run out of the old Del Monte building in China Basin, in San Francisco's industrial east.

Calvin Welch, who had already been a housing activist in San Francisco for a long time, writes of the far-reaching consequences of that program. Hearst's father tried just dumping groceries: "It was a disorganized disaster. Scores of people were injured as panicked workers threw boxes of food off moving trucks as huge crowds of people unexpectedly showed up for the food. The size of the crowds shocked the media and so upset Gov. Ronald Reagan that he stated, 'It's just too bad we can't have an epidemic of botulism.'"

The SLA responded by demanding that food distribution be managed by a community organization named the Western Addition Project Area Committee. WAPAC had ties both to Jim Jones's Peoples Temple and to the Black Liberation Army. According to one biographer of Jones, one of the BLA/Peoples Temple leaders involved in WAPAC had helped torture to death a member of the Panthers—which is to say that it was all tangled up in the mess that was the 1970s. Nevertheless, the Western Addition group was heading back into useful community politics. The sheer modesty and practicality of WAPAC's endeavors forms an instructive contrast with the SLA. The course of action didn't lead to revolution as it was imagined then, but it did lay the groundwork for decades of radical change.

First they handed out more than 100,000 bags of groceries at sixteen locations in four Bay Area counties. The program ran efficiently, and the Community Coalition morphed into the Coalition to Register 100,000 Voters, and those voters elected progressive Mayor George Moscone and helped return the city to district elections (whereby neighborhoods would elect their own representatives rather than vote in citywide races for supervisors; this was the shift that made Harvey Milk's 1977 victory possible.) Welch writes of this organizing coalition:

> Within two years, some had begun the creation of community-based non-profit housing development corporations, building affordable housing for many of the people in those long lines seeking free food. Others went on to transform the urban environmental movement in San Francisco, redirecting it toward limiting high-rise development and demanding developer payments for child care and public transit. The "neighborhood movement" that dominated the political agenda of San Francisco through the early 1990s was born during those two insane months in 1974.

"The arc of the moral universe is long but it bends toward justice," Martin Luther King had said in 1963, and what began as the madness of the SLA ended with the civil, public, inclusive campaign of Harvey Milk (who was opposed by some in the Castro District as a compromiser, as one who would turn the queer sexual revolution into mere reform). Milk was both a visionary and a moderate, one who defended small businesses and cared about city policy, and who saw that what seemed like an outrageous agenda—the acceptance of gays and lesbians within the mainstream—would open the door for their ordinariness. The tape he made to be played in case of his assassination was the opposite of paranoid: it was practical, naming his preferred successors, asking that there be no violence, and ending with "You gotta give 'em hope."

NO MORE HEROES

A few other things that mattered began the year Milk was elected. The Abalone Alliance, whose name was inspired by New England's antinuclear Clamshell Alliance, began protesting Diablo Canyon Power Plant on the central California coast. At the August 7, 1977, demonstration against the poorly designed nuclear reactor, 1,500 people showed up; a year later 5,000 people showed up. By 1981, there was a large and effective antinuclear movement—focused then on the dangers of nuclear power (confirmed by another 1970s disaster, the Three Mile Island nuclear power plant near-meltdown in 1979).

This movement was organized by anarchist means—without hierarchy or authority—with consensus-based decision-making. Radicals were learning to self-govern without charismatic leaders or coercion, in a shift initiated in large part by feminists. Anarchy became the politics of punk, and punk became the gateway through which a generation decided to embrace anarchism. Abalone Alliance and the activism that came after was committed to nonviolence and worked openly, which undid much of the paranoia of the 1970s. This non-authoritarian and largely nonviolent means of organizing is still central to radical movements everywhere—including Britain, Eastern Europe, India, and Argentina—that have done much to change the world in the last few decades, picking up from the 1960s civil rights movement, the half of that decade that actually worked well.

Those smitten with the conventional notion of revolution had hung onto the notion of vanguards. They believed in the idea that the few would lead the many; thus a lot of college students without a clue of how to get along with the proletariat fantasized that they would bring it into armed revolt. The idea of vanguards—or avant-gardes—had been important in the art world too. A military term presuming linear narrative, the phrase suggests humanity as an army of sorts that someone was leading forward.

If the 1970s accomplished anything, it was the realization that we actually wanted to go in a lot of different directions, not one. We never had been anything as neatly assembled and homogenized as an army, and we shouldn't trust leaders. This meant, for art and for revolution, no more avant-gardes, though there might be prophetic and influential elements in both culture and politics. In 1977, the Stranglers released what might be the most anthemic of punk songs, "No More Heroes." Heroes were leaders; leaders begot followers; following was demonstrated to be literally fatal and otherwise troublesome in that era in which so many followed their leaders down strange and malevolent paths.

To go to or stay in California had always meant to choose to be outside the mainstream, the orthodoxy, to choose other influences and a less Eurocentric point of view. This could mean cults, but it more often meant a little useful distance, literally and otherwise, from the status quo at the center of cultural power. You were further from the culture police—that's why a painter like David Park could drive all his abstract expressionist paintings to the dump in 1949 and begin to paint in the style that would be called Bay Area Figurative. Artists such as Bruce Conner and Jess made a conscious choice to stay outside the market and the mainstream by settling in California and abandoning the reigning aesthetics.

In the 1970s, the art world would go "pluralist," which means only that New York abandoned its dominant narrative of an avant-garde and admitted to the variety of artists and directions that had always been there. While race was talked about by the New York–based national media as though it were a black/white division well into the 1990s, Californians had, since the Gold Rush, inhabited a region where indigenous, Asian, and Latino presences mattered. To be in California was to braid together various possibilities and to unravel the main thread. Further away from Europe and the notion of an elite white lineage, those under the big black sun of the Golden State were closer to all sorts of fecund things—Asian, Latin, and indigenous traditions; esoteric subcultures and the burgeoning countercultures of Buddhists, bikers, communes, foodies, druggies, Diggers, and more—as well as to the vastness of deserts and mountains, the untamed landscape.

More of what began as 1960s revolution became part of everyday life. Communes mostly failed, but organic farming, food co-ops, and attention to food as politics, health, and pleasure spread. Arenas like health care were democratized (a comment that only makes sense to those who know that before feminists took on the medical establishment in the 1970s, doctors were autocratic figures who made decisions for you, including whether you should know your diagnosis and prognosis). Queer people advanced astonishingly in both legal standing and cultural acceptance. The conservative movement has made its own inroads, particularly in the economic organization of the country, but the genies of reproductive rights, women's rights, queer rights, and the rights of people of color are not going back into any bottle. The SLA's food program failed; Milk was assassinated; many visible projects failed; many subterranean forces moved onward; everything changed. In the 1970s, many things blew up spectacularly (and sometimes literally), but a lot of seeds were quietly planted.

"You can go your own way," sang L.A.-based British émigré band Fleetwood Mac in 1977, the year that the Avengers sang an ironic "We Are the One." Music was unraveling into several strands that year when hip-hop was being born in the Bronx. In his 1977 hit "Disco Heat," San Francisco queer black disco king Sylvester sang, "Dancing's total freedom / Be yourself and choose your feeling." The 1970s were as generative as they were terrible.

2010

CONCRETE IN PARADISE

Some Pictures of Coastal California

Et in Arcadia Ego, says the famous inscription on the tomb in Nicolas Poussin's paintings of that title. Even in Paradise there am I. He twice painted a group of shepherds and a woman who looks like a goddess standing around a tomb in a pastoral setting, as though he were wrestling with the meanings himself. The phrase was sometimes thought to be spoken by death itself: even in Arcadia death is present. Other interpretations suggest that it is instead spoken by the dead shepherd whose tomb is being inspected. Whether the text refers to death itself or to one dead friend, the tomb is two kinds of intrusion into the landscape.

One, often remarked on, is mortality in a beautiful landscape. But *growing* is always also dying, even in Arcadia, even in springtime, where the new grass pushes through the old, where the trees and flowers feed on the soil made out of life and digested deaths, where mortality itself, of lambs and shepherds alike, gives it the poignancy that heaven lacks. And Poussin's Arcadia is a little rough and rustic, not tender shoots, but lean trees and, in the distance, sharp crags. What isn't remarked on often is the architectural intrusion of the big, heavy, rectilinear stone monument in the landscape, a trace of industry, of a labor far harder than herding, of altering the material world, of making stone itself work for men and their intentions, and of making something permanent in a landscape of change.

We have our own tombs throughout the coastal San Francisco Bay Area, each of which could readily be inscribed *et in Arcadia ego*. Even in the paradises I have hiked so often, there is, along with the smell of coastal sage and the sea shining silver or green or gray to the horizon or not shining at all on foggy days, death, in the form of deer carcasses, the pellets of coyote, and fox spoor in which the fur of mice and rabbits is compressed, squashed salamanders, and countless vultures soaring and swinging around the hills on the lookout for carrion. And every spring's green grass turns gold and then gray. The ordinary realm of natural death is present one way or another in every landscape. But there is also the violent death of war, in thought if not in deed, commemorated in the seventy or so bunker complexes whose blunt concrete forms are an apt modern echo of that shepherd's tomb.

There they are, along the beaches, roads, and the trails of this superlatively beautiful landscape, to be stumbled upon by hikers and day-trippers, who will stop for a moment like Poussin's shepherds to contemplate monuments and death. The bunkers were becoming outdated as they were being built, and so they were becoming monuments to a particular imagination of danger and fear even as they were erected. And in a way, they are honorable monuments to the idea that wars would involve direct confrontation and that the United States would face the dangers it imposed on other nations. Soldiers sat in them waiting for ships to appear on the horizon and waiting to receive orders to fire on those ships and to be fired upon. It has not turned out that way, however.

"We are here because wars are now fought in outer space," said Headlands Center for the Arts director Jennifer Dowley in the 1980s, when the center was still a fresh arrival in what was a fairly new national park, the Golden Gate National Recreation Area (GGNRA), and the Star Wars missile defense system was being actively pursued not far away, at Lawrence Livermore National Laboratory. The park is unusual because it's a large amount of open space—almost 75,000 acres—in one of the major metropolitan areas in the country. It's also unusual because its focus is neither historical nor natural but an uneasy melding of the two. The history is rarely examined, though its evidence is everywhere in the chunks of concrete embedded throughout the landscape of the park. These are the dozens of bunkers and related structures, crumbling souvenirs of the wars that never were, or that were elsewhere. And yet, war is here in a thousand ways. Even in the headlands there is war.

Dowley spoke in Building 944, a spacious military barracks built in 1907, when the Headlands was an extension of the Pacific headquarters of the U.S. Army across the Golden Gate at San Francisco's Presidio and Fort Mason. From those headquarters U.S. military action was directed, from the Indian Wars to the Korean and Vietnam Wars; during the Second World War alone, more than a million soldiers were said to have embarked from Fort Mason for the Pacific theater of war. The barracks and the other handsome buildings arrayed in a horseshoe tucked into a valley in the Headlands were used for housing and training soldiers who'd be deployed elsewhere. The Bay Area has always been militarized, always involved with wars, though the actual wars have been, since the 1860s, fought elsewhere.

If you walk down Building 944's worn, handsome wooden staircase and out the big doors and head west, past the old bowling alley and chapel, the eucalyptuses and the Monterey cypresses, you come to the Nike missile launch site tucked into a depression that the road curves around. It was designed to fire nuclear-tipped weapons at incoming missiles, but by that time the targets were imagined as incoming intercontinental ballistic missiles fired from overseas. In the 1950s the threat was thought to be Russia, but by the late 1960s the nuclear war fantasies that generated the preventative architecture and weapons included China, and the idea that a missile could take out a missile was itself something of a fantasy. There was no particular reason to situate missile depots directly on the coast. The Marin County Planning Department put together a staff report in 1969 (probably written by my father) that wondered "whether the probable risk of accident isn't greater than the probable risk from the kind of attack these missiles are supposed to defend against." Fortunately, neither accident nor attack ever came before the warheads were taken away. What remains are industrial structures surrounded by cyclone fencing.

So ignore the Nike facility and keep walking. You can take the narrow, uneven trail that takes you through tall green banks of willows, coyote bush, brambles, and poison oak, on past the lagoon that the pelicans, ducks, seagulls and other birds frequent, to the sand of Rodeo Beach, the cove beyond the lagoon, and between two high shoulders of coastline. If you go left, or south, you'll come to the bunkers. If you go north, you'll pass the many buildings of Fort Cronkhite and arrive at the old road that leads to more bunkers. They are embedded in the landscape like shrapnel or buckshot in a body, the ruins of old fears and old versions of war, the architecture of a violence that was first of all a violence against the earth, with concrete poured dozens of feet deep into slopes that were also home to rare species and prone to erosion when disrupted.

These welts of concrete have shifted, cracked, crumbled, and in some cases slid down eroded hillsides into the surf, but the majority of them are still in place. If you imagine them as an assault on the earth, then the earth has fought back, with foliage that has half-hidden and choked some of them, with the forces of water and temperature that forced cracks in the massive structures, with erosion that has dislodged and tilted some at crazy angles. But they have a harsh beauty of their own, in the simple geometry of the domes and semicircular walls and cylindrical pits of the gun emplacements, in the steps that take you up to the roofs of some of the structures, and particularly in the long tunnels that frame views of land, sea, and sky.

They have the shapes of art-school exercises in drawing cubes, spheres, cones, and cylinders with shading, and they are the color of old pencil sketches. Poussin with his passion for simple monumental form would have loved them, though he would have inscribed them all "et in Arcadia ego" lest the hasty hiker miss the point. And they have the seduction of all ruins, the seduction of the past, of lost history, of irrecoverable time, of the sense that something happened here and then ceased. In Poussin's landscape it's the tomb, not the trees, that invites contemplation. It's only when you imagine the dreary discomfort of soldiers stationed in them, the actual big guns that pointed toward the bay, and what a war might have looked like on these shores, whether like the bombardment of Fort Sumner at the beginning of the Civil War or the Normandy Invasion toward the end of the Second World War, that the romance diminishes. Or does it?

As Dowley put it, wars are now fought in outer space. A nation under attack is usually attacked inside its national borders. Troops may surge across a border, as they did at the outset of both of the Bush wars on Iraq— across their border, not ours—but both of those were accompanied by the aerial bombardment that goes far inside the country. And aerial bombardment is often directed at civilians. Thus war from Mussolini's bombing of North Africa and the Fascist bombing of Guernica became profoundly asymmetrical. The old idea of a confrontation between two sides is blown away; in its place is an attacker who cannot be attacked directly, though the blows can be parried.

Missiles and more monstrous new inventions like pilotless drones are even directed from afar, often from within the attacking nation. Afghanistan cannot fire missiles back at the headquarters of the drone operators near Las Vegas, Nevada, though in the all-out nuclear wars imagined during the Cold War era, both the United States and the USSR would send nuclear bombs to strategic targets, military and civilian, within the other nation's boundaries while trying to intercept the incoming missiles. The heroic idea of combat, of bodily skill and equal engagement, of Achilles or Roland or even Wellington and Grant facing risk with physical courage, has some relevance to the ground troops in some places, but nothing to do with the death rained from the skies by these men whose daily lives more resemble those of video gamers. The bunkers are, among other things, an old daydream of an enemy you would face, one who could only hurt you by confronting you, by showing up.

They were built to defend us from wars that never quite arrived on these shores. Central California has been attacked by foreigners a few times, starting with invading Spanish and Mexican attacks on the Native peoples, which consisted largely of skirmishes and one-sided brutalities. (The big campaigns against the Native Californians were elsewhere and later, run by Yankees in events such as the Modoc War and the Bloody Island Massacre.) The indigenous peoples responded, with attacks on the Missions, raids on ranchos, and other acts of self-defense and survival, including an incursion on Mission San Rafael. Events resembling European war with all its pageantry and weaponry came later, when the Spanish-speaking nominal citizens of Mexico had become part of the population to be invaded and displaced.

Commodore Thomas ap Catesby Jones's fleet arrived in Monterey—then the capital of the Mexican province—on October 19, 1842. He demanded surrender and got it without firing a shot. Perhaps the fearsome arsenal of the five ships with a total of 116 big guns convinced the small

Californiano population that resistance would be unpleasant. The next day 150 Marines marched up the hill to the fort, while the bands played "Yankee Doodle." The invasion was premature and based on rumors of British competition for the northernmost portion of Mexico. A couple of days later, Jones withdrew his proclamation and acknowledged Mexican sovereignty before the soldiers dispatched from Los Angeles could make much progress up the coast.

Less than four years later, on June 16, 1846, the Bear Flag Revolt began inland with the attack on Sonoma and the raising of a primitive version of what would become the California state flag. A few weeks into the skirmishes by invading Yankees against resident Mexicans, Army Captain John C. Frémont—one of the few government men involved in the revolt—took twelve men with him on an American ship, the *Moscow*, that sailed south in the Bay to the Presidio of San Francisco. It had been abandoned, and there was no conflict, though there were some squabbles when they marched onward to the hamlet of Yerba Buena and took a few captives. There were larger battles further south as the revolt merged with the war on Mexico, but the Bay Area remained unscathed by major conflict. The newly American region was prepared for defense against coastal attack in the 1850s and 1860s, but the Civil War led to no violence—beyond duels such as the Broderick-Terry duel of 1859—in the locale. The fortifications then and a century later were built for conflicts that never arrived. They are the architecture of grim anticipation, of imagination of things to come that never came.

During the Second World War, there were some grounds to fear Japanese attack. In the wake of the 1941 attack on Pearl Harbor, Hawaii, seven enemy submarines patrolled the Pacific Coast, but Japan decided against a mainland attack for fear of reprisals. A false alert the following May caused the USS *Colorado* and the USS *Maryland* to sail out from the Golden Gate to defend the coast from attacks that never came. Late in the war, a Japanese fire balloon—a kind of incendiary device that floated across the Pacific—was shot down by a Lockheed P-38 Lightning fighter plane near Santa Rosa with no major damage reported. (Others landed in various places in the American West, and a few inflicted actual damage and a total of six deaths—of a pregnant woman with her five children, out on a picnic: *et in arcadia*.) War was in the skies, and coastal fortifications were anachronistic.

But the Lockheed P-38 Lightning fighter was made by Lockheed when it was based in Burbank on the fringes of Los Angeles, back when Los Angeles was producing the airplanes to fight the war and the Bay Area was turning out a warship a day in its furiously productive shipyards. If we think of war as combat and casualties, then it has with small exceptions, such as the Ohlone and Miwok resistance to the missions and the land grabs, been fought elsewhere. But if we think of it as a mind-set, an economy, a way of life—a lot of things that add up to a system—then two things become as evident as a thirty-foot-thick chunk of concrete embedded amid the sticky monkey flower and coast sage of the Headlands.

One is that the Bay Area is entrenched in and crucial to this system, with UC Berkeley running the nation's nuclear weapons programs since their inception, with defense contractors such as Lockheed Martin (makers, once upon a time, of the Nike missile) clustered in Silicon Valley, with the ring of old bases around the Bay—Mare Island, Hunter's Point, Alameda, Treasure Island, Hamilton, and the Presidio. The other is that this system is mad. Its madness was perhaps most perfectly manifested in the soldiers or national guardsmen in camouflage who patrolled the Golden Gate Bridge at one phase of the GWOT, the Global War on Terror, a war that in its very name declared hostility not to a group or a nation but to an emotion while seeking—with, for example, heavily armed men in civilian spaces such as Penn Station or the Golden Gate Bridge—to induce that very emotion in the public. That their desert camouflage only made them stand out and that the threats to the bridge were sketchy and remote, while the men with semiautomatic weapons were evident and unnerving, articulates something about war as a state of being. The enemy may be remote, invisible, or even conceptual, but we ourselves as a society devoted to war see ourselves in a thousand mirrors, of which the bunkers are one.

The bunkers were both prophylactics against physical damage by an alien military and part of the damage that is the mind-set of war, the mind-set that induces fear and suspicion, that countenances sacrifices, destructions, and the willingness to engage in acts of violence, that damages a society before the enemy ever touches it. The military left radioactive waste behind at Hunter's Point Naval Shipyards; dozens of rusting, leaking warships in the Mothball Fleet near Benicia; PCBs at 100,000 times the acceptable level, along with dioxins and other chemicals on Treasure Island; and more. The Headlands and much of the rest of the GGNRA got off lightly, larded only with cement and rust, not with chemicals and radiation. What all these areas have in common is their status as monuments to public expenditure by those in charge of protecting us. There is, for example, the *Sea Shadow*, a stealth ship built at extraordinary expense in the 1980s and then abandoned without ever being used or even useful. The prototype is in the Mothball Fleet. It is a corollary to the lack of money for libraries and schools in towns like Richmond, whose African-American population mostly arrived in World War II for shipyard jobs and stayed even when the economy withered, despite the growth of the Chevron refineries there that have been refining Iraqi crude since early in the war there. Chevron, whose board member Condoleezza Rice became our secretary of state and led us into that war, Rice, who is back at Stanford, Stanford that helped generate Silicon Valley, Silicon Valley that has done so much to develop the new technologies of war. War is everywhere for those who have eyes to see, but in some places it's hard to miss.

It is good that the bunkers are in the beautiful open space of the coast and good that one of the region's native sons, Alex Fradkin, has photographed them so eloquently. They should be there; we should pause amid the myriad pleasures that this Mediterranean climate and protected landscape afford to contemplate the presence of death and our own implication in the business. Until something profound changes in the United States, war will never be far away, and even on the most paradisical meander we do well to pause and remember this.

2011

CLIMATE CHANGE IS VIOLENCE

If you're poor, the only way you're likely to injure someone is the old traditional way: artisanal violence, we could call it—by hands, by knife, by club, or maybe modern hands-on violence, by gun or by car.

But if you're tremendously wealthy, you can practice industrial-scale violence without any manual labor on your own part. You can, say, build a sweatshop factory that will collapse in Bangladesh and kill more people than any hands-on mass murderer ever did, or you can calculate risk and benefit about putting poisons or unsafe machines into the world, as manufacturers do every day. If you're the leader of a country, you can declare war and kill by the hundreds of thousands or millions. And the nuclear superpowers—the United States and Russia—still hold the option of destroying quite a lot of life on Earth.

So do the carbon barons. But when we talk about violence, we almost always talk about violence from below, not above.

Or so I thought when I received a press release from a climate group announcing that "scientists say there is a direct link between changing climate and an increase in violence." What the scientists actually said, in a not-so-newsworthy article in *Nature* a few years ago, is that there is higher conflict in the tropics in El Niño years and that perhaps this will scale up to make our age of climate change also an era of civil and international conflict.

The message is that ordinary people will behave badly in an era of intensified climate change. All this makes sense, unless you go back to the premise and note that climate change is itself violence. Extreme, horrific, long-term, widespread violence.

Climate change is anthropogenic—caused by human beings, some much more than others. We know the consequences of that change: the acidification of oceans and decline of many species in them, the slow disappearance of island nations such as the Maldives, increased flooding, drought, crop failure leading to food-price increases and famine, increasingly turbulent weather. (Think Hurricane Sandy and the recent typhoon in the Philippines and heat waves that kill elderly people by the tens of thousands.)

Climate change is violence.

So if we want to talk about violence and climate change, then let's talk about climate change as violence. Rather than worrying about whether ordinary human beings will react turbulently to the destruction of the very means of their survival, let's worry about that destruction—and their survival. Of course, water failure, crop failure, flooding, and more will lead to mass migration and climate refugees—they already have—and this will lead to conflict. Those conflicts are being set in motion now.

You can regard the Arab Spring, in part, as a climate conflict: the increase in wheat prices was one of the triggers for that series of revolts that changed the face of northernmost Africa and the Middle East. On the one hand, you can say, how nice if those people had not been hungry in the first place. On the other, how can you not say, how great is it that those people stood up against being deprived of sustenance and hope? And then you have to look at the systems that created that hunger—the enormous economic inequalities in places such as Egypt and the brutality used to keep down the people at the lower levels of the social system, as well as the weather.

People revolt when their lives are unbearable. Sometimes material reality creates that unbearableness: droughts, plagues, storms, floods. But food and medical care, health and well-being, access to housing and education—these things are also governed by economic means and government policy. That's what the revolt called Occupy Wall Street was against.

Climate change will increase hunger as food prices rise and food production falters, but we already have widespread hunger on Earth, and much of it is due not to the failures of nature and farmers, but to systems of distribution. Almost 16 million children in the United States now live with hunger, according to the U.S. Department of Agriculture, and that is not because the vast, agriculturally rich United States cannot produce enough to feed all of us. We are a country whose distribution system is itself a kind of violence.

Climate change is not suddenly bringing about an era of equitable distribution. I suspect people will be revolting in the coming future against what they revolted against in the past: the injustices of the system. They should revolt, and we should be glad they do, if not so glad that they need to. (Though one can hope they'll recognize that violence is not necessarily where their power lies.) One of the events prompting the French Revolution was the failure of the 1788 wheat crop, which made bread prices skyrocket and the poor go hungry. The insurance against such events is often thought to be more authoritarianism and more threats against the poor, but that's only an attempt to keep a lid on what's boiling over; the other way to go is to turn down the heat.

The same week during which I received that ill-thought-out press release about climate and violence, Exxon Mobil Corporation issued a policy report. It makes for boring reading, unless you can make the dry language of business into pictures of the consequences of those acts undertaken for profit. Exxon says, "We are confident that none of our hydrocarbon reserves are now or will become 'stranded.' We believe producing these assets is essential to meeting growing energy demand worldwide."

Stranded assets that mean carbon assets—coal, oil, gas still underground—would become worthless if we decided they could not be extracted and burned in the near future. Because scientists say that we need to leave most of the world's known carbon reserves in the ground if we are to go for the milder rather than the more extreme versions of climate change. Under the milder version, countless more people, species, and places will survive. In the best-case scenario, we damage the Earth less. We are currently wrangling about how much to devastate the Earth.

In every arena, we need to look at industrial-scale and systemic violence, not just the hands-on violence of the less powerful. When it comes to climate change, this is particularly true. Exxon has decided to bet that we can't make the corporation keep its reserves in the ground, and the company is reassuring its investors that it will continue to profit off the rapid, violent, and intentional destruction of the Earth.

That's a tired phrase, the destruction of the Earth, but translate it into the face of a starving child and a barren field—and then multiply that a few million times. Or just picture the tiny bivalves: scallops, oysters, Arctic sea snails that can't form shells in acidifying oceans right now. Or another superstorm tearing apart another city. Climate change is global-scale violence against places and species, as well as against human beings. Once we call it by name, we can start having a real conversation about our priorities and values. Because the revolt against brutality begins with a revolt against the language that hides that brutality.

2014

DRY LANDS

The Colorado River and Hydrological Madness of the West

The supply of stories has perhaps been the American West's only reliable bounty. The difficult thing has been finding people to notice them, let alone tell them well. The Indian wars, still unfinished as tribes continue to struggle for rights, territory, and cultural survival; the resource rushes, the Gold Rush in particular, which turned San Francisco into a cosmopolitan city standing alone in the wilderness; the once astonishingly abundant salmon runs that sustained soil and trees, as well as birds, bears, and humans; the timber wars; the rangeland wars; the radical labor and environmental movements; the attitudes people adopted toward a harsh, unfamiliar, often-sublime landscape; the evolution of European cultures in a non-European terrain; and the arrival of Asian and Latin American immigrants to shape a hybrid culture: all these have had their occasional historians, though most Americans were raised to believe that history happened somewhere else. The San Francisco Public Library has an overflowing case of books on the East's Civil War, but only a handful on the war that transferred a million square miles or so of Mexico to the United States, including California and most of what we now call the West.

The central thread in this story of the West is the story of the Colorado River and the attempts to determine what dreams it licenses and which must be left unwatered as it snakes through much of the major nonfiction of the West. The river begins in Colorado with tributaries reaching up into Wyoming, and they gather force and volume as they rush through the magnificent canyons they carved in Utah and Arizona, through Nevada's southern tip and down California's backside to—well, thanks to Yankee rapacity, the river doesn't usually reach the Gulf of California or water much of Mexico anymore. It's the story of the intermountain West: could it be domesticated for agriculture and settlement, or would its inhabitants become feral, nomadic peoples scattered lightly in a belt of un-European terrain that would divide the West Coast from the sedentary, verdant East? It's the story of the Hoover Dam and the rise of the extraordinary hydraulic engineering that since the 1920s has come to alter the world from Iceland to India, largely for the worse. Of the rise of industrial tourism as the Grand Canyon became part of the railroad-based restaurant and hotel empire of Fred Harvey. Of the rise of the modern environmental movement: the evolution of ideas about landscape, aesthetics, the public good, and the battles between a boomtown, resource-rush mentality and a minority more interested in long-term planning.

And it's the story of the rise of the big cities of the Southwest, notably Phoenix and Las Vegas, whose optimism is inscribed in their names (the immortal bird whose name will surely become ironic during the course of this century and the *vegas*, or meadows, watered by an aquifer that Vegas sucked dry early in its short history). And of the City of Angels, whose situation is not quite as precarious as that of the desert towns, but whose thirst has long outstripped its regional resources and reached the Colorado River, far to its east.

T. S. Eliot's Mississippi was a "strong brown god." The Colorado River is more like a ruddy writhing serpent. Or was, since the snake has now been chopped into segments by dams, notably by Glen Canyon Dam above the Grand Canyon and Hoover Dam south of Vegas, each with a gigantic reservoir backed up behind it. Even its red color, its *colorado*, has changed; the sandstone sediment settles behind Glen Canyon Dam, and what was once a hot red river emerges as a cool green one, too cool for many of its species of endangered fish. Occasionally a thunderstorm over a tributary sends down enough sediment to turn it red again for a day or two. Along the way, the river is grabbed and squeezed for water to make the cities explode in the dry lands and to allow the endless arid-land agriculture to produce iceberg lettuces and rice and alfalfa and cotton fields, though in some of those places there is hardly enough rainfall to raise an agave plant. | *61*

The water is heavily subsidized so that farmers—mostly large-scale agribusiness enterprises, not Jeffersonian yeomen—can also collect subsidies to grow stuff that would grow better in lusher places elsewhere. Eighty percent of the Colorado River's water goes to agriculture. Twenty percent of California's agricultural water goes to grow low-value alfalfa. The river, in its climate change–driven decline, will strangle all these projects and make a mockery of the two great dams and the reservoirs that were once signs of triumph over it and over nature. The reservoirs and dams are failing now, long on silt, short on water, products of the shortsightedness that has made the West a place littered with projects that seemed like a good idea at the time.

No one holds a monopoly, but Americans have proved very good at junk science. It's a specialty field, in which the claims about Iraq's weapons of mass destruction, aluminum "centrifuge" tubes and the like, are only the most widely noted. The Panglossian "rain follows the plow" was the motto used to dispatch hapless would-be farmers to the arid lands of the American West, where rainfall is inadequate to raise crops, and irrigation started as a corruption racket and ended up as an environmental disaster. Its agenda is short-term convenience. Its methodology is lies. An atmospheric scientist once told me that he had checked Edward Teller's projections of the amount of fallout that would reach Americans during the years of above-ground nuclear testing in southern Nevada. The great genius had somehow left off some zeros, reducing the impact a hundred- or a thousandfold, while other scientists created arbitrary standards of exposure safety and schoolchildren were taught to duck and cover to protect themselves from atomic blasts. Scientific facts about the environment—water flow, radioactive half-lives, principles of containment, et cetera—were jiggled until they could be used to justify the dumping of nuclear waste near the atomic test site.

Junk science might be too generous a label for the way conclusions have been reached about the water of the Colorado River—how much there is and how much and how securely it can change the arid landscape around it. The water has transformed that landscape. Without it, Arizona and southern Nevada would still be barely populated, and a lot of the agriculture in the Southwest wouldn't exist. But the supply was always precarious and overcommitted, and it is already running out. Water limitations were noticed from the beginning, when Major John Wesley Powell and his crew became the first white men to float down the Colorado. Powell's 1875 *Exploration of the Colorado River and Its Canyons*, an expansion of his magazine reports, is still in print. It is a gorgeous book about adventure, geology, anthropology, and hydrology, with illustrations carrying captions like "The Great Unconformity at the Head of the Grand Canyon" and chapters such as "From Flaming Gorge to the Gate of Lodore." But it was the sobering *A Report on the Lands of the Arid Region of the United States, with a More Detailed Account of the Lands of Utah* of 1878 that makes Powell matter even today. A Civil War veteran and government explorer, he saw that there wasn't enough water to irrigate people's visions of a big agricultural society and that the limits on water would ultimately be the limit on everything else. Ignoring Powell has been the basis of almost everything that has come since, except the literature on the river, which Powell presides over as a kind of god.

James Lawrence Powell's *Dead Pool: Lake Powell, Global Warming, and the Future of Water in the West* tells the story of the Colorado well and moves it forward to speculate on what the era of climate change will bring. He isn't optimistic—in his account, climate change is just one more factor that the engineers and hydrologists who are responsible for plotting the river's fate refuse to face. He begins with two crises at Glen Canyon Dam—one of a sudden abundance of water that nearly destroyed the dam in the 1980s, and another in 2005, when the water level fell lower than the official scientists had calculated it would ever go. (A disaster for water managers, it was a miracle for explorers, who got to see canyons and cliff faces that were thought to have been lost forever.) *Dead Pool* then doubles back to begin the story at the beginning, with Major Powell and his warnings on the finitude of the Southwest's water:

> To a man of Powell's principles and background, that his nation encouraged thousands of poor farmers to move to lands so dry that the settlers were bound to fail was a tragedy. He would spend most of the rest of his career trying to save them from that fate. . . . By March 1888 one of Powell's scientific facts was undeniable: the West had too little water to irrigate all

the land. To collect and best use what water did exist would require a system of dams and reservoirs.

Building those dams and reservoirs would, in theory, be a cooperative enterprise; in practice, it was a big-government project for the benefit of Westerners who for the most part considered themselves individualists and independents. This delusion of self-sufficiency, along with the fantasy that enough water could be found to supply the region, launched the eco-tragedy now unfolding.

Toward the end of his book, Powell points out that the U.S. Bureau of Reclamation has decided not to take climate change into account when planning water management and allocation for the twenty-first century. Instead, it has been basing its projections on what we now know was the unusually wet twentieth century. No shortage, no problems to plan for. The author points out that climate change is not something that *may happen* to the American West or that is now happening only in the Arctic. It is here, now. And at the end of *Dead Pool* he describes what a post–climate change Southwest might look like—the book's title, incidentally, is the term used to describe a reservoir when its water level drops too low to feed the intake valves for hydropower generators.

"Mistakes were made" is the locution politicians like to use, and it could be used for a lot of the plans for the Southwest, which have left follies in their wake. The Salton Sea, for example, a little west of the tail end of the Colorado, became the biggest lake in California when it was accidentally created around the time the Tulare Lake was drained into nonexistence. It was the result of an attempt early in the last century to divert a little irrigation water. The whole river raged into the new canal, ripped it into a broad channel, and for two years emptied itself into the low point that in another climatological era had been a lake and now became one again, full of the salts of the desert. Only one force in the West was mighty enough to do battle with the river: the Southern Pacific Railroad (SP), the monster corporation that dominated California politics and land for decades. It took the SP two years to stuff enough rubbish into the gap to send the river back into its usual bed. The Salton Sea is recharged by farm runoff and other filthy waters; it has become a major bird sanctuary because their old wetland habitat, the delta where the Colorado runs into the sea, has largely dried up. Most of the attempts to develop resorts around the lake have turned into ruins; the most famous site there is Salvation Mountain, a folksy one-man religious complex made of concrete poured a few bags at a time and painted with discarded house paint.

The Salton Sea is already a conundrum, a toxic bird sanctuary in a place where water doesn't belong, and the reservoir-dam systems will go the same way. But not all the strange phenomena that have arisen from the long wrestling match with the Colorado are situated near it. Take the San Francisco–based, family-owned Bechtel Corporation, which is to the United States what the Bin Laden construction firm is to Saudi Arabia—a colossus itself and a maker of colossi. Bechtel emerged from the building of the Hoover Dam to become a major force in reshaping the West and then the world: it is responsible for nuclear power plants and infrastructure for mining in hitherto roadless jungle and for triggering Bolivia's water war earlier this decade when its attempts to privatize Cochabamba's water backfired. And it was one of the more visibly problematic contractors in Bush's Iraq. (The bin Laden family was earlier this decade a "substantial investor," with $10 million in a private equity fund owned by Bechtel, but that's another story.)

No one opposed the Hoover Dam, built at the height of the Depression and the height of hope in technology, but Glen Canyon Dam, built thirty years later, was controversial from the outset. Furious about the development, the Sierra Club transformed from a genteel regional mountaineering society into the most powerful environmental group in the country. The canyon that would be dammed was one of the most beautiful places in the Southwest. Although the Sierra Club knew this, it originally signed off on it as a replacement for a dam upstream. But then the club changed its course and began to fight—in vain, ultimately—to save the canyon and the river ecology downstream. Yet the struggle produced soul-searching and rabble-rousing, out of which came the modern environmental movement. | 65

The logic for the dam was hard to find, but the junk science was not: basic errors were made concerning the rate of evaporation (creating a big lake in a desert entails giving a lot of the water to the sky); cost figures were squirrelly; the estimates for how much water the river collects annually were off. In his book, James Lawrence Powell concludes that the dam and Lake Powell exist because a powerful Colorado representative wanted them and because the Bureau of Reclamation "needed new dams to burnish its reputation and justify its funding and staff levels."

The battle over the damming of Glen Canyon is one of the great epics of twentieth-century America, and out of it came two classics. One was Eliot Porter's elegiac photographic book, *The Place No One Knew: Glen Canyon on the Colorado*, a book that helped create the genre of color nature photography. The other was by John McPhee, the *New Yorker*'s science writer. *Encounters with the Archdruid* recounts what transpired when McPhee managed to get the dam's chief advocate, Floyd Dominy, and its bitterest opponent, Porter's publisher and the Sierra Club's executive director, David Brower, to float together down the Grand Canyon below the dam, arguing all the way. Neither of them imagined the fate the dam now faces. But others hoped. Two classics, or maybe three. In his 1975 novel, *The Monkey Wrench Gang*, the insurrectionary environmental writer Edward Abbey coined the verb "monkey-wrenching" for a certain kind of ecological sabotage: its four central characters plot to float a houseboat full of explosives to the dam. The book helped prompt the formation of the radical environmental group Earth First!, which announced its arrival on the scene in 1981, when some of its founders unfurled a vast line of black plastic resembling a crack down the 700-foot-high face of Glen Canyon Dam. "Surely no man-made structure in modern American history has been so hated for so long by so many with such good reason," said Abbey, speaking to a crowd in a parking lot with a good view of the dam and the prank. It was Earth First! that came up with the optimistic bumper sticker about all this: "Nature Bats Last." But Bechtel keeps the profits.

The docks and ramps at both reservoirs have had to be relocated and rebuilt in pursuit of the fleeing waterline, and one dock simply closed. One ramp at Lake Powell grew to 1,300 feet long, another to more than 1,500 feet, new additions to the collection of landscape follies across the American West. Phoenix and Vegas seem fated, the book argues, to become dusty ruins, for the water to sustain them is already vanishing (though

Vegas has a murderous scheme to drain much of the rest of Nevada for its golf courses and casino fountains, to the detriment of rural communities and wildlife). If the lack of water doesn't get them, climate change might: the author predicts that summer temperatures in the 120s (above 48°C) will be routine in Phoenix. Aridity, he proposes, could well kill off much of the agriculture and two of the biggest cities of the Southwest by the middle of this century. (In California, my local paper reports that a severe drought, now into its third year, is forcing state and federal water agencies to cut water deliveries to farmers in the Central Valley, perhaps the world's single richest agricultural region, by "85 to 100 percent." A 100 percent cut would be a death sentence in this Mediterranean climate without rain between May and October.)

"When all the rivers are used, when all the creeks in the ravines, when all the brooks, when all the springs are used, when all the reservoirs along the streams are used, when all the canyon waters are taken up, when all the artesian waters are taken up, when all the wells are sunk or dug that can be dug in all this arid region, there is still not sufficient water to irrigate all this arid region," Major Powell told an audience gathered in support of large-scale irrigation in Los Angeles in 1893. Booed and shouted down, the major retorted: "I tell you, gentlemen, you are piling up a heritage of conflict and litigation over water rights, for there is not sufficient water to supply these lands." The day he spoke, Las Vegas did not yet exist; Los Angeles had 50,000 residents, and Phoenix, a tenth of that. The other Powell, the author of *Dead Pool*, confirms that the Earth First! bumper sticker is correct.

The waters that are insufficient for this desert civilization will continue to flow anyway. The river that carved a canyon a mile deep will eventually remove all the concrete in its way and scour out the massive piles of silt built up behind both megadams. The process will be catastrophic at some point, but in geological time, it will mean restoration of the live, continuous river. Long before then, Phoenix will be like Jericho or Ur of the Chaldees, with the shriveled relics of golf courses and the dusty hulls of swimming pools added on. The snake may break up into dead pools in this century, but unlike Phoenix, it will rise again.

2009

DETROIT ARCADIA

Exploring the Post-American Landscape

Until recently there was a frieze around the lobby of the Hotel Pontchartrain in downtown Detroit, a naively charming painting of a forested lakefront landscape with Indians peeping out from behind the trees. The hotel was built on the site of Fort Pontchartrain du Détroit, the old French garrison that three hundred years ago held a hundred or so pioneer families inside its walls while several thousand Ottawas and Hurons and Potawatomis went about their business outside, but the frieze evoked an era before even that rude structure was built in the lush woodlands of the place that was not yet Michigan or the United States. Scraped clear by glaciers during the last ice age, the landscape the French invaded was young, soggy, and densely forested. The river frontage that would become Detroit was probably mostly sugar maple and beech forest, with black ash or mixed hardwood swamps, a few patches of conifers, and the occasional expanse of what naturalists like to call wet prairie—grasslands you might not want to walk on. The Indians killed the trees by girdling them and planted corn in the clearings, but the wild rice they gathered and the fish and game they hunted were also important parts of their diet. One pioneer counted badger, bear, fisher, fox, mink, muskrat, porcupine, rabbit, raccoon, weasel, wildcat, wolf, and woodchuck among the local species, and cougar and deer could have been added to the list. The French would later recruit the Indians to trap beaver, which were plentiful in those once-riverine territories—*détroit* means "strait" or "narrows," but in its thirty-two-mile journey from Lake St. Clair to Lake Erie, the Detroit River also had several tributaries, including Parent's Creek, which was later named Bloody Run after some newly arrived English soldiers managed to lose a fight they picked with the local Ottawas.

Fort Pontchartrain was never meant to be the center of a broad European settlement. It was a trading post, a garrison, and a strategic site in the scramble between the British and the French to dominate the North American interior. Cadillac, the ambitious Frenchman who established the fort in 1701, invited members of several Indian nations to surround the fort in order to facilitate more frequent trading, but this led to clashes not just between nations but also between races. Unknown Indians set fire to Fort Pontchartrain in 1703, and the Fox skirmished there in 1712. After the English took over in 1760, deteriorating relations with the local tribes culminated in the three-year-long, nearly successful Ottawa uprising known as Pontiac's Rebellion.

This is all ancient history, but it does foreshadow the racial conflicts that never went away in Detroit, though now white people constitute the majority who surround and resent the 83 percent black city. It's as if the fort had been turned inside out—and, in fact, in the 1940s a six-foot-tall concrete wall was built along Eight Mile Road, which traces Detroit's northern limits, to contain the growing African-American population. And this inversion exposes another paradox. North of Eight Mile, the mostly white suburbs seem conventional, and they may face the same doom as much of conventional suburban America if sprawl and auto-based civilization die off with oil shortages and economic decline. South of Eight Mile, though, Detroit is racing to a far less predictable future.

It is a remarkable city now, one in which the clock seems to be running backward as its buildings disappear and its population and economy decline. The second time I visited Detroit I tried to stay at the Pontchartrain, but the lobby was bisected by drywall, the mural seemed doomed, and the whole place was under some form of remodeling that resembled ruin, with puddles in the lobby and holes in the walls, few staff people, fewer guests, and strange grinding noises at odd hours. I checked out after one night because of the cold water coming out of the hot-water tap and the generally spooky feeling generated by trying to sleep in a 413-room high-rise hotel with almost no other guests. I was sad to see the frieze on its way out, but, still, as I have explored this city over the last few years, I have seen an oddly heartening new version of the landscape it portrays, a landscape that is not quite post-apocalyptic but that is strangely—and sometimes even beautifully—post-American.

This continent has not seen a transformation like Detroit's since the last days of the Maya. The city, once the fourth largest in the country, is now so depopulated that some stretches resemble the outlying farmland, and others are altogether wild. Downtown still looks like a downtown, and all of those high-rise buildings still make an impressive skyline, but when you look closely at some of them, you can see trees growing out of the ledges and crevices, an invasive species from China known variously as the ghetto palm and the tree of heaven. Local wisdom has it that whenever a new building goes up, an older one will simply be abandoned, and the same rule applies to the blocks of new condos that have been dropped here and there among the ruins: why they were built in the first place in a city full of handsome old houses going to ruin has everything to do with the momentary whims of the real estate trade and nothing to do with the long-term survival of cities.

The transformation of the residential neighborhoods is more dramatic. On so many streets in so many neighborhoods, you see a house, a little shabby but well built and beautiful. Then another house. Then a few houses are missing, so thoroughly missing that no trace of foundation remains. Grass grows lushly, as though nothing had ever disturbed the pastoral verdure. Then there's a house that's charred and shattered, then a beautiful house, with gables and dormers and a porch, the kind of house a lot of Americans fantasize about owning. Then more green. This irregular pattern occurs mile after mile, through much of Detroit. You could be traveling down Wabash Street on the west side of town or Pennsylvania or Fairview on the east side of town or around just about any part of the State Fair neighborhood on the city's northern border. Between the half-erased neighborhoods are ruined factories, boarded-up warehouses, rows of storefronts bearing the traces of failed enterprise, and occasional solid blocks of new town houses that look as though they had been dropped in by helicopter. In the bereft zones, solitary figures wander slowly, as though in no hurry to get from one abandoned zone to the next. Some areas have been stripped entirely, and a weedy version of nature is returning. Just about a third of Detroit, some forty square miles, has evolved past decrepitude into vacancy and prairie—an urban void nearly the size of San Francisco.

It was tales of these ruins that originally drew me to the city a few years ago. My first visit began somberly enough, as I contemplated the great neoclassical edifice of the train station, designed by the same architects and completed the same year as Grand Central station in Manhattan. Grand Central thrives; this broken building stands alone just beyond the grim silence of Michigan Avenue and only half a mile from the abandoned Tiger Stadium. Rings of cyclone fence forbid exploration. The last train left on January 5, 1988—the day before Epiphany. The building has been so thoroughly gutted that on sunny days the light seems to come through the upper stories as though through a cheese grater; there is little left but concrete and stone. All the windows are smashed out. The copper pipes and wires, I was told, were torn out by the scavengers who harvest material from abandoned buildings around the city and hasten their decay.

On another visit, I took a long walk down a sunken railroad spur that, in more prosperous times, had been used to move goods from one factory to another. A lot of effort had gone into making the long channel of brick and concrete about twenty feet below the gently undulating surface of Detroit, and it had been abandoned a long time. Lush greenery grew along the tracks and up the walls, which were like a museum of spray-can art from the 1980s and 1990s. The weeds and beer cans and strangely apposite graffiti decrying the 1993 passage of the North American Free Trade Agreement seemed to go on forever.

I took many pictures on my visits to Detroit, but back home they just looked like snapshots of abandoned Nebraska farmhouses or small towns farther west on the Great Plains. Sometimes a burned-out house would stand next to a carefully tended twin, a monument to random fate; sometimes the rectilinear nature of city planning was barely perceptible, just the slightest traces of a grid fading into grassy fields accented with the occasional fire hydrant. One day after a brief thunderstorm, when the rain had cleared away and chunky white clouds dotted the sky, I wandered into a neighborhood, or rather a former neighborhood, of at least a dozen square blocks where trees of heaven waved their branches in the balmy air. Approximately one tattered charred house still stood per block. I could hear the buzzing of crickets or cicadas, and I felt as if I had traveled a thousand years into the future.

To say that much of Detroit is ruins is, of course, to say that some of it isn't. There are stretches of Detroit that look like anywhere in the U.S.A.— blocks of town houses and new condos, a flush of gentility spreading around the Detroit Institute of Arts, a few older neighborhoods where everything is fine. If Detroit has become a fortress of urban poverty surrounded by suburban affluence, the city's waterfront downtown has become something of a fortress within a fortress, with a convention center, a new ballpark, a new headquarters for General Motors, and a handful of casinos that were supposed to be the city's economic salvation when they were built a decade ago. But that garrison will likely fend off time no better than Fort Detroit or the Hotel Pontchartrain.

Detroit is wildly outdated, but it is not very old. It was a medium-size city that boomed in the first quarter of the twentieth century, became the "arsenal of democracy" in the second, spent the third in increasingly less gentle decline, and by the last quarter was a byword for urban decay, having made a complete arc in a single century. In 1900, Detroit had a quarter of a million people. By midcentury the population had reached nearly 2 million. In recent years, though, it has fallen below 900,000. Detroit is a cautionary tale about one-industry towns: it shrank the way the old boomtowns of the gold and silver rushes did, as though it had been mining automobiles and the veins ran dry, but most of those mining towns were meant to be ephemeral. People thought Detroit would go on forever.

Coleman Young, Detroit's first African-American mayor, reigned from 1974 to 1993, the years that the change became irreversible and impossible to ignore, and in his autobiography he sounds like he is still in shock:

> It's mind-boggling to think that at mid-century Detroit was a city of close to two million and nearly everything beyond was covered with corn and cow patties. Forty years later, damn near every last white person in the city had moved to the old fields and pastures—1.4 frigging million of them. Think about that. There were 1,600,000 whites in Detroit after the war, and

1,400,000 of them left. By 1990, the city was just over a million, nearly eighty percent of it was black, and the suburbs had surpassed Detroit not only in population but in wealth, in commerce—even in basketball, for God's sake.

The Detroit Pistons are now based in Auburn Hills. According to the 2000 census, another 112,357 whites left the city in the 1990s, and 10,000 more people a year continue to leave. Even three hundred bodies a year are exhumed from the cemeteries and moved because some of the people who were once Detroiters or the children of Detroiters don't think the city is good enough for their dead. Ford and General Motors, or what remains of them—most of the jobs were dispatched to other towns and nations long ago—are in trouble, too. Interestingly, in this city whose name is synonymous with the auto industry, more than a fifth of households have no cars.

"Detroit's Future Is Looking Brighter," said a headline in the *Detroit Free Press*, not long after another article outlined the catastrophes afflicting the whole state. In recent years, Michigan's household income has dropped more than that of any other state, and more and more of its citizens are slipping below the poverty line. David Littmann, a senior economist for the Michigan think tank the Mackinac Center for Public Policy, told the paper, "As the economy slows nationally, we're going to sink much farther relative to the other states. We've only just begun. We're going to see Michigan sink to levels that no one has ever seen."

In another sense, the worst is over in Detroit. In the 1980s and 1990s, the city was falling apart, spectacularly and violently. Back then the annual pre-Halloween arson festival known as Devil's Night finished off a lot of the abandoned buildings; it peaked in 1984 with 810 fires in the last three days of October. Some of the arson, a daughter of Detroit's black bourgeoisie told me, was constructive—crack houses being burned down by the neighbors; her own respectable aunt had torched one. Between 1978 and 1998, the city issued 9,000 building permits for new homes and 108,000 demolition permits, and quite a lot of structures were annihilated without official sanction.

Even Ford's old Highland Park headquarters, where the Model T was born, is now just a shuttered series of dusty warehouses with tape on the windows and cyclone fences around the cracked pavement. Once upon a time, the plant was one of the wonders of the world—on a single day in 1925 it cranked out 9,000 cars, according to a sign I saw under a tree next to the empty buildings. Detroit once made most of the cars on earth; now the entire United States makes not even one in ten. The new Model T Ford Plaza next door struck my traveling companion—who, like so many white people born in Detroit after the war, had mostly been raised elsewhere—as auspicious. But the mall was fronted by a mostly empty parking lot and anchored by a Payless ShoeSource, which to my mind did not portend an especially bright future.

When I came back, a year after my first tour, I stopped at the Detroit Institute of Arts to see the Diego Rivera mural commissioned in 1932 by Henry Ford's son, Edsel. The museum is a vast Beaux-Arts warehouse— "the fifth-largest fine arts museum in the United States," according to its promotional literature—and the fresco covered all four walls of the museum's central courtyard. Rivera is said to have considered it his finest work.

It's an odd masterpiece, a celebration of the River Rouge auto plant, which had succeeded the Highland Park factory as Ford's industrial headquarters, painted by a Communist for the son of one of the richest capitalists in the world. The north and south walls are devoted to nearly life-size scenes in which the plant's gray gears, belts, racks, and workbenches surge and swarm like some vast intestinal apparatus. The workers within might be subsidiary organs or might be lunch, as the whole churns to excrete a stream of black Fords.

Rivera created this vision when the city was reveling in the newfound supremacy of its megafactories, but Detroit had already reached its apex. Indeed, the River Rouge plant—then the largest factory complex in the world, employing more than 100,000 workers on a site two and a half times the size of New York City's Central Park—was itself built in suburban Dearborn. In 1932, though, capitalists and Communists alike shared a belief that the most desirable form of human organization—indeed, the inevitable form—was not just industrial but this kind of industrial: a Fordist system of "rational" labor, of centralized production in blue-collar cities, of eternal prosperity in a stern gray land. Even the young Soviet Union looked up to Henry Ford.

But Detroit was building the machine that would help destroy not just this city but urban industrialism across the continent. Rivera painted, in a subsidiary all-gray panel in the lower right corner of the south wall, a line of slumped working men and women exiting the factory into what appears to be an endless parking lot full of Ford cars. It may not have looked that way in 1932, but a lot of the gray workers were going to buy those gray cars and drive right out of the gray city. The city-hating Ford said that he wanted every family in the world to have a Ford, and he priced them so that more and more families could. He also fantasized about a post-urban world in which workers would also farm, seasonally or part-time, but he did less to realize that vision. Private automobile ownership was a double blow against the density that is crucial to cities and urbanism and against the Fordist model of concentrated large-scale manufacture. Ford was sabotaging Detroit and then Fordism almost from the beginning; the city had blown up rapidly and would spend the next several decades simply disintegrating.

Detroit was always a rough town. When Rivera painted his fresco, the Depression had hit Detroit as hard as or harder than anywhere, and the unemployed were famished and desperate, desperate enough to march on the Ford Motor Company in the spring of 1932. It's hard to say whether ferocity or desperation made the marchers fight their way through police with tear-gas guns and firemen with hoses going full bore the last stretch of the way to the River Rouge plant. Harry Bennett, the thug who ran Ford more or less the way Stalin was running the Soviet Union, arrived, and though he was immediately knocked out by a flying rock, the police began firing on the crowd, injuring dozens and killing five. The battle of the Hunger March or the huge public funeral afterward would've made a good mural.

It wasn't cars alone that ruined Detroit. It was the whole improbable equation of the city in the first place, the "inherent contradictions." The city was done in by deindustrialization, decentralization, the post–World War II spread of highways and freeways, government incentives to homeowners, and disinvestment in cities that aided and abetted large-scale white flight into the burgeoning suburbs of those years. Chunks of downtown Detroit were sacrificed early, in the postwar years, so that broad arterial freeways—the Edsel Freeway, the Chrysler Freeway—could bring commuters in from beyond city limits.

All of this was happening everywhere else too, of course. The manufacturing belt became the Rust Belt. Cleveland, Toledo, Buffalo, and other cities clustered around the Great Lakes were hit hard, and the shrinking stretched down to St. Louis and across to Pittsburgh, Philadelphia, and Newark. Now that it has entered a second gilded age, no one seems to remember that New York was a snowballing disaster forty or fifty years ago. The old textile district south of Houston Street had emptied out so completely that in 1962 the City Club of New York published a report on it and other former commercial areas titled "The Wastelands of New York City." San Francisco went the same way. It was a blue-collar port city until the waterfront dried up and the longshoremen faded away.

Then came the renaissance, but only for those cities reborn into more dematerialized economies. Vacant lots were filled in, old warehouses were turned into lofts or offices or replaced, downtowns became upscale chain outlets, janitors and cops became people who commuted in from downscale suburbs, and the children of that white flight came back to cities that were not exactly cities in the old sense. The new American cities trade in information, entertainment, tourism, software, finance. They are abstract. Even the souvenirs in these new economies often come from a sweatshop in China. The United States can be mapped as two zones now: a high-pressure zone of economic boom times and escalating real estate prices, and a low-pressure zone, where housing might be the only thing that's easy to come by.

This pattern will change, though. The forces that produced Detroit—the combination of bitter racism and single-industry failure—are anomalous, but the general recipe of deindustrialization, depopulation, and resource depletion will likely touch almost all the regions of the global north in the next century or two. Dresden was rebuilt, and so was Hiroshima, and so were the cities destroyed by natural forces—San Francisco and Mexico City and Tangshan—but Detroit will never be rebuilt as it was. It will be the first of many cities forced to become altogether something else.

The Detroit Institute of Arts is in one of those flourishing parts of Detroit; it is expanding its 1927 building, and when I said goodbye to the Rivera mural and stepped outside into the autumn sunshine, workmen were installing slabs of marble on the building's new facade. I noticed an apparently homeless dog sleeping below the scaffolding, and as I walked past, three plump white women teetered up to me hastily, all attention focused on the dog. "Do you have a cell phone?" the one topped by a froth of yellow hair shrilled. "Call the Humane Society!" I suggested that the dog was breathing fine and therefore was probably okay, and she looked at me as though I were a total idiot. "This is downtown *Detroit*," she said, in a tone that made it clear the dog was in imminent peril from unspeakable forces, and that perhaps she was, I was, we all were.

I had been exploring an architectural-salvage shop near Rosa Parks Boulevard earlier that day, and when I asked the potbellied and weathered white man working there for his thoughts on the city, the tirade that followed was similarly vehement: Detroit, he insisted, had been wonderful—people used to dress up to go downtown, it had been the Paris of the Midwest!—and then it all went to hell. Those people destroyed it. My traveling companion suggested that maybe larger forces of deindustrialization might have had something to do with what happened to the city, but the man blankly rejected this analysis and continued on a tirade about "them" that wasn't very careful about not being racist.

On the Web you can find a site, Stormfront White Nationalist Community, that is even more comfortable with this version of what happened to the city and even less interested in macroeconomic forces like deindustrialization and globalization: "A huge non-White population, combined with annual arson attacks, bankruptcy, crime, and decay, have combined to make Detroit—once the USA's leading automotive industrial center—into a ruin comparable with those of the ancient civilizations—with the cause being identical: the replacement of the White population who built the city, with a new non-White population." It could have been different. "In more civilized environs, these facilities might have easily been transformed into a manufacturing and assembly center for any number of industrial enterprises," writes the anonymous author.

A few months before the diatribe in the salvage yard, I'd met a long-haired counterculture guy who also told me he was from Detroit, by which he, like so many others I've met, meant the suburbs of Detroit. When I asked him about the actual city, though, his face clenched like a fist. He recited the terrible things they would do to you if you ventured into the city, that they would tear you apart on the streets. He spoke not with the voice of a witness but with the authority of tradition handed down from an unknown and irrefutable source. The city was the infernal realm, the burning lands, the dragon's lair at the center of a vast and protective suburban sprawl.

The most prominent piece of public art in Detroit is the giant blackened bronze arm and fist that serve as a monument to heavyweight boxing champion Joe Louis, who grew up there. If it were vertical it would look like a Black Power fist, but it's slung from cables like some medieval battering ram waiting to be dragged up to the city walls.

Deindustrialization dealt Detroit a sucker punch, but the knockout may have been white flight—at least economically. Socially, it was a little more complex. One African-American woman who grew up there told me that white people seemed to think they were a great loss to the city they abandoned, "but we were glad to see them go and waved bye-bye." She lived in Ann Arbor—the departure of the black middle class being yet another wrinkle in the racial narrative—but she was thinking of moving back, she said. If she had kids, raising them in a city where they wouldn't be a minority had real appeal.

The fall of the paradise that was Detroit is often pinned on the riots of July 1967, what some there still refer to as the Detroit Uprising. But Detroit had a long history of race riots—there were vicious white-on-black riots in 1833, 1863, 1925, and 1943. And the idyll itself was unraveling long before 1967. Local 600 of the United Auto Workers broke with the union mainstream in 1951, sixteen years before the riots, to sue Ford over decentralization efforts already under way. They realized that their jobs were literally going south, to states and nations where labor wasn't so organized and wages weren't so high, back in the prehistoric era of "globalization."

The popular story wasn't about the caprices of capital, though; it was about the barbarism of blacks. In 1900, Detroit had an African-American population of 4,111. Then came the great migration, when masses of southern blacks traded Jim Crow for the industrialized promised land of the North. Conditions might have been better here than in the South, but Detroit was still a segregated city with a violently racist police department and a lot of white people ready to work hard to keep black people out of their neighborhoods. They failed in this attempt at segregation, and then they left. This is what created the blackest city in the United States, and figures from Joe Louis and Malcolm X to Rosa Parks and the bold left-wing Congressman John Conyers—who has represented much of the city since 1964—have made Detroit a center of activism and independent leadership for African Americans. It's a black city, but it's surrounded.

Surrounded, but inside that stockade of racial divide and urban decay are visionaries, and their visions are tender, hopeful, and green. Grace Lee Boggs, at ninety-one, has been politically active in the city for more than half a century. Born in Providence to Chinese immigrant parents, she got a Ph.D. in philosophy from Bryn Mawr in 1940 and was a classical Marxist when she married the labor organizer Jimmy Boggs, in 1953. That an Asian woman married to a black man could become a powerful force was just another wrinkle in the racial politics of Detroit. (They were together until Jimmy's death, in 1993.) Indeed, her thinking evolved along with the radical politics of the city itself. During the 1960s, the Boggses were dismissive of Martin Luther King Jr. and ardent about Black Power, but as Grace acknowledged when we sat down together in her big shady house in the central city, "The Black Power movement, which was very powerful here, concentrated only on power and had no concept of the challenges that would face a black-powered administration." When Coleman Young took over city hall, she said, he could start fixing racism in the police department and the fire department, "but when it came time to do something about Henry Ford and General Motors, he was helpless. We thought that all we had to do was transform the system, that all the problems were on the other side."

As the years went by, the Boggses began to focus less on putting new people into existing power structures and more on redefining or dismantling the structures altogether. When she and Jimmy crusaded against

Young's plans to rebuild the city around casinos, they realized they had to come up with real alternatives, and they began to think about what a local, sustainable economy would look like. They had already begun to realize that Detroit's lack of participation in the mainstream offered an opportunity to do everything differently—that instead of retreating back to a better relationship to capitalism, to industry, to the mainstream, the city could move forward, turn its liabilities into assets, and create an economy entirely apart from the transnational webs of corporations and petroleum. Jimmy Boggs described his alternative vision in a 1988 speech at the First Unitarian-Universalist Church of Detroit:

> We have to get rid of the myth that there is something sacred about large-scale production for the national and international market. We have to begin thinking of creating small enterprises which produce food, goods, and services for the local market, that is, for our communities and for our city. . . . In order to create these new enterprises, we need a view of our city which takes into consideration both the natural resources of our area and the existing and potential skills and talents of Detroiters.

That was the vision, and it is only just starting to become a reality. "Now a lot of what you see is vacant lots," Grace told me. "Most people see only disaster and the end of the world. On the other hand, artists in particular see the potential, the possibility of bringing the country back into the city, which is what we really need." After all, the city is rich in open space and—with an official unemployment rate in the mid-teens—people with time on their hands. The land is fertile, too, and the visionaries are there.

In traversing Detroit, I saw a lot of signs that a greening was well under way, a sort of urban husbandry of the city's already occurring return to nature. I heard the story of one old woman who had been the first African-American person on her block and is now, with her grandson, very nearly the last person of any race on that block. Having a city grow up around you is not an uncommon American experience, but having the countryside return is an eerier one. She made the best of it, though. The city sold her the surrounding lots for next to nothing, and she now raises much of her own food on them.

I also saw the lush three-acre Earth Works Garden, launched by Capuchin monks in 1999 and now growing organic produce for a local soup kitchen. I saw a 4-H garden in a fairly ravaged east-side neighborhood, and amid the utter abandonment of the west side, I saw the handsome tiled buildings of the Catherine Ferguson Academy for Young Women, a school for teenage mothers that opens on to a working farm, complete with apple orchard, horses, ducks, long rows of cauliflower and broccoli, and a red barn the girls built themselves. I met Ashley Atkinson, the young project manager for The Greening of Detroit, and heard about the hundred community gardens they support and the thousands more food gardens that are not part of any network. The food they produce, Atkinson told me, provides food security for many Detroiters. "Urban farming, dollar for dollar, is the most effective change agent you can ever have in a community," she said. Everywhere I went, I saw the rich soil of Detroit and the hard work of the gardeners bringing forth an abundant harvest any organic farmer would envy.

Everyone talks about green cities now, but the concrete results in affluent cities mostly involve curbside composting and tacking solar panels onto rooftops while residents continue to drive, to shop, to eat organic pears flown in from Argentina, to be part of the big machine of consumption and climate change. The free-range chickens and Priuses are great, but they alone aren't adequate tools for creating a truly different society and ecology. The future, at least the sustainable one, the one in which we will survive, isn't going to be invented by people who are happily surrendering selective bits and pieces of environmentally unsound privilege. It's going to be made by those who had all that taken away from them or never had it in the first place.

After the Panic of 1893, Detroit's left-wing Republican mayor encouraged his hungry citizens to plant vegetables in the city's vacant lots and went down in history as Potato Patch Pingree. Something similar happened in Cuba when the Soviet Union collapsed and the island lost its subsidized oil and thereby its mechanized agriculture; through garden-scale semi-organic agriculture, Cubans clawed their way back to food security and got better food in the bargain. Nobody wants to live through a depression, and it is unfair, or at least deeply ironic, that black people in Detroit are being forced to undertake an experiment in utopian post-urbanism that appears to be uncomfortably similar to the sharecropping past their parents and grandparents sought to escape. There is no moral reason why they should do and be better than the rest of us—but there is a practical one. They have to. Detroit is where change is most urgent and therefore most viable. The rest of us will get there later, when necessity drives us too, and by that time Detroit may be the shining example we can look to, the post-industrial green city that was once the steel-gray capital of Fordist manufacturing.

Detroit is still beautiful, both in its stately decay and in its growing natural abundance. Indeed, one of the finest sights I saw on my walks around the city combined the two. It was a sudden flash on an already bright autumn day—a pair of wild pheasants, bursting from a lush row of vegetables and flying over a cyclone fence toward a burned-out building across the street. It was an improbable flight in many ways. Those pheasants, after all, were no more native to Detroit than are the trees of heaven growing in the skyscrapers downtown. And yet it is here, where European settlement began in the region, that we may be seeing the first signs of an unsettling of the very premises of colonial expansion, an unsettling that may bring a complex new human and natural ecology into being.

This is the most extreme and long-term hope Detroit offers us: the hope that we can reclaim what we paved over and poisoned, that nature will not punish us, that it will welcome us home—not with the landscape that was here when we arrived, perhaps, but with land that is alive, lush, and varied all the same. "Look on my works, ye mighty, and despair!" was Shelley's pivotal command in his portrait of magnificent ruins, but Detroit is far from a "shattered visage." It is a harsh place of poverty, deprivation, and a fair amount of crime, but it is also a stronghold of possibility.

That Rivera mural, for instance. In 1932 the soil, the country, the wilderness, and agriculture represented the past; they should have appeared, if at all, below or behind the symbols of industry and urbanism, a prehistory from which the gleaming machine future emerged. But the big panels of workers inside the gray chasms of the River Rouge plant have above them huge nude figures—black, white, red, yellow, lounging on the bare earth. Rivera meant these figures to be emblematic of the North American races and meant their fistfuls of coal, sand, iron ore, and limestone to be the raw stuff of industrialism. To my eye, though, they look like deities waiting to reclaim the world, insistent on sensual contact with the land and confident of their triumph over and after the factory that lies below them like an inferno.

2007

ONE NATION UNDER ELVIS

Environmentalism for Everyone

The biggest wilderness I've ever been in—a roadless area roughly the size of Portugal with about fifty contiguous watersheds and the whole panoply of charismatic macrofauna doing their thing undisturbed—is another story. This one is about what happened afterward, when I and the Canadian environmentalists I'd been traveling with arrived at the nearest settlement, a logging town in the far northeast corner of British Columbia consisting of a raw row of buildings on either side of the highway to Alaska.

We were celebrating two weeks of rafting down the central river in that ungulate- and predator-rich paradise at the outpost's big honky-tonk-ish nightclub, where the DJ kept playing country songs, to which all the locals would loop around gracefully, clasped together. But my compadres kept making faces of disgust at the music and asking the DJ to put on something else. He'd oblige with reggae, mostly, and we'd wave our limbs vaguely, dancing solo and free-form as white people have danced to rock-and-roll since the mid-1960s. Everyone else would sit down to wait this other music out. It was not a great movement-building exercise. How far were you going to get with a community when you couldn't stand their music or even be diplomatic about it? I've been through dozens of versions of that scene over the years and got reminded of it last year by a letter I received from Dick.

He really was named Dick. From a return address in the exorbitantly expensive near–San Francisco countryside, he sent me a typewritten note about a section in a recent book of mine. He declared, "The country music parts of the U.S. you love so much are also home of the most racist, reactionary, religiously authoritarian (i.e., Dominionist) people in the country. You don't have to go far: just look at voting patterns among rednecks (descendants of the white yeomanry, if you wish to be polite) in the Central Valley. They love Bush and are very backward people by the standards of the Enlightenment. The Q might be, what is the correlation between country music and political backwardness, if any?"

My first question for Dick might be: which country music? You could cite Johnny Cash's long-term commitment to Native American rights and stance against the Vietnam War (he called himself "a dove with claws") or the song about interracial love that Merle Haggard wrote (but his record company refused to release at the time, though the minor country star Tony Booth had a hit with "Irma Jackson" in 1970) or "I Believe the South Is Gonna Rise Again," boldly sung by Tanya Tucker in 1974:

Our neighbors in the big house called us redneck
'Cause we lived in a poor share-croppers shack
The Jacksons down the road were poor like we were
But our skin was white and theirs was black
But I believe the South is gonna rise again
But not the way we thought it would back then

Or you could just mention medium-sized country star Charley Pride (thirty-six *Billboard* number-one country hits), who also doesn't fit Dick's redneck designation because he is African American.

In terms of political orientation, you could cite the Texas-based Dixie Chicks, who refused to back down from criticizing Bush on the brink of the current war. They were, as their later hit had it, "Not Ready to Make Nice." Though corporate country stars like Toby Keith stampeded to support the so-called war on terror, alt-country musicians like Steve Earle charged just as hard in the opposite direction. Country music is a complex beast, sometimes in resistance to or mockery of the mainstream and the rural South, sometimes a mirror of or hymn to it, the product of many voices over many eras, arisen from a culture that was never pure anything, including white. (And its current listening territory includes much of the English-speaking world.)

Another set of questions might be why Dick despises the people and places that spawned the music, and what larger rifts his attitude reveals.

Answering them requires digging into the deep history of American music and American race and class wars, and into the broad crises of environmentalism in recent years.

Those wars about race and class are peculiarly evident in the stories we tell about Elvis. I was raised on the tale that Elvis stole his music from black people. The story told one way makes Elvis Presley a thief rather than someone who bridged great divides by hybridizing musical traditions and brought the lush energetic force of African-American music into white ears and hearts and loins. It ignores his many white influences, from bluesy Hank Williams to schmaltzy Perry Como, his genius in synthesizing multiple American traditions into something unprecedented, and the raw power of his own voice and vocal style. It ignores, too, the lack of an apartheid regime in American roots music. White country blues and white gospel were part of the rich river of sound that came out of the South long before Presley. Despite segregation, black and white musicians learned from each other and influenced each other. (Another view of Elvis, from *Billboard* magazine in 1958, stated, "In one aspect of America's cultural life, integration has already taken place.")

The particular song Elvis was supposed to have stolen from R&B singer Big Mama Thornton, "Hound Dog," was written by two New York Jews, Jerry Leiber and Mike Stoller. Elvis's first single featured a cover of the song "That's All Right Mama" by Delta blues singer Arthur Crudup, but the B-side was a cover of bluegrass star Bill Monroe's "Blue Moon of Kentucky," as perfect a mix of southern musical traditions as you can find. Elvis was repeatedly charged with being a racist—most famously in rapper Chuck D's 1990 song—on the basis of a comment he never actually made. James Brown and Muhammad Ali thought otherwise, and some Native Americans claim the reputedly part-Cherokee Elvis as their own.

The story that Elvis stole his music from African Americans as told by, for example, my now-deceased, über-leftie, America-hating, and otherwise wonderful aunt painted rock-and-roll as a mostly white child miraculously born to a purely black family. It was a way of saying that cool and correct white people could love rock-and-roll—white music with roots in the South—but dodge the sense that they had any affinities with white southerners; they could imagine them as wholly other and hate them with ease, with a fervor and disdain that spilled over pretty easily to all blue-collar rural people, to the white American peasantry, basically. That hate had and has wide currency. Ask Dick.

The story that racism belongs to poor people in the South is a little too easy, though. Just as not everybody up here, geographically and economically, is on the right side of the line, so not everyone down there is on the wrong side. But the story allows middle-class people to hate poor people while claiming to be on the side of truth, justice, and everything else good.

I grew up surrounded by liberals and leftists who liked to play the idiot in fake southern accents, make jokes about white trash and trailer trash, and, like the Canadian enviros, made gagging noises whenever they heard Dolly Parton or anything like her. If Okies from Muskogee thought they were being mocked, they were right, in part. This mockery was particularly common during the 1970s and 1980s, but it has yet to evaporate altogether—after all, Dick, who judging by his typewriter was around then, wrote me in this era, not some other.

My own conversion to country music came all of a sudden in 1990, around another campfire, also in Nevada. The great Western Shoshone anti-nuclear and land-rights activist Bill Rosse, a decorated World War II vet and former farm manager, unpacked his guitar and sang Hank Williams and traditional songs for hours. I was enchanted as much by the irreverent rancor of some of the songs as by the pure blue yearning of others. I'd had no idea such coolness, wit, and poetry was lurking in this stuff I was taught to scorn before I'd met it.

Hating white southerners, particularly poor white southerners, and often, by extension, any poor rustic whites, seems to be a legacy of the civil rights movement. So far as I can tell (I came later), well-meaning people outside the South were horrified by the culture of Jim Crow, with its segregation, discrimination, and violence—and rightly so. Over the past couple of years, I've spent time in New Orleans and on the Gulf Coast, and I myself was horrified by the racial violence that transpired during the chaos of Katrina and some of the everyday apartheid and racist vileness that persists in the region. But I also recently ran into raging white racists on the periphery of Detroit, Michigan, right across the river from Canada. And the last ostentatious racists I met were the middle-aged heir of a fabulously wealthy family—whose hallowed name is smeared all over the Northeast—and his yachting buddy, right here in left-coast ultra-urban San Francisco. Racism is pervasive. The pretense that it belongs solely to poor people who talk slow lets the rest of us off the hook.

So on the one hand, we have white people who hate black people. On the other hand, we have white people who hate other white people on the grounds that they hate black people. But that latter hatred accuses many wrongfully, and it serves as a convenient cover-up for the racism that is all around us. The reason it matters is that middle-class people despising poor people becomes your basic class war, and the ongoing insults seem to have been at least part of what has weakened the environmental movement in particular and progressive politics in general.

Right-wing politicians may serve the super-rich with tax cuts and deregulation and privatization galore, but they also dress up expertly in a heartland all-Americanism that has, at least until Bush's plummeting popularity, allowed a lot of rural Americans to see them as allies rather than opponents. The right has also done a superb job of portraying the left as elite and hostile to working-class interests, and the class war going on inside and outside leftist and environmentalist circles did this propaganda battle a great service. The result of all this has been a marginalized environmental movement—more specifically, an environmental movement that has alienated the people who often live closest to "the environment."

Of course dreadlocks and ragged clothes weren't exactly diplomatic outreach tools either. I spent some of the 1990s with and around activists in the national forests of the West, and a lot of the supposedly most radical had a remarkable knack for going into rural communities and insulting practically everyone with whom they came into contact. It became clear to me that in their eyes the worst crimes of the locals did not involve chainsaws and voting choices but culture and what gets called lifestyle. It was a culture war that got pretty far from who was actually doing what to the earth and how anyone might stop it.

Grubby, furry, childless pseudo-nomads who could screw up all they wanted and live hand to mouth—until something went wrong and the long arm of middle-class parents reached out to rescue them—scorned the tough economic choices of people with kids, mortgages, and no bail-out plan or white-collar options. Some of them did great things for trees, but their approach wasn't always, to say the least, coalition-building. It also wasn't ubiquitous. There were some broad-minded people in the movement and some who even hailed from these rural and poor cultures, and Earth First! always had a self-proclaimed redneck contingent—but the scorn was widespread enough to be a major problem. And it seemed to be part of the reason a lot of rural people despise environmentalists.

I remember talking to a young rancher in an anti-environmental bar in Eureka, Nevada, who humbly presumed that environmentalists, including me and the group I was with, loathed him. His hat was large and his heart was good. Whatever you think of arid-lands ranching, he seemed to be doing it pretty well. He boasted of grass up to his cows' bellies, talked about moving the cows around to prevent erosion, and deplored the gold mines that are doing far worse things to the region. We were clearly on the wrong track—the environmental movement as a whole, if not the Nevada activists I worked with, who did a decent job of bridging the divide. But why was there a divide? The bar in Eureka, as of last July, still sold T-shirts emblazoned with the acronym WRANGLERS (Western Ranchers Against No-Good Leftist Environmentalist Radical Shitheads), a slogan about as diplomatic as my letter from Dick.

The socialism and progressivism that thrived through the 1930s saw farmers, loggers, fisheries workers, and miners as its central constituency along with longshoremen and factory workers. Where did it go? You can see missed opportunities again and again. Some of the potential for a broad, blue-collar left was trampled by the virulent anti-communism and anti-labor-union mood of the postwar era. More of it was undermined by the culture clash that came out of the civil rights movement. By the 1980s, when I was old enough to start paying attention, the divide was pretty wide. And environmentalists were typically found on one side.

The environmental justice movement set out in part to rectify that. The founding notion was to address the way that environmental hazards—refineries, incinerators, toxic dumps—are often sited in poor communities and communities of color. But class, and thereby poor white people, very quickly vanished from the formula. Toxic dumping in a rural North Carolina African-American community is said to have launched the environmental justice movement in 1982, but the prototypical environmental injustice had been exposed a few years earlier, in the mostly white community at Love Canal in western New York. It wasn't an anomaly either. The 1972 Buffalo Creek flood occurred when a coal-slurry impoundment dam on a mountaintop in West Virginia burst and killed 125 people, left 4,000 homeless, destroyed many small communities, and devastated the survivors—almost all of whom were white. And modern-day coal mining continues to ravage poor, mostly white regions of the South in what environmental journalist Antrim Caskey calls "the government-sanctioned bombing of Appalachia." Caskey describes how "coal companies turn communities against each other by telling their employees that the environmentalists want to take away their jobs."

The right wooed rural white people (and then screwed them), the left neglected them at best, and the electoral maps everyone made so much noise about in the 2004 election weren't about red states and blue states; they were about urban islands of blue surrounded by oceans of red. The anti-environmental and often corporate-backed Sagebrush Rebellion of the 1970s and the Wise Use Movement of the 1980s did their part to deepen the divide by convincing rural whites that their livelihoods were threatened by environmentalists and persuading them to embrace pro-corporate, pro–extractive industry positions. And small-scale farmers losing their land were receptive to right-wing rhetoric that claimed to feel their pain and pinned the blame on liberals or immigrants or environmentalists, rather than corporate consolidation, globalization, or other macroeconomic forces. During the Clinton era when rural right-wingers feared the United Nations and "world government" (remember the black helicopters?), and the militia movement was strong, I wished that the anti–corporate globalization movement could have done a better job of reaching out to these descendants of the old Progressives, Wobblies, and agrarian insurgents to tell them that there were indeed schemes for scary world domination, but they involved the World Trade Organization, not the UN. An environmental movement, or a broader progressive movement, that could speak to these communities would be truly powerful. And truly just.

Pieces of it are here. The Quivira Coalition and many other groups across the West have found common ground with ranchers; land trust organizations and others have forged alliances with farmers; and the whole premise that the people who actually produce the resources are the enemies of the rest of us who use them is fading away. I think of the fantastic work being done by good-old-boy-like activists I've met in the South—a land preservationist getting lots of conservation easements from the local Charleston-area gentry and a big red-faced drawling guy doing extraordinarily great environmental justice work with the African-American community in New Orleans's Lower Ninth Ward. And of people like Oakland's Van Jones, who are thinking about how jobs and the environment can come together as a goal. The argument that a healthy environment can bring more revenue into rural communities through recreation and other benefits has more credence nowadays, and hardly radical constituencies, such as the lobstermen of Maine, have recognized the relationship between their livelihoods and the health of the oceans. But much remains to be done.

The environmental movement's founding father, John Muir, was himself a Wisconsin farm boy, and he did not so much flee the farm for the wilderness as invent wilderness as a counterimage to the farm on which his brutal father nearly worked him to death. Muir worked later as a shepherd and lumber-miller in the Sierra Nevada and much later married into an orchard-owning family, but he didn't have much to say about work, and what little he did say wasn't positive. The wilderness he sought was solitary, pure, and set apart from human society, corporeal sustenance, and human toil— which is why he had to forget about the Indians who were still subsisting on the land there. This apartness and forgetting so beautifully codified in Ansel Adams's wilderness photographs has shaped the vision of much of the environmental movement since them.

The Sierra Club, which Muir cofounded with a group of lawyers and University of California professors in 1892, saw nature as not where one lived or worked but where one vacationed. And traditional American environmentalism still largely imagines nature as vacationland and as wilderness, ignoring the working landscapes and agricultural lands, whose beauties and meanings are widely celebrated in European art. More recently, as environmentalists have found themselves dealing with more systemic problems—pesticides, acid rain—they've begun to shed the sense that the rural and urban, human and wild, are separate in ecological terms, but that awareness has done little to actually connect rural and urban people and issues.

Today, rural citizens see themselves in an unappreciated, fast-shrinking middle zone between wilderness and development (even though agriculture is often the best bulwark against sprawl). In many ways, rural culture is dying, and that seems to push many rural people into near-paranoia. During the water-scarcity crises in the Klamath River region on the California-Oregon border, farmers spoke of "rural cleansing" and seemed to believe that environmentalists wanted to empty out the countryside. Some of them do. Rural life—other than sentimental fantasies of an idyllic past, cowboy fetishism, or the pseudo-ruralism of people who live in rustic-looking settings but commute to work in the white-collar economy—is largely invisible to most of us most of the time. It's true that agriculture and wilderness are sometimes in competition—the farmers of the Klamath Basin are competing with salmon for water, for example. But if rural culture and rural life were positive values also being defended, the negotiations might go better.

Wallace Stegner wrote forty-seven years ago: "Something will have gone out of us as a people if we ever let the remaining wilderness be destroyed." And something else will go out of us if the resourcefulness, rootedness, and richness of rural culture disappears. It's why the environmentalist-rancher coalitions are so noteworthy, and the new alliances forged to resist the Bush-era oil and gas leases across the arid West. But they are only a small part of a culture and a movement that need to do a lot more.

One step would be to stop letting the right wing frame the debate. More significantly, we need to seek ways to sustain both rural life and wildlife. The small solutions—fencing riparian habitat, allowing wildlife corridors, reorienting farms toward sustainable agriculture and local markets and away from chemical-heavy industrial production—can be cooperative rather than competitive. The large solution is a culture that values all of its fulfilling landscapes—the ones that sustain us bodily as well as imaginatively, the tilled lands as well as the wild. Of course one complication is that rural life itself has been increasingly industrialized in ways that produce, rather than a picturesque farm scene, a sort of food factory operated largely by exploited and transient workers and run by offsite profiteers. Reforming this will be good for both human rights and the environment—as well as our health and our tables.

If, at the start of this story, the great divide was manifest in musical taste and distaste, that too has begun to close, as musical genres bleed into each other and no longer provide the airtight identities they once did. The young don't seem to care who owns what music, and a lot of them have distinctly downwardly mobile tastes—garnished with irony, but not with scorn. (After all, a lot of them *are* downwardly mobile in this ruthless economy.) Race has gotten a lot more complicated in their lifetimes (and ours), both in abstract ideologies and in actual liaisons and general hybridizations, and so has music, above and beyond all those suburban white boys who wanted to be rappers in the 1990s.

The twenty-something music aficionado Steven Leckart wrote me about the splendidly hybrid music and tastes of his generation. "I get the sense that the phrase 'everything but country'—which was rather popular when I was a teenager—is starting to go out of fashion," he said. "When Jack White of the White Stripes produced Loretta Lynn's last record and was nominated for a Grammy, that may not have been on teenagers' radars, but it's certainly reflected online. So you have a thirteen-year-old who happens to like Beck navigating with a click to the White Stripes and then to Loretta Lynn, and if he likes what he hears with Loretta even just a little, he will continue to explore those roots." The Farm Aid lineups over the last decade suggest another kind of crossover: everyone from Billy Joel and B. B. King to Dave Matthews has played alongside Willie Nelson and a regular array of country musicians. Maybe the music that once divided us could unite us as we wander this unfenced aural landscape.

Happily, I think Dick might be a relic. There are particular organizations as well as general tendencies that make me hopeful. Among them are the resurgent interest in where food actually comes from, the growing tendency to condemn less and build coalitions more, and a stronger capacity for thinking systemically. And then climate change is an issue that could unite us in new ways as it makes clear how interdependent everything on this planet is and the extent to which privilege and consumption are part of the problem. The solutions will involve modesty as well as innovation.

The anti-environmentalist right has shot itself in both feet in recent years, losing credibility and constituency, and a smart and fast-moving left could make hay out of this, to mix a few fairly rural metaphors. It would mean giving up vindication for victory—that is, giving up on triumphing over the wickedness of one's enemies and looking at them as unrecruited allies instead. It might mean giving up on the environmental movement as a separate sector and thinking more holistically about what we want to protect and why, including people, places, traditions, and processes outside the wilderness. It might even mean getting over the notion that left and right are useful or even adequate ways to describe who we are and what we long for (or even over the notion of rural and urban, as food gardens proliferate in the latter and sprawl becomes an issue in the former). We must also talk about class again, loudly and clearly, without backing down or forgetting about race. This is the back road down which lie stronger coalitions, genuine justice, a healthier environment, and maybe even a music that everyone can dance to.

2008

WINGED MERCURY AND THE GOLDEN CALF

Heavy Metal Histories

I

For a while in the middle of the twentieth century, economists liked to model their subject as hydrology. They built elaborate systems of pipes, pumps, and reservoirs through which water traveled, allegedly modeling the movements of money, wealth, capital. They were funny devices, stuck halfway between literal-mindedness and metaphor, and they begged many questions about the nature of economies and the nature of water. Since that time, water contamination and scarcity have become global issues, and water privatization an even more heated one. But even if you left aside all the strange things we do to water, water was never exactly a good model for economies, since the implication was that the flow of capital is natural, that money moves like water.

Even water doesn't move like water in our systems. Our economies produce lots of strange uphill pumping (as Los Angeles does with the Colorado River's water, as the Bush tax cuts do with the nation's wealth), hoarding, flooding, squandering, as well as false droughts and unnecessary thirsts unto death. What model explains the 100-foot yachts and fifth homes U.S. captains of industry accumulate while hunger, homelessness, lack of access to medical care, and general precariousness overtake more and more of the population? Or Bechtel Corporation privatizing the water supply in a Bolivian town and jacking up prices to the point that the poor were expected to do without—what kind of economic model is that? Could we model as a flood the uprising that forced Bechtel out?

But there's another problem with the attempt to represent wealth as water, which is that wealth was for millennia embodied for monetary societies not by the two-hydrogen-one-oxygen molecule that makes life on earth possible, but by a true element, a heavy metal, and a fairly useless one: gold. The real movement of wealth and poverty through an economy or at least our economy might better be modeled by the movement of gold out of the California ecosystem in the Gold Rush and by the diversion and contamination of water and release of deadly mercury into the same system during the same rush.

The gold was the point. The mercury was the secret. The former yielded a one-time profit and was thereafter mostly sequestered, made into coins, or worn as ornaments, not even much of a speculative commodity during that century when the price of gold was fixed, not fluctuant. The latter was dispersed in all the streams in which and near which gold was mined, mercury being useful in securing the gold with the old technologies of ore refinement. Even today, more than a century and a half later, the mercury continues to spread, pervading thousands of miles of stream and river, continually flowing via the rivers of the Gold Rush into the San Francisco Bay and outward into the great ocean. Mercury travels from other mining operations into other water systems from the Salmon River in Idaho to the Amazon in Brazil. In stream, river, bay, and ocean, it enters the bodies of aquatic creatures, moves up the food chain into bigger fish and then into other predators, including our own species, where it particularly affects the mental capacities and nervous systems of young children and unborn children, so that you can say that at least indirectly gold dims the minds and drains the futures of the youngest among us. The gathering of gold then and now is the spread of mercury. The making of wealth along this extractive model is also often a far more widespread and long-lived generation of poverty.

In the popular version of the California Gold Rush, every man is free to seek his fortune, and flannel-shirted miners panning for gold in mountain streams strike it rich. This picturesque version of the bearded prospector with his pick and pan is still reenacted at places like Knott's Berry Farm Amusement Park near Disneyland in Orange County and celebrated in tourist-dependent towns up and down Route 49, which runs through the old Mother Lode, the gold-bearing belt in the Sierra Nevada. It's a vision of natural riches naturally distributed, a laissez-faire and free-market system in which all start out even, with the implication that all thereby have equal opportunity to benefit. It was almost nearly briefly true, if you ignore the racist laws and the violence that deprived Asians and Latinos of mining access and basic rights. Foreigners, particularly Chinese miners, were subject to special taxes, denied the right to stake claims or work them independently, intimidated, lynched, driven off the richest sites, and barred from legal remedies, but their lot was far more pleasant than that of the Native Californians. For years, it was open season against them, with bounties paid for scalps or ears brought in, with no legal or treaty rights. (A large number of California's Indian treaties were suppressed by Congress in the nineteenth century and settled with a pitiful cash payment in the mid-twentieth; though they owned the Mother Lode from which the gold came, most received from the rush nothing but ruin.) Disease, deracination, starvation, despair, and outright murder reduced the indigenous population by about four-fifths in those early years of the Gold Rush. So if you imagine a world in which everyone is a young white man, you can picture the gorges, ridgelines, and canyons in which the Gold Rush unfolded as the level playing field of which free-market enthusiasts sing.

Distinguished historians once endorsed this version of the Gold Rush as a paradise of opportunity: California historian and former *Nation* editor Carey McWilliams wrote in 1949, a century after the rush began, "Few could conquer with Pizarro or sail with Drake, but the California gold rush was the great adventure for the common man. Since there was no 'law of mines' in 1848, the California miners adopted their own rules and regulations in which they were careful to safeguard the equality of opportunity which had prevailed at the outset." But within a decade of James Marshall's January 1848 discovery of gold on the American River, mining in the Mother Lode shifted from simple pans and sluice boxes to complex mechanical systems. The mining organizations built larger washing devices to get the gold out of the streams, introduced hydraulic mining—the use of high-powered jets of water—to hose it out of the nearby landscape, and launched hard-rock mining operations whose tunnels and shafts still riddle the Sierra landscape to get underground ore that could then be processed in stamp mills (a sort of crushing machine).

The technological changes were paralleled by a shift from individual endeavor to increasingly industrialized large-scale processes requiring capitalization and eventually producing stockholders and distant profiteers, as well as bosses and employees. By that point, it took wealth to get wealth. Charles Nordhoff in his 1873 guidebook to California mentions a 3,000-foot tunnel dug near the Yuba River at a cost of $250,000, completed before "a cent's worth of gold could be taken out of the claim," not the kind of investment option available to everyone. Some of the earlier photographs are astonishing. Whole rivers were diverted so that men could pick more easily at the bed, and if the economy is imagined as flowing like water, these evicted rivers provide some interesting metaphors.

Many of the men who joined the scramble for gold spent much to get to California only to become destitute or die by malnutrition, disease, violence, suicide, accident, or other typical mining-camp misfortune. Many others became ordinary laborers working for ordinary wages, with no chance of striking it rich. It was a colorful world, with lurid newspapers published seemingly in every small town, touring singers, theaters, and even opera in San Francisco, writers like Joaquin Miller and Bret Harte, a tsunami of alcohol consumed in taverns with concomitant brawls, delirium tremens, brothels—ranging from courtesan palaces to child-rape mills—and a lot of vigilante injustice. Maybe it's all evident in the names of their mining camps. Murderer's Bar, Hangtown, Rough and Ready, and Sucker Flat all existed by 1849.

Of course the division of labor and inequality were there from the beginning. Walter Colton, a Protestant minister who had settled in Monterey when it was still part of Mexico, wrote on August 12, 1848, "Four citizens of Monterey are just in from the gold mines on Feather River, where they worked in company with three others. They employed about thirty wild Indians, who are attached to the rancho owned by one of the party. They worked precisely seven weeks and three days, and have divided $76,844—nearly $11,000 to each." If you leave out the thirty who likely worked for trade goods and food. Or leave out that the Feather River ran through the territory of the Maidu, who had not sold or surrendered their land by treaty, so that all riches extracted and lands ravaged were done so illegally. Today's equivalent, the gold rush that would make Nevada, were it an independent nation, the world's third largest gold producer, is taking place on land never quite obtained from the Western Shoshone. Picture the terrain of gold rushes as a level playing field riddled with mineshafts and poisoned waters.

II

Just as one of those useful commentators from another culture or galaxy might perceive the purpose of drinking heavily to be achievement of a splitting headache and furry tongue in the morning, so she might perceive mining as a way of ravaging great swathes of the land, water, and air about as thoroughly as it is possible to do. For from an ecological point of view, mining produces large-scale, long-term poverty of many kinds, while producing short-term wealth for a small minority. When it comes to iron, aluminum, copper, and other metals necessary for industrial society, you can argue that the mining is necessary, but about 80 percent of the world's current gold production is made into jewelry destined for India and China. The soft yellow metal has had few practical uses throughout history. The U.S. government even now has 8,134 tons hidden away and recently recommitted itself not to sell, helping to buoy up the metal's current high price. (After dropping to about $200 in the 1990s, it has recently soared to more than $600 an ounce.)

Gold was itself money and money was gold throughout most of Near Eastern, European, and American history, right until August 15, 1971, when President Richard Nixon took the wartime United States off the gold standard for various then-expedient reasons, and most of the world followed. Until then the bills that circulated were essentially receipts for gold held in vaults, and the gold coins still in circulation into the twentieth century were literally worth their weight in gold. During the long era of the gold standard, the metal was the means by which all else was quantified, the measure of all other things. Its value when extracted and abstracted from the landscape was obvious. The difficulty of quantifying the true cost of extracting it is the basic failure to account for environmental impact. Contemporary accounting does sometimes speak of "externalized costs," those borne by others than the profiteers, and by this measurement the gold rush was very expensive.

Today's environmental and social justice advocates would like to see "true cost" accounting, in which the price, value, or cost of an item takes into account its entire impact from creation to disposal or recycling. Moves to measure costs in this way are increasing as communities begin to recognize the ways that a corporation, industry, or enterprise may bring specific benefits to their region, but may also potentially wreak more pervasive or long-term damage, social or ecological. Similar analyses could be performed on many enterprises previously framed as profitable, simply by asking, "For whom? And who pays? For how long?" You can look at an individual automobile, for example, as conveying profit to the seller and usefulness to the buyer and noxious fumes and climate change to the larger community. And you can see that we are still paying for the Gold Rush that began 158 years ago.

The California Gold Rush clawed out of the foothills of the Sierra Nevada considerable gold—93 tons or 2.7 million troy ounces in the peak year of 1853 alone, an estimated 973 tons or 28.4 million ounces by 1858, more than 3,634 tons or 10.6 million troy ounces to date. In the course of doing so, everything in the region and much downstream was ravaged. Wildlife was decimated. Trees were cut down to burn for domestic and industrial purposes and to build the huge mining infrastructures that were firmly in place by the 1870s. That infrastructure included huge log dams to make water available for use on demand—the photographer Carleton Watkins took some pictures of them, looking alarmingly precarious as they stoppered deep valleys full of water. According to environmental historian Michael Black, "Within its first five years of operation, California's hydraulic cavalry dismembered whole forests to construct five thousand miles of ditches and flumes. This figure was doubled by the close of the decade." The earth was dug into desolation and later hosed out by the high-powered water-jets of hydraulic mining, so that some landscapes—notably the Malakoff Digging and San Juan Ridge near Nevada City—are still erosive badlands of mostly bare earth. But most of all, the streams and rivers were devastated. The myriad waterways of the Sierra Nevada were turned into so much plumbing, to be detoured, dammed, redirected into sluices high above the landscape, filled with debris and toxins. Water as an industrial agent was paramount, and water as a source of life for fish, riparian life, downstream drinkers, farmers, and future generations was ignored.

By 1853, the Sacramento River's once-prodigious salmon run was in steep decline, and so were those of most of the rest of the streams and rivers that flow into San Francisco Bay. Black continues, "Three years later, an exasperated commissioner reported that owing to mining, fish runs on the Feather, the Yuba, and the American rivers were dead." In 1853, an Indian agent wrote of the Native peoples in the region,

> They formerly subsisted on game, fish, acorns, etc. but it is now impossible for
> them to make a living by hunting or fishing, for nearly all the game has been
> driven from the mining region or has been killed by the thousands of our
> people who now occupy the once quiet home of these children of the forest.
> The rivers or tributaries of the Sacramento formerly were clear as crystal
> and abounded with the finest salmon and other fish. . . . But the miners
> have turned the streams from their beds and conveyed the water to the dry
> diggings and after being used until it is so thick with mud that it will scarcely
> run it returns to its natural channel and with it the soil from a thousand hills,
> which has driven almost every kind of fish to seek new places of resort where
> they can enjoy a purer and more natural element.

There was no new place of resort; the fish mostly just died off.

At the time, the costs of the Gold Rush were perfectly apparent to its witnesses; only later was it reconfigured as a frolic. As Nordhoff wrote in 1873,

> At Smartsville, Timbuctoo, and Rose's Bar I suppose they wash away into
> the sluices half a dozen acres a day, from fifty to two hundred feet deep;
> and in the muddy torrent which rushes down at railroad speed through the
> channels prepared for it, you may see large rocks helplessly rolling along. . . .
> Of course the acres washed away must go somewhere, and they are filling up
> the Yuba River. This was once, I am told by old residents, a swift and clear
> mountain torrent; it is now a turbid and not rapid stream, whose bed has been
> raised by the washings of the miners not less than fifty feet above its level in
> 1849. It once contained trout, but I now imagine a catfish would die in it.

The volume of mercury-tainted soil washed into the Yuba was three times that excavated during construction of the Panama Canal, and the riverbed rose by as much as eighty feet in some places. So much of California was turned into slurry and sent downstream that major waterways filled their own beds and carved new routes in the elevated sludge again and again, rising higher and higher above the surrounding landscape and turning ordinary Central Valley farmlands and towns into something akin to modern-day New Orleans: places below water level extremely vulnerable to flooding. Hydraulic mining washed downstream 1.5 billion cubic yards of rock and earth altogether. Most of it—1.14 million cubic yards—reached the San Francisco Bay. "Nature here reminds one of a princess fallen into the hands of robbers who cut off her fingers for the jewels she wears," said one onlooker at a hydraulic mine.

The gold rush was a huge giveaway of public or indigenous resources to private profiteers, a mass production of long-term poverty disguised as a carnival of riches. Which is to say that the profit the mining operations made was contingent on a very peculiar, if familiar, form of enterprise that might be a mistake to call free: one in which nature and the public domain could be squandered for private gain, in which the many were impoverished so that a few could be enriched, and no one was free to stop them in the name of the public, or almost no one.

Only one great battle was fought against the mining, by downstream farmers. They too were invaders transforming the landscape, but in that pre-pesticide era of farming with horse and plow, their impact was at least comparatively benign, and they had, unlike any miners anywhere, an interest in the long-term well-being of the place and a useful product. The farmers took the hydraulic mining operations of the Central Sierra to court for polluting the rivers, raising their beds, and rendering farms extremely vulnerable to flooding, and they won in 1884. Robert L. Kelley, in his 1959 history of the lawsuit, called it "one of the first successful attempts in modern American history to use the concept of general welfare to limit free capitalism."

III

Gold is heavy, and it sinks to the bottom of a pan, a rocker, a long tom, or whatever device you might have used to get the metal out of the stream in the early days of the California Gold Rush. Some of the gold always slipped away—unless you added mercury, also known as quicksilver, to the water and silt in your pan. The mercury amalgamates with the gold, making it easier to capture, but some of the mercury inevitably washes downstream. With hydraulic mining, the same methods were used on far larger scales. You hosed out riverbanks, hillsides, mountainsides, breaking the very landscape down into slush and slurry that you then washed for the gold that sinks to the bottom. Then you poured mercury, one flask— seventy-five pounds—at a time, into the washing device. This was one of the most extravagant uses of mercury, and much of it traveled downstream. With hard rock mining, as the 1858 *California Miner's Own Handbook* describes it, you put pulverized ore into "an 'amalgamating box' containing quicksilver, and into which a dash-board is inserted that all the water, gold, and tailings may pass through the quicksilver." Here too the mercury helped capture the gold. You dissolved the amalgamation by heating it so that the mercury vaporized, leaving the gold behind, and tried to capture the vapor in a hood for reuse. Inevitably some of it would be atmospherically dispersed, and breathing mercury fumes was one of the more deadly risks of the process.

During the California gold rush, an estimated 7,600 tons or 15.2 million pounds of mercury was thus put into the watersheds of the Sierra Nevada. The U.S. Geological Survey estimates that placer, or stream-based, mining alone put 10 million pounds of the neurotoxin into the environment, while hard-rock mining accounted for another 3 million pounds. Much of it is still there—a Fish and Wildlife biologist once told me that he and his peers sometimes found globules the size of a man's fist in pristine-looking Sierra Nevada streams—but the rest of it traveled downstream, where it ended up lining the bottom of the San Francisco Bay. Some of it is still traveling: the *San Jose Mercury News*—named after the old mercury mines there— reports that 1,000 pounds of the stuff comes out of gold-mining country and into the Bay every year, and another 200 pounds comes from a single mercury mine at the south end of the Bay into the Bay annually. Some of this mercury ends up in the fish, and as you move up the food chain, the mercury accumulates. According to the San Francisco Estuary Institute, "Fish at the top of the food web can harbor mercury concentrations in their tissues over one million times the mercury concentration in the water in which they swim." All around the edges of the bay, warning signs are posted, sometimes in Spanish, Tagalog, and Cantonese as well as English, but people fish, particularly poor and immigrant people, and some eat their catch. They are paying for the gold rush too.

Overall, approximately ten times more mercury was put into the California ecosystem than gold was taken out of it. There is something fabulous about this, or at least fablelike. Gold and mercury are brothers and opposites, positioned next to each other, elements 79 and 80, in the periodic table of elements. Gold has been prized in part because it does not rust, change, or decay, while mercury is the only metal that is liquid at ordinary temperatures, and that liquid is, for those who remember breaking old thermometers to play with the globules, something strange, congealing into a trembling mass or breaking into tiny spheres that roll in all directions, ready to change, to amalgamate with other metals, to work its way into the bodies of living organisms. The miners called it quicksilver, for its color and its volatility. Half gold's goodness is its inertness; it keeps to itself; mercury's problem is its protean promiscuity.

Gold was never more than a material and occasionally a curse in the old stories, but Mercury was the deity who shared with his namesake element the elusive fluctuant qualities still called mercurial, and it is as the god of commerce and thieves that he intersects with the gold that is money. Perhaps in tribute to the element's talent for engendering fetal abnormalities, the mythological Mercury is also the father of Hermaphrodite, though mercury-generated birth defects are never so picturesque. Many other modern industrial processes, notably coal-fired power plants, disperse mercury in the biosphere, but mining did it far earlier.

At least from Roman times onward, mercury was critical for many of the processes used to isolate both gold and silver from ore. Thus mercury was a crucial commodity, not valued in itself, but necessary for obtaining the most valued metals. Sources of mercury were far rarer than those of gold, and one of the great constraints on extracting wealth from the New World was the supply of mercury. (In forested parts of the world, heat could be used in gold refining, but in the fuel-poor deserts, mercury was the only means.) The Almaden Mine in Spain and then the Santa Barbara Mine in Hauncavelica, Peru, were the two major mercury sources in the Western world from the sixteenth century until the mid-nineteenth, and when the Spanish colonies gained their independence, they (except for Peru, of course) lost easy access to this supply of mercury.

So dire was this lack that the Mexican government offered a reward— $100,000 by one account—to whoever could discover a copious supply. In the northwesternmost corner of old Mexico, in 1845, a staggeringly rich mercury lode was discovered by one Captain Don Andres Castillero. Located near San Jose at the southern end of the San Francisco Bay, it became famous as the New Almaden Mine. By the time the mine was developed, it was well within the territory seized by the United States. Only days before the February 2, 1848, treaty giving Mexico $16 million for its northern half was signed, gold was also discovered in California. Thus began the celebrated Gold Rush, which far fewer know was also a mercury rush, or that the two were deeply intertwined.

An anonymous 1857 visitor to the mine Castillero discovered published his (or her?) observations in *Harper's* magazine a few years later. "One of the most curious circumstances connected with the New Almaden Mine is the effect produced by the mercurial vapors upon the surrounding vegetation," said the report.

> Despite the lofty chimneys, and the close attention that has been devoted to the secret of effectually condensing the volatile matter, its escape from the chimneys withers all green things around. Every tree on the mountainside above the works is dead, and some of more sensitive natures farther removed exhibit the influence of the poison in their shrunken and blanched foliage. . . . Cattle feeding within half a mile of the hacienda sicken, and become salivated; and the use of waters of a spring rising near the works is guarded against. . . . The workmen at the furnaces are particularly subjected to the poisonous fumes. These men are only able to work one week out of four, when they are changed to some other employment, and others take their place for a week. Pale, cadaverous faces and leaden eyes are the consequences of even these short spells; and any length of time continued at this labor

effectually shortens life and impregnates the system with mercury. . . . In such an atmosphere one would seem to inhale death with every respiration.

Without the torrent of toxic mercury that poured forth from this and a few smaller mercury mines in the Coast Range, the California Gold Rush would probably been dampened by foreign monopolies on the stuff. Though the mining operation closed more than thirty years ago, the mercury is still leaching out of New Almaden into the San Francisco Bay and out of hundreds of other mercury mines in the state. A series of Gold-Rush-era mercury mines has gravely contaminated Clear Lake 120 miles or so to the north, where the local Pomo people have seven times as much mercury in their systems as the regional normal. In many places, mercury contamination of water forces Native North Americans who have traditionally relied on marine animals and fish as primary food sources to choose between tradition and health.

Gold is the paradise of which the bankers sang; mercury is the hell hidden in the fine print. The problem is not specific to the California Gold Rush, which only realized on a particularly epic scale in a particularly lush and pristine landscape the kinds of devastation gold and mercury can trigger. The current gold rush in northeastern Nevada, which produces gold on a monstrous scale—7 million ounces in 2004 alone—is also dispersing dangerous quantities of mercury. This time it's airborne. The forty-mile-long Carlin Trend on which the gigantic open-pit gold mines are situated is a region of "microscopic gold," dispersed in the soil and rock far underground, imperceptible to the human eye, unaffordable to mine with yesteryear's technology. To extract the gold, huge chunks of the landscape are excavated, pulverized, piled up, and plied with a cyanide solution that draws out the gold. The process, known as cyanide heap-leach mining and banned in Montana, also releases large amounts of mercury, which is often found along with the gold, into the biosphere. Wind and water meet the materials at each stage and create windblown dust and seepage, and thus the mercury and other heavy metals begin to travel.

As the Ban Mercury Working Group reports, "Though cumulatively coal fired power plants are the predominant source of atmospheric mercury emissions, the three largest point sources for mercury emissions in the United States are the three largest gold mines there." The Great Salt Lake, when tested in 2004, turned out to have astonishingly high mercury levels, as did wild waterways in Idaho, and Nevada's gold mines seem to be the culprit. The *Reno Gazette-Journal* reported that year:

> The scope of mercury pollution associated with Nevada's gold mining industry wasn't discovered until the EPA changed rules in 1998 to add mercury to the list of toxic discharges required to be reported. When the first numbers were released in 2000, Nevada mines reported the release of 13,576 pounds in 1998. Those numbers have since been revised upward to an estimated 21,098 pounds, or more than 10 tons, to make Nevada the nation's No. 1 source of mercury emissions at the time.

Glen Miller, a longtime Nevada environmentalist and professor of natural resources and environmental science at the University of Nevada, Reno, estimates that since 1985, the eighteen major gold mines in the state have released between 70 and 200 tons of mercury into the environment.

Maybe some of this is already evident in the Greek myth of King Midas. Bacchus, the god of wine and revelry, gave Midas a single wish and regretted the mortal's foolish choice: the ability to turn anything he touched into gold. The rest is familiar. The king transformed all he touched so that what he tried to drink became gold when it touched his lips, and his thirst grew intolerable. Worse yet, he touched his daughter and his greed turned her to inanimate metal, and it was with this that he begged the god to take back his gift, resigned his crown and power, and became a rural devotee of the god Pan. In this ancient tale, gold is already associated with contaminated water and damaged children. Gold is a curse in Exodus too, when the Israelites, having lost faith during their forty years in the desert, come to worship the Golden Calf made out of melted-down jewelry. Moses comes down from the mountaintop, grinds the golden idol into powder, throws it into a stream, and forces them to drink it. For us, perhaps the Golden Calf is the belief that the current economic system produces wealth rather than poverty. It's the focus on the gold to the exclusion of the mercury.

Midas and the Golden Calf are myth, but true tales of gold as a horror checker the history of the Americas. There is an extraordinary print from Girolamo Benzoni's 1565 *La historia del Mondo Nuovo*, a report by an embittered witness to fifteen years of Spanish colonization. In the image, unclothed Native men, tired of being savagely forced to produce gold, pour the molten metal down the throat of a captive Spaniard in pantaloons. Thus literal fulfillment of a hunger for wealth leads to death, and thus revenge for the brutality of the gold economy begins in the Americas. Another tale comes from the Death Valley Forty-Niners, seeking an easy route but finding a hard one to the California gold fields. On their parched sojourn across the desert, one goldseeker abandoned $2,500 in gold coins to lighten his load in the hopes that thus unburdened he might make it to water and life. Another of these desperadoes snapped at his companion that he had no interest in what looked like gold-bearing ore on the route through the dry lands: "I want water; gold will do me no good." Something similar became the slogan of an anti-gold-mining struggle in Washington State in the 1990s. Pointing out that the water the mine was contaminating had value and, if bottled and sold, more short-term monetary value than the gold, they proclaimed, "Pure water is more precious than gold."

2006

OIL AND WATER

The BP Spill in the Gulf

New Orleans's Saint Charles Avenue is lined with oak trees whose broad branches drip Spanish moss and Mardi Gras beads from the pre-Lenten parades, and behind the oaks are beautiful old houses with turrets, porches, balconies, bay windows, gables, dormers, and lush gardens. There are no refineries for miles, hardly even gas stations on the stretch I was on in mid-June, and the Deepwater Horizon rig that exploded on April 20, 2010, and the oil welling up a mile below it were dozens of miles away as the bird flies. So there was no explanation for the sudden powerful smell of gasoline that filled my car for several blocks or for the strange metallic taste in my mouth when I parked at the Sierra Club offices uptown, except that since the BP spill, such incidents have been common. By mid-July, the spill was supposed to be plugged at last, except that the plug is temporary at best, and the millions of gallons of oil are out there in the ocean, on the coast—and in the air.

The Centers for Disease Control and Prevention and the Environmental Protection Agency have an unhelpful handout for the BP era that says that the effects of such toxic taste

> should go away when levels go down or when a person leaves the area.
> The low levels that have been found are not expected to cause long-term harm. . . . If you smell a "gas station" like odor . . . it may be volatile organic compounds, or VOCs. The key toxic VOCs in most oils are benzene, toluene, ethylbenzene and xylene.

When I went out on the sea from Grand Isle, which is hardly more than a great sandbar at the end of the watery land south of the city, 109 miles from it by car, the taste was much stronger, and one of my companions on the boat had run into far worse. Drew Wheelan, a birdwatcher from the American Birding Association, told us that he had walked into a patch of fumes so intense his body seemed to react automatically and fling him away. "I hit a cloud so concentrated," he wrote on his blog, "that 20 hours later my mouth and tongue still feel as though they've been burned by a hot liquid."

A pregnant friend wondered if she should have left New Orleans altogether, and another friend warned his pregnant girlfriend to stay indoors on the more pungent days. The smells were just part of the ominous, uncertain atmosphere of the Gulf in the wake of the BP spill. The whole region had become something like the Western Front, a place where you might run into pockets of poison gas, except that this wasn't a battlefront: it's home, for pregnant women, for children, for old people who've spent their entire lives here, for people who love the place passionately, for people who don't know anyplace else on earth and don't want to go anywhere, and for people who can't, at least economically. And for countless birds, fish, crustaceans, cetaceans, and other ocean life. The spill has hit them all hard.

If *spill* is the right word for this oil that didn't pour down but welled up like magma from the bowels of the earth. It's also called the Macondo blowout, and maybe *blowout* is a better word. The blowout is about global capital, and about policy, and about the Bush-era corruption that turned the Minerals Management Service into a crony-ridden camp that didn't do its job, and about Big Oil, and about a host of other things. But it is also about the destruction we've all seen in the images, which are horrible in a deep and primordial way. I went out on boats twice and saw an oiled pelican through binoculars and some faint oily traces on wetlands grass and couldn't quite make out the oiled terns in the distance. And I saw what everyone else could see too, the photographs and footage from those who went to ground zero of this catastrophe.

Mary Douglas said that dirt is matter out of place, and petroleum is out of place everywhere above ground. We design our lives around not seeing it even when we pump it into our cars and burn it; and when we do encounter it, it's repulsive stuff with a noxious smell, a capacity to cause conflagrations, and a deadly impact. Nature kindly put a huge amount of the earth's carbon underground, and we have for the past two hundred years been putting it back into the atmosphere faster and faster, even though we now know that this is a project for which words like "destructive" are utterly inadequate.

There's a YouTube video shot by an oil-rig diver in which huge brown globs of oil float underwater like colossal clots of phlegm. From the surface, the chunky brown stuff looks like vomit. "Just globs of death out there," one diver, Al Walker, says in a southern accent. "Oil so thick it blocks out almost all the light below," says another diver. An AP photograph by Dave Martin shows one of the gentle little waves of the Gulf Coast in close-up, a wave on Orange Beach that's brownish gold with spots of orange and black oil on it, water acting just like water and looking just like paint thinner or gasoline.

And then there's the aerial footage taken by John Wathen, or Hurricane Creekkeeper, that's gone viral on YouTube, Facebook, other facets of the Internet, and the media, including CNN. It shows great plumes of smoke rising from the sea, as the oil is burned off the surface. The flames are invisible, but the columns of smoke rise up and float away: burning water, like the famous incident in 1969 when the Cuyahoga River in Cleveland caught fire from having so much industrial contaminant. That was one river in an industrial region; the flat calm blue ocean burning is apocalyptic, a world turned upside-down, rules broken, taboos violated, something as unnatural as nuclear fission and fallout, something nightmarishly wrong, and it extends for hundreds of miles, on water and under it, on shore and in the air.

In the Sierra Club offices, Darryl Malek-Wiley, the club's local environmental justice organizer, showed us a map of the Gulf, checkerboarded with gas leases, and peppered, as though the map had been hit with buckshot, with oil platforms, 4,000 of them. A news story a week later mentioned the 27,000 old oil wells also out there in the territory the maps show, some probably leaking, but no one is monitoring them. Darryl, a big white-haired guy with a southern accent and a slight Santa affect, showed me another map—an aerial photograph of a portion of the Louisiana coast—

on which you could see all the channels the oil and gas industry has cut through the wetlands, creating straight routes through which water can move fast and hard, cutting the channels wider and eroding this coast still further. "Nature meanders but time is money," a bayou-dweller told me. About a football field of coastline erodes away every forty-five minutes, and a third map of Darryl's showed how much land has been lost in the past several decades, since the petroleum industry came to the Gulf, an area about the size of Delaware, or 2,500 square miles.

Oil and gas channels are responsible for nearly half of this erosion of land that is for the most part sediment laid down by the Mississippi over the eons before it was tamed. When you look at the remnant land on a map, it looks like tattered lace, a frail smear of soil pitted and pocketed and veined by fresh and salt water, if the map is up to date. (Mostly we see out-of-date maps that make the coast look more solid and extensive than it is.) From the flat ground you can't see much of this texture, but water is everywhere, and anything can flood. Most structures rebuilt since 2005 are on stilts a dozen feet or more high, ready for the next surge, flood, or sea-level rise, if not for the continuing erosion that will leave a lot of these structures literally out at sea. Sometimes traveling through this country you see drowned old structures whose underpinnings the sea has already reclaimed.

Another source of coastal erosion is the channelization of the Mississippi, which no longer delivers sediment in the quantities it did when it was building up the delta. The place had a lot of problems before BP, really. Shrimping was being undermined by cheap, ecologically horrendous shrimp farms in Asia and Central America, and the Mississippi was delivering its own form of death to the ocean: nitrogen from synthetic fertilizers in the corn belt of the Midwest washes into the river and out to the delta, where it feeds algae blooms that die, decay, and take much of the oxygen out of the seawater. The dead zone is about 8,500 square miles. About a third of the corn is supposed to be for ethanol, the not-very-green alternative to petroleum, so you can see the Gulf being throttled by a pair of energy-economy hands. Inland are the refineries and chemical plants that have given a swathe of the region the nickname Cancer Alley.

Louisiana is in many ways a semi-tropical Third World country with a resource-extraction economy that subsidized splendid social programs in the era of Huey Long, a lot of subsistence lifestyles in remote and roadless places, and corruption and incompetence galore. The current conservative senator, David Vitter, has been mixed up with prostitutes while preaching family values; the Democratic congressman from New Orleans had to resign after he was found to have an unexplained $90,000 in his freezer (in an interesting twist, the disarray he created in the large African-American population allowed the much smaller Vietnamese-American population to send its first representative to the House, Anh "Joseph" Cao, the congressman who in June suggested that BP's president should be given a knife to commit hara-kiri).

People like to say that New Orleans is not a particularly poor, corrupt American city, but rather the rich northern capital of the Caribbean, with its vibrant African-descended cultures, Carnival, sweet gregariousness, and warm weather conducive to living in public. It is rich in cultural creation and continuity in a way no other place in the United States is. Before Katrina, it had the most stable population of any American city: people stayed in one neighborhood, sometimes one house, for generations; they knew their music, their food, their history, and their neighbors, and they celebrated their rituals, which are complex and frequent in this Catholic bacchanal of a port town that has a second-line jazz parade with dancing in the streets forty Sundays a year and a plethora of social organizations, mostly segregated.

It also suffers from racism and hurricanes. Hurricanes make and unmake the landscape. In Hurricane Rita, Chevron's deepwater platform, cleverly named Typhoon, drifted dozens of miles from its position. Another platform was carried sixty-six miles by Katrina and washed up on Dauphin Island. A rig owned by Shell broke free from the Mars platform and dragged a twelve-ton anchor that crushed oil pipelines. The hurricane destroyed seven platforms, damaged twenty-four, and created underwater mudslides that dislodged more than a hundred pipelines. When you travel around the coast, signs everywhere warn you not to dredge or even cast anchor because of the underwater pipelines.

This place was already a toxic mess before the Macondo blowout, thanks to oil.

Eight million gallons of petroleum were spilled in Hurricane Katrina alone, and other spills in the Gulf include the colossal Mexican oil-well blowout of 1979 that sent oil all the way up the Texas coast. That one is over, and maybe it's evidence that a region can recover, if the most directly affected town, Ciudad del Carmen, did recover—what was once a shrimping economy there is now based on petrojobs.

Before the blowout, Katrina seemed like the worst thing that could have happened. Now people mention the hurricane to explain how much worse the blowout is. Not in terms of immediate loss of human life or social conflict, but in terms of clarity and solutions. Hurricanes come in; they wreck and flood; they're over; you clean up. This thing—when will it be over and how can you clean up? Technological disasters—meltdowns, contaminations, toxic spills—tend to be more traumatic than natural disasters, because their consequences are hard to measure and hard to recover from. If you've just been irradiated or poisoned, you don't know if you're going to die of it in twenty years' time or have kids with birth defects; you don't know if it can be cleaned up or how or what clean or safe means; your home might be permanently contaminated and you don't know. You're also likely to have the liable corporation lying to you, whether the incident is Three Mile Island or Bhopal or the *Exxon Valdez*.

Uncertainty has been central to the horror of the spill: unlike a hurricane or an earthquake, the spill has no clear termination, no precedent. There's little that ordinary people can do to respond and no imaginable end to its consequences. "People have a feeling their way of life is disappearing," Darryl at the Sierra Club told me. "What if a really big storm comes right at the rig? Is BP gonna give me one check? Two checks? The next twenty years while we can't fish? Sometimes I don't wanna think about it. I drink a beer, maybe more than one."

"It was already poor and now it's gonna be fuckin' destitute," Henry Rhodes, the tattoo artist who called the first big demonstration against BP in New Orleans and then cofounded the organization Murdered Gulf, told me. "I don't even eat seafood anymore, because that shit's fucked up."

A native New Orleanian, the blond, goateed, and heavily inked man spoke passionately, mournfully, about what he saw as the destruction of his homeland. And he said the moratorium on deepwater rigs on top of the destruction of the seafood industry means "100 billion annually that's just gone."

Margaret Dubuisson, the communications director for the local branch of Catholic Charities, spoke with me at the crisis center in the Vietnamese community in New Orleans East. A huge portion of the immigrant Vietnamese population either fish or process seafood for a living, she said. They are not well educated, and often their English is negligible: "They have Ph.D.s in fishing, but some of them did not go to high school—did not go to grade school. The skills don't transfer. Oyster fishermen especially. If that closes, you can't go a hundred miles up the bayou. It's not transferable." Oystermen here work like farmers, with designated beds they tend and harvest; if your bed is contaminated, you're out of luck. Fresh Mississippi river water redirected to keep oil away from the oyster seedbeds has devastated the saltwater organisms, and the $330 million industry is in big trouble.

It's said that Corexit, the dispersant now being used on the oil, causes birth defects and testicular and reproductive damage, particularly the old batch of more toxic Corexit 9527 that's been used along with the new formula, Corexit 9500. The 407 dead sea turtles may have drowned because of neurological damage from the oil or the dispersant—or in shrimp nets operated by fishermen desperate to get their last catches. About 2 million gallons of dispersant are said to have been poured into the sea.

Why BP has been using dispersant at all is a question whose answer seems to be about a policy of disguising, repressing, and hiding the damage. One cleanup worker quit because she said they were told to remove only the surface sand: the BP supervisors just wanted the beach to *look* clean. One BP contractor, ex-soldier Adam Dillon, was fired for questioning the cleanup after working for months to keep the media at bay. He describes thick oil and disgruntled workers from whom he kept journalists away. BP has created a no-fly zone; the cooperative Coast Guard keeps boats at a distance, their captains afraid of huge penalties if they cross into restricted waters. Workers were obliged to sign non-disclosure contracts; others had all recording technologies confiscated, and data on worker exposure were suppressed. Scientists were not allowed data. Birders were allowed to band but not put transmitters on rescued birds, according to Drew Wheelan. And data on the spill were constantly spun so the volume of gas upwelling was smaller, the impact was less, the facts were unavailable. A vast area of the ocean is now the scene of a cover-up. Even Anderson Cooper, the star anchor on CNN, has spoken out vehemently against this oceanic lock-down that treats scientists and journalists as the enemy.

BP rules the waves and a lot of Louisiana. I met one boat's captain who'd been trying to get information from the Coast Guard but was re-peatedly passed on to BP, which also seemed to be calling the shots on land about who could go where, controlling media access and even air traffic to the area of the spill. Police, sheriffs, National Guardsmen, and politicians seemed to be taking their orders from the corporation whose power, rather than shrinking, has in a strange way grown from its folly and destruction. BP has also taken over virtual space, buying up ads on the Internet and spending a great deal of money to ensure that its own propaganda sites come up first in searches for topics related to the spill. BP's hegemony is part of the helplessness people here feel. BP negligently created a blowout but has intentionally staged a coup. Of course Big Oil has been running American politics for more than a century, an achievement that peaked with the Bush administration. Much of the criticism of Obama is for not sufficiently reining in what his predecessor wrought.

The blowout was not only the biggest oil spill in American history by far: it's a story that touches on everything else—taints everything, like the black glop on sandy beaches, on pelicans, terns, boats, sea turtles, marsh-lands, and dolphins. It's about climate change, peak oil, the energy future, the American presidency; about corporate power and the corrosive effect of Big Oil on global politics. It's also about technology, geology, biology, oceanography, ornithology, the rich, and deeply entrenched cultures of the Gulf; about human health and risk management; about domestic violence, despair, drinking, unemployment, and bankruptcy; about British pension funds, the wake-up call to shareholders, and the class action suit brought by the New Orleans chef Susan Spicer of the restaurant Bayona because contamination, scarcity, or outright loss of the primary ingredients in the region's cuisine—shrimp, crab, fish, and crayfish—is one current and probably continuing outcome of the blowout.

Drill, baby, drill, Sarah Palin's petro chant, is not going to be heard again soon. If the BP blowout had to happen, it happened at an opportune time. Weeks earlier, Obama had said that offshore oil wells were safe and that he was going to open up for exploration and drilling portions of the Atlantic and northern coast of Alaska, much of it for the first time. Shell was preparing to drill in the fragile Beaufort and Chukchi sea regions of the Alaskan Arctic. All of that got put on hold. Timing is everything. If the global economy had waited a month longer to collapse in 2008, there's a good chance John McCain would have become president and Sarah Palin would have been even harder to get rid of.

The blowout also happened at an interesting moment in global history. On the one hand, the conversations about climate change, after the post-Copenhagen hangover, got a little jolt of urgency from this reminder of how brutal, humanly and ecologically, petroleum extraction is. In an essay for TomDispatch.com posted in May, Michael Klare reminded us that the Deepwater Horizon blowout is an augury of the age of extreme extraction to come: "While poor oversight and faulty equipment may have played a critical role in BP's catastrophe in the Gulf, the ultimate source of the disaster is Big Oil's compulsive drive to compensate for the decline in its conventional oil reserves by seeking supplies in inherently hazardous areas—risks be damned." The disaster furthers the arguments for moving away from a carbon economy sooner by putting on display how grotesque these systems—gigantic offshore rigs and drills that go miles below the deep ocean floor—are even when they work.

Horrendous as the spreading oil is, the overall effect on the environment—more climate change—would have been even more irreversibly destructive had the stuff been collected and burned as planned: the biggest disaster, a number of scientists say, is the invisible one we all add to every day with our airplanes and cars, steaks and air conditioners, overseas goods and coal-fired power plants. When everything goes exactly as planned, a deepwater drilling platform is profoundly destructive, polluting, toxic, and dirty: waste goes directly into the surrounding water, drilling releases heavy metals from the sea floor into the sea, and other toxins enter the water. Deepwater drilling releases colossal quantities of methane hydrates, thus releasing methane, a greenhouse gas at least twenty times as potent a climate changer as carbon dioxide. I don't know if this has been a wake-up call to the horrors of the carbon economy, but I haven't heard much from the climate-change deniers lately.

In the wake of the economic collapse of 2008, a new anti-corporate rage has seized the United States, and the BP disaster has focused hatred on the oil companies. If there was a left with the capacity to focus this rage into reform, we might be arguing about the abolition of their huge tax dodges or even the end of corporate personhood—the granting of human and even constitutional individual rights to these behemoths—or the nationalization à la Venezuela of the oil industry. But we're not. Things are dying from BP, but not much is being born that I can see.

Still, the $20 billion claims fund and the $100 million for worker compensation constitute a fairly unprecedented assault on the citadel of corporate profit, a pre-emptive payment. Exxon was able to fight out compensation for the 1989 *Exxon Valdez*'s Prince William Sound spill in court, dragging the process out for decades, outlasting its opponents, and finally settling in 2008 for a pittance compared to the destruction and suffering the corporation's spill had created. As Antonia Juhasz wrote in 2009, in *The Tyranny of Oil*,

> Big Oil gets sued a lot, and its greatest defense is its financial might—its ability to outspend any and all challengers (whether it's a single gasoline consumer in Illinois or the federal government) and ride cases out for five, ten or even 20 years. . . . Chevron alone has 300 in-house lawyers and an annual budget of $100 million for farming out litigation to private firms. It employs some 450 law firms globally.

"This is the biggest thing to happen to Big Oil in a hundred years," Juhasz told me on June 26, just after the local iteration of the national Hands Across the Sand solidarity demonstrations at Ocean Beach in San Francisco. "That is, since the Standard Oil monopoly was broken up. And maybe bigger," she added. The damage of the spill remains to be seen in the Gulf and in the way it may reshape or dismantle Britain's single largest corporation, encourage the regulation of the oil industry and perhaps corporate accountability, and affect the significant but subtler business of public opinion. The recently radicalized Sierra Club used the blowout as an occasion to call for an end to U.S. dependency on oil within twenty years.

Obama compared the blowout to 9/11, which brings up all kinds of possibilities, notably the one that BP is the new al-Qaida, and once you speculate about that, all sorts of interesting ways of mapping the situation arise. Osama bin Laden's inherited wealth was also oil money, or rather construction money from building the infrastructure for the Saudi oil empire, and fifteen of his nineteen hijackers on September 11 were Saudis too. The blowout is really just part of what you could call the contemporary oilscape, which includes the war in Iraq, the presence of the United States in Kuwait and formerly in Saudi Arabia (this was one of bin Laden's grievances), and the role of Big Oil in American politics—which was not long ago dominated by a president, vice president, secretary of state, and others direct from the industry.

The cleanup's lack of safety measures also recalls 9/11. After that disaster, Rudy Giuliani and the Bush administration, anxious to get business back in business and to assert their capacity to handle the situation, suppressed information about the toxicity of the burning heap of rubble that had been the World Trade Center. Asbestos, plastics, heavy metals, PCBs, and other toxins were all going up in smoke and into the lungs of anyone nearby, but the Environmental Protection Agency was pressured into turning scary scientific analysis into reassuring press releases, and thousands of workers worked for months without respirators. "World Trade Center cough" is a widespread disorder among New York City firemen today, and more than 10,000 people have sought treatment after inhaling the fumes.

Similarly, in the Gulf many of the cleanup workers have been sent into toxic situations without protective clothing or respirators. "When I visited a Louisiana Parish Work Release jail this past Friday, it was early evening, and the inmates were returning from their twelve-hour workday shoveling oil-soaked sand into trash bags," my friend Abe Louise Young, whom I met through her Katrina oral history project nearly five years earlier, wrote to me.

Wearing BP uniforms and rubber boots (nothing identifying them as inmates), they were driven in an unmarked white van, and looked dog-tired. The majority of beach workers are African American. It's a striking sight in the Louisiana coastal towns where eight out of ten people are white—and the only telltale sign of their incarceration. In the first few days after the blowout, cleanup workers could be seen wearing scarlet pants and white T-shirts with "Inmate Labor" printed in large red block letters. Outrage flared among local officials and newly unemployed residents desperate for work. Those explicit outfits disappeared in a matter of days. The clothing change is no accident—it's an effort at concealing the nature of BP's labor force. Work-release prisoners have no choice in their job assignments. After arriving in BP uniforms, the inmates suit up in Tyvek head-to-toe coveralls.

Forced labor in toxic conditions. Cheap prison labor undercutting cleanup income for unincarcerated, unemployed Gulf residents. Dead sea turtles by the hundred. Turtles being burned. Plumes of smoke rising up from the burning ocean. Dead whales. Pelicans soaked in oil. Fourteen thousand Vietnamese fishermen out of work in New Orleans Parish alone after having survived Katrina, Rita, and Gustav, after surviving the Vietnam War and exile. A way of life dead, at least temporarily, for the Vietnamese, Cajun, white, black, and indigenous communities of the waterlands. Rebuilt homes in a landscape suddenly without jobs. Derrick Evans of Turkey Creek Community Initiatives told me, as we traveled through the oil-smeared islands of marsh grass in Grand Bayou, that a bayou dweller named Mike had told him: "Osama fuckin' bin Laden could not have imagined, planned or executed more devastation than BP has."

I met Evans at Grand Bayou, out on the road to Port Sulphur and Venice. Think of southern Louisiana as a hand whose fingers are the remnants of the eroded land, pointing south into the sea. New Orleans is somewhere in the palm of that hand, and the easternmost finger has one road running down its length. More than halfway down, past the giant mountain of coal and a few of the countless refineries in the region, there's a tiny sign for Grand Bayou where you turn off onto a dirt road running west. When I did, a beat-up truck passing in the other direction paused, and the dark-skinned driver rolled down his window to say that the party we were looking for was standing by the road just up ahead. Apparently not a lot of people come down that road.

The road soon petered out into a set of boat docks, an abandoned house, and cane marshes, into which flocks of little blue crabs with big right claws scurried when I approached. We found the sailors we were looking for: Rosina Philippe and her brothers Danny and Maurice, members of the Atakapa-Ishak tribe. She told me that their name was Choctaw for "cannibal people," a long-ago slur they hung onto in case it made the small group seem like more impressive opponents. There had been twenty-three families living in Grand Bayou before Katrina; the Amish and the Mennonites helped them rebuild their houses on stilts, but only nine families remained. Some of the evacuees come when they can, she says: "Vacation time, summer time they come back. We make up pallets on the floor. They wanna come back. I didn't get home until August 2009."

As Danny, her younger brother, the one with the *God Is My Hero. And He Rocks* black T-shirt, steered the flat-bottomed boat, Rosina Philippe, a strong woman with a thick dark braid down to her waist, told me, "This situation with the oil will be with us for at least another decade. How to move forward? Our primary food source is from the water. Not only is our source of revenue cut off from us, but our food supply. Maybe three people here work in the [petroleum] industry, but it's not a conflict because they're not the decision-makers."

As the boat went down the wide channels between the flat islands of grass she added, "This area was forested. My father passed last year, at eighty-six. When he was a boy you could cross from one side to another of the channels on foot." The word *bayou* means moving water in a flat, low-lying area, a place that is neither swamp nor stream, and once most of the bayous were wetland forests. Like Grand Bayou, many places still called bayous have eroded into something else.

Ibises flew overhead—young birds who retained their brown markings—and the wind blew through the grasses, and the sky overhead was stormy, and it seemed impossibly peaceful if you could forget it had all just been contaminated, parts of it were dying or dead, and more might be doomed. Rosina Philippe said, "This is nursery for shrimp and fish and crabs—when the oil is all along the banks and into the grasses, everything dies. What's happening in the Gulf right now is death."

Andrea Schmidt, who had just wrapped up an al-Jazeera documentary on the spill when I spoke to her, told me that everyone kept comparing the relationship between fishing and oil extraction to a marriage. Oil was the bellicose husband; fishing was the battered wife; but divorce was not in the works. They are the two economies of coastal Louisiana. This is why the moratorium that's laid off thousands of oil workers and more workers in support industries is not popular locally. In the minds of a lot of people a disaster that's trashed half the economy is not a good reason to shut down the other half.

It was on a trip to Grand Isle (we never got to Queen Bess or any other bird island, thanks to prohibitions against getting within sixty-five feet of a boom) that we met Drew Wheelan, the birder, who saw far more than we did. He wrote on his blog:

> What we found on Queen Bess was oil-soaked sorbent boom tossed into the colony by the waves, and that about 85 percent of all young royal terns on the windward side of the island were oiled on most of their plumage. Many of these birds were severely oiled, and could barely stand. There were at least 45 young royal terns that if I had my say would need immediate rescue and care, though at this point I would have to think that many would succumb to the effects of this oil and weather regardless of care received. The Coast Guard has imposed new rules on these colonies to keep people out, which include criminal trespass, a felony, which could be punishable by 15 years in jail and up to a $450,000 fine. No one I know is prepared to save a bird with that kind of a risk attached.

A major disaster brings in outsiders, some like Drew, some not so altruistic or not so competently engaged with the facts on the ground. Or at sea. At its best, it's like Katrina, which brought an unprecedented wave of volunteers—probably more than a million—to the Gulf and particularly to New Orleans to rebuild, to clean, to cook, and to tend. At its worst, it's a fund-raising and travel opportunity for the self-serving. We went to lunch down the road from Grand Bayou, at Ann's Restaurant and Catering, a collection of trailers by the side of the road in Port Sulphur, with the Reverend Tyronne Edwards of the Zion Travelers Cooperative Center, a dark-skinned man in a light-colored linen jacket and trousers, and Byron Encalade, the African-American president of the Louisiana Oystermen Association, an organization announced on his orange T-shirt. We ordered versions of deep-fried seafood that came in a series of Styrofoam containers, and we washed it down with the over-sweetened iced tea that is the totemic drink of the South. (Was the seafood contaminated? Everyone ate it.) The oysterman and the preacher talked about all the outsiders who were going to be using the Gulf blowout to raise funds, then use the funds to augment their existing programs or meet payroll, a syndrome they'd grown acquainted with after Katrina. They had many complaints about outsiders, politicians, and BP. They wanted everything managed locally.

The reverend talked about all the local African Americans who were disaffected with Obama, including his aged mother. "We wanna support him but man . . . he's really lost a lot of respect. I feel sorry for the president. He's got people around him making him fail. I'm still a supporter of the president, but it's gotten so hard."

Encalade said, "It's the unknown things. Even after Katrina, you assessed where you stood. Here you don't know what your damages are and how long it's gonna last." And he spoke of the Vietnamese refugees and the American veterans of the war that made them refugees who had come here: "That's all any of them ever wanted to do is come home, get a trawler. That was peace by them. I've been talking to the VA." He'd told the Veterans' Administration he was worried about old trauma resurfacing. He talked about the crews on his three boats, now fighting the spill. Later, when we had followed him on the ferry that takes cars across the river to the eastern side of the peninsula, where he kept his boats, he stood on a dock and talked about getting his first boat when he was thirteen, about working in the petroleum industry himself: "But you're always coming back to fishing. We got salt water in our veins and we can't get it out. We ain't trying to. We don't know what's going to happen and that's the thing. Seems like we're down to the last try." | *123*

The Macondo well was capped, though the cap is only temporary. A lot of people will be ready to say the story is over, but that's like saying that you put the bottle of poison down after drinking only a pint of it. The oil is out there, and the consequences will be felt for the foreseeable future. A little more than a week after my trip, I went to the national disaster studies conference in Colorado, where I hung out with a guy who's been studying the *Exxon Valdez* spill for twenty-one years. He told me that the herring industry there never recovered and fishermen were hard hit. The Gulf, in his view, can look forward to the death of the shrimping industry, massive unemployment, an outmigration of those who can go, leaving behind the elderly, indigent, and infirm, a loss of trust and social capital, a lot of despair, and a lot of medical consequences of the chronic stress of living in a ruined world. And to living in a poisoned environment. That this is the Gulf—a place of deeply rooted families and cultures, as well as wildlife— means that there's a lot to lose. Nothing now suggests it won't be lost.

July 2010

IN HAITI, WORDS CAN KILL

Soon after almost every disaster the crimes begin: ruthless, selfish, indifferent to human suffering, and generating far more suffering. The perpetrators go unpunished and live to commit further crimes against humanity. They care less for human life than for property. They act without regard for consequences.

I'm talking, of course, about those members of the mass media whose misrepresentation of what goes on in disasters often abets and justifies a second wave of disaster. I'm talking about the treatment of sufferers as criminals, both on the ground and in the news, and the endorsement of a shift of resources from rescue to property patrol. They still have blood on their hands from Hurricane Katrina, and they are staining themselves anew in Haiti.

Within days of the Haitian earthquake, for example, the *Los Angeles Times* ran a series of photographs with captions that kept deploying the word "looting." One was of a man lying face down on the ground with this caption: "A Haitian police officer ties up a suspected looter who was carrying a bag of evaporated milk." The man's sweaty face looks up at the camera, beseeching, anguished.

Another photo was labeled: "Looting continued in Haiti on the third day after the earthquake, although there were more police in downtown Port-au-Prince." It showed a somber crowd wandering amid shattered piles of concrete in a landscape where, visibly, there could be little worth taking anyway.

A third image was captioned: "A looter makes off with rolls of fabric from an earthquake-wrecked store." Yet another: "The body of a police officer lies in a Port-au-Prince street. He was accidentally shot by fellow police who mistook him for a looter."

People were then still trapped alive in the rubble. A translator for Australian TV dug out a toddler who'd survived sixty-eight hours without food or water, orphaned but claimed by an uncle who had lost his pregnant wife. Others were hideously wounded and awaiting medical attention that wasn't arriving. Hundreds of thousands, maybe millions, needed food, shelter, and first aid. The media in disaster bifurcates. Some step out of their usual "objective" roles to respond with kindness and practical aid. Others bring out the arsenal of clichés and pernicious myths and begin to assault the survivors all over again.

The "looter" in the first photo might well have been taking that milk to starving children and babies, but for the news media that wasn't the most urgent problem. The "looter" stooped under the weight of two big bolts of fabric might well have been bringing it to now homeless people trying to shelter from a fierce tropical sun under improvised tents.

The pictures do convey desperation, but they *don't* convey crime. Except perhaps for that shooting of a fellow police officer—his colleagues were so focused on property that they were reckless when it came to human life, and a man died for no good reason in a landscape already saturated with death.

In recent days, there have been scattered accounts of confrontations involving weapons, and these may be a different matter. But the man with the powdered milk? Is he really a criminal? There may be more to know, but with what I've seen I'm not convinced.

WHAT WOULD YOU DO?

Imagine, reader, that your city is shattered by a disaster. Your home no longer exists, and you spent what cash was in your pockets days ago. Your credit cards are meaningless because there is no longer any power to run credit-card charges. Actually, there are no longer any storekeepers, any banks, any commerce, or much of anything to buy. The economy has ceased to exist.

By day three, you're pretty hungry and the water you grabbed on your way out of your house is gone. The thirst is far worse than the hunger. You can go for many days without food, but not water. And in the improvised encampment you settle in, there is an old man near you who seems on the edge of death. He no longer responds when you try to reassure him that this ordeal will surely end. Toddlers are now crying constantly, and their mothers infinitely stressed and distressed.

So you go out to see if any relief organization has finally arrived to distribute anything, only to realize that there are a million others like you stranded with nothing, and there isn't likely to be anywhere near enough aid anytime soon. The guy with the corner store has already given away all his goods to the neighbors. That supply's long gone by now. No wonder, when you see the chain pharmacy with the shattered windows or the supermarket, you don't think twice before grabbing a box of PowerBars and a few gallons of water that might keep you alive and help you save a few lives as well.

The old man might not die, the babies might stop their squalling, and the mothers might lose that look on their faces. Other people are calmly wandering in and helping themselves, too. Maybe they're people like you, and that gallon of milk the fellow near you has taken is going to spoil soon anyway. You haven't shoplifted since you were fourteen, and you have plenty of money to your name. But it doesn't mean anything now.

If you grab that stuff, are you a criminal? Should you end up lying in the dirt on your stomach with a cop tying your hands behind your back? Should you end up labeled a looter in the international media? Should you be shot down in the street, since the overreaction in disaster, almost *any* disaster, often includes the imposition of the death penalty without benefit of trial for suspected minor property crimes?

Or are you a rescuer? Is the survival of disaster victims more important than the preservation of everyday property relations? Is that chain pharmacy more vulnerable, more a victim, more in need of help from the National Guard than you are, or those crying kids, or the thousands still trapped in buildings and soon to die?

It's pretty obvious what my answers to these questions are, but it isn't obvious to the mass media. And in disaster after disaster, at least since the San Francisco earthquake of 1906, those in power, those with guns and the force of law behind them, are too often more concerned for property than human life. In an emergency, people can, and do, die from those priorities. Or they get gunned down for minor thefts or imagined thefts. The media not only endorses such outcomes, but regularly, repeatedly, helps prepare the way for, and then eggs on, such a reaction.

IF WORDS COULD KILL

We need to banish the word *looting* from the English language. It incites madness and obscures realities.

Loot, the noun and the verb, is a word of Hindi origin meaning the spoils of war or other goods seized roughly. As historian Peter Linebaugh points out, "At one time loot was the soldier's pay." It entered the English language as a good deal of loot from India entered the English economy, both in soldiers' pockets and as imperial seizures.

After years of interviewing survivors of disasters, and reading first-hand accounts and sociological studies from such disasters as the London Blitz and the Mexico City earthquake of 1985, I don't believe in looting. Two things go on in disasters. The great majority of what happens you could call *emergency requisitioning*. Someone who could be you, someone in the kind of desperate circumstances I outlined above, takes necessary supplies to sustain human life in the absence of any alternative. Not only would I not call that looting, I wouldn't even call that theft.

Necessity is a defense for breaking the law in the United States and other countries, though it's usually applied more to, say, confiscating the car keys of a drunk driver than feeding hungry children. Taking things you don't need is theft under any circumstances. It is, says the disaster sociologist Enrico Quarantelli, who has been studying the subject for more than half a century, vanishingly rare in most disasters.

Immediate personal gain is the last thing most people are thinking about in the aftermath of a disaster. In that phase, the survivors are almost invariably more altruistic and less attached to their own property, less concerned with the long-term questions of acquisition, status, wealth, and security, than just about anyone not in such situations imagines possible. (The best accounts from Haiti of how people with next to nothing have patiently tried to share the little they have and support those in even worse shape than them only emphasize this disaster reality.) Crime often drops in the wake of a disaster.

The media are another matter. They tend to arrive obsessed with property (and the headlines that assaults on property can make). Media outlets often call everything looting and thereby incite hostility toward the sufferers as well as a hysterical overreaction on the part of the armed authorities. Or sometimes the journalists on the ground do a good job and the editors back in their safe offices cook up the crazy photo captions and the wrongheaded interpretations and emphases.

They also deploy the word *panic* wrongly. Panic among ordinary people in crisis is profoundly uncommon. The media will call a crowd of people running from certain death a panicking mob, even though running is the only sensible thing to do. In Haiti, they continue to report that food is being withheld from distribution for fear of "stampedes." Do they think Haitians are cattle?

The belief that people in disaster (particularly poor and nonwhite people) are cattle or animals or just crazy and untrustworthy regularly justifies spending far too much energy and far too many resources on control— the American military calls it "security"—rather than relief. A British-accented voiceover on CNN calls people sprinting to where supplies are being dumped from a helicopter a "stampede" and adds that this delivery "risks sparking chaos." The chaos already exists, and you can't blame it on these people desperate for food and water. Or you can, and in doing so help convince your audience that they're unworthy and untrustworthy.

Back to looting: of course you can consider Haiti's dire poverty and failed institutions a long-term disaster that changes the rules of the game. There might be people who are not only interested in taking the things they need to survive in the next few days but also things they've never been entitled to own or things they may need next month. Technically that's theft, but I'm not particularly surprised or distressed by it; the distressing thing is that even before the terrible quake they led lives of deprivation and desperation.

In ordinary times, minor theft is often considered a misdemeanor. No one is harmed. Unchecked, minor thefts could perhaps lead to an environment in which there were more thefts and so forth, and a good argument can be made that, in such a case, the tide needs to be stemmed. But it's not particularly significant in a landscape of terrible suffering and mass death.

A number of radio hosts and other media personnel are still upset that people apparently took TVs after Hurricane Katrina hit New Orleans in August 2005. Since I started thinking about and talking to people about disaster aftermaths, I've heard a lot about those damned TVs. Now, which matters more to you, televisions or human life? People were dying on rooftops and in overheated attics and freeway overpasses, they were stranded in all kinds of hideous circumstances on the Gulf Coast in 2005 when the mainstream media began to obsess about looting, and the mayor of New Orleans and the governor of Louisiana made the decision to focus on protecting property, not human life.

A gang of white men on the other side of the river from New Orleans got so worked up about property crimes that they decided to take the law into their own hands and began shooting. They seem to have considered all black men criminals and thieves and shot a number of them. Some apparently died; there were bodies bloating in the September sun far from the region of the floods; one good man trying to evacuate the ruined city barely survived; and the media looked away. This vigilante gang claimed to be protecting property, though its members never demonstrated that their property was threatened. They boasted of killing black men. And they shared values with the mainstream media and the Louisiana powers that be.

Somehow, when the Bush administration subcontracted emergency services—like providing evacuation buses in Hurricane Katrina—to cronies who profited even while providing incompetent, overpriced, and much-delayed service at the moment of greatest urgency, we didn't label that *looting*.

Or when a lot of wealthy Wall Street brokers decide to tinker with a basic human need like housing . . . Well, you catch my drift.

Woody Guthrie once sang that "some will rob you with a six-gun, and some with a fountain pen." The guys with the six-guns (or machetes or sharpened sticks) make for better photographs, and the guys with the fountain pens not only don't end up in jail, they end up in McMansions with four-car garages and, sometimes, in elected—or appointed—office.

LEARNING TO SEE IN CRISES

Last Christmas a priest, Father Tim Jones of York, started a ruckus in Britain when he said in a sermon that shoplifting by the desperate from chain stores might be acceptable behavior. Jones told the Associated Press: "The point I'm making is that when we shut down every socially acceptable avenue for people in need, then the only avenue left is the socially unacceptable one."

The response focused almost entirely on why shoplifting is wrong, but the claim was also repeatedly made that it doesn't help. In fact, food helps the hungry, a fact so bald it's bizarre to even have to state it. The means by which it arrives is a separate matter. The focus remained on shoplifting, rather than on why there might be people so desperate in England's green and pleasant land that shoplifting might be their only option, and whether unnecessary human suffering is itself a crime of sorts.

Right now, the point is that people in Haiti need food, and for all the publicity, the international delivery system has, so far, been a visible dud. Under such circumstances, breaking into a U.N. food warehouse—food assumedly meant for the poor of Haiti in a catastrophic moment—might not be "violence," or "looting," or "law-breaking." It might be logic. It might be the most effective way of meeting a desperate need.

Why were so many people in Haiti hungry before the earthquake? Why do we have a planet that produces enough food for all and a distribution system that ensures more than a billion of us don't have a decent share of that bounty? Those are not questions whose answers should be long delayed.

Even more urgently, we need compassion for the sufferers in Haiti and media that tell the truth about them. I'd like to propose alternative captions for those *Los Angeles Times* photographs as models for all future disasters.

Let's start with the picture of the policeman hogtying the figure whose face is so anguished: "Ignoring thousands still trapped in rubble, a policeman accosts a sufferer who took evaporated milk. No adequate food distribution exists for Haiti's starving millions."

And the guy with the bolt of fabric? "As with every disaster, ordinary people show extraordinary powers of improvisation, and fabrics such as these are being used to make sun shelters around Haiti."

For the murdered policeman: "Institutional overzealousness about protecting property leads to a gratuitous murder, as often happens in crises. Meanwhile countless people remain trapped beneath crushed buildings."

And the crowd in the rubble labeled looters? How about: "Resourceful survivors salvage the means of sustaining life from the ruins of their world."

That one might not be totally accurate, but it's likely to be more accurate than the existing label. And what is absolutely accurate in Haiti right now, and on Earth always, is that human life matters more than property, that the survivors of a catastrophe deserve our compassion and our understanding of their plight, and that we live and die by words and ideas, and it matters desperately that we get them right.

January 2010

ICEBERGS AND SHADOWS

Further Adventures in the Landscape of Hope

After the Macondo well exploded in the Gulf of Mexico, it was easy enough (on your choice of screen) to see a flaming oil platform, the very sea itself set afire with huge plumes of black smoke rising, and the dark smear of what would become 5 million barrels of oil beginning to soak birds and beaches. Infinitely harder to see and less dramatic was the vast counterforce soon at work: the mobilizing of tens of thousands of volunteers, including passionate locals from fishermen in the Louisiana Oystermen's Association to an outraged tattoo-artist-turned-organizer; from visiting scientists, activist groups, and Catholic Charities reaching out to Vietnamese fishing families to the journalist and oil-policy expert Antonia Juhasz and Rosina Philippe of the Atakapa-Ishak tribe in Grand Bayou. And don't forget the ceaseless toil of the Sierra Club's local environmental justice organizer, the Gulf Coast Restoration Network, the New Orleans–born poet-turned-investigator Abe Louise Young, and so many more than I can list here.

I think of one ornithologist I met in Grand Bayou who had been dispatched to the Gulf by an organization but had decided to stay on even if his funding ran out. This mild-mannered man with a giant pair of binoculars seemed to have some form of pneumonia, possibly induced by oil-fume inhalation, but that didn't stop him. He was among the thousands whose purpose in the Gulf had nothing to do with profit. The force he represented mattered there, as it does everywhere—a force that has become ever more visible to me as I live and journey among those who dedicate themselves to their ideals and act on their solidarities. Only now, though, am I really beginning to understand the full scope of its power.

Long ago, Adam Smith wrote about the "invisible hand" of the free market, a phrase which always brings to my mind horror movies and

Gothic novels in which detached and phantasmagorical limbs go about their work crawling and clawing away. The idea was that the economy would somehow self-regulate and so didn't need to be interfered with further—or so still go the justifications for capitalism, even though it took an enormous armature of government interventions to create the current mix of wealth and poverty in our world. Your tax dollars pay for wars that make the world safe for giant oil corporations, and those corporations hand over huge sums of money to their favorite politicians (and they have so many favorites!) to regulate the political system to continue to protect, reward, and enrich themselves. But you know that story well.

What really interests me aren't the corrosions and failures of this system, but the way another system, another invisible hand, is always at work in what you could think of as the great, ongoing, Manichean arm-wrestling match that keeps our planet spinning. The invisible claw of the market may fail to comprehend how powerful the other hand—the one that gives rather than takes—is, but neither does that open hand know itself or its own power. It should. We all should.

THE ICEBERG ECONOMY

Who wouldn't agree that our society is capitalistic, based on competition and selfishness? As it happens, however, huge areas of our lives are also based on gift economies, barter, mutual aid, and giving without hope of return (principles that have little or nothing to do with competition, self-ishness, or scarcity economics). Think of the relations between friends and between family members. Think of the activities of volunteers or those who have chosen their vocation on principle rather than for profit.

Think of the acts of those—from daycare worker to nursing home aide—who do more, and do it more passionately, than they are paid to do. Think of the armies of the unpaid who are at work counterbalancing and cleaning up after the invisible hand and making every effort to loosen its grip on our collective throat. Such acts represent the relations of the great majority of us some of the time and a minority of us all the time. They are, as the two feminist economists who published together as J. K. Gibson-Graham noted, the nine-tenths of the economic iceberg that is below the waterline.

Capitalism is only kept going by this army of anti-capitalists, who constantly exert their powers to clean up after it and at least partially compensate for its destructiveness. Behind the system we all know, in other words, is a shadow system of kindness, the other invisible hand. Much of its work now lies in simply undoing the depredations of the official system. Its achievements are often hard to see or grasp. How can you add up the foreclosures and evictions that don't happen, the forests that aren't leveled, the species that don't go extinct, the discriminations that don't occur?

The official economic arrangements and the laws that enforce them ensure that hungry and homeless people will be plentiful amid plenty. The shadow system provides soup kitchens, food pantries, and giveaways; takes in the unemployed, evicted, and foreclosed upon; defends the indigent; tutors the poorly schooled; comforts the neglected; and provides loans, gifts, donations, and a thousand other forms of practical solidarity, as well as emotional support. In the meantime, others seek to reform or transform the system from the inside and out, and in this way, inch by inch, inroads have been made on many fronts over the past half century.

The terrible things done, often in our name and thanks in part to the complicity of our silence or ignorance, matter. They are what wells up daily in the news and attracts our attention. In estimating the true makeup of the world, however, gauging the depth and breadth of this other force is no less important. What actually sustains life is far closer to home and more essential, even if deeper in the shadows, than market forces, and much more interesting than selfishness.

Most of the real work on this planet is not done for profit: it's done at home, for each other, for affection, out of idealism, and it starts with the heroic effort to sustain each helpless human being for all those years before fending for yourself becomes feasible. Years ago, when my friends started having babies, I finally began to grasp just what kind of labor goes into sustaining one baby from birth just to toddlerhood.

If you do the math, with nearly 7 billion of us on earth right now, that means more than 7 billion years of near-constant tending only to get children upright and walking, a labor of love that adds up to more than the age of this planet. That's not a small force, even if it is only a force of maintenance. Still, the same fierce affection and determination pushes back everywhere at the forces of destruction.

Though I'm not sure I could bring myself to watch yet again that Christmas (and banking) classic *It's a Wonderful Life*, its premise—that the effects of what we do might best be gauged by considering what the world would be like without us—is still useful. Erase all the groups at work on the environment, hardly noticed by the rest of us, and there would be far more disasters we'd notice.

THE ALTERNATIVES TO "THERE IS NO ALTERNATIVE"
We not only have a largely capitalist economy but an ideological system that justifies this as inevitable. "There is no alternative," as former British prime minister Margaret Thatcher used to like to say. Many still argue that this is simply the best that human nature, nasty to the core, can possibly hope to manage.

Fortunately, it's not true. Not only is there an alternative, but it's here and always has been. Recently, I had dinner with Renato Redentor Constantino, a climate and social justice activist from the Philippines, and he mentioned that he never cared for the slogan "Another world is possible." That other world is not just possible, he pointed out, it's always been here.

We tend to think revolution has to mean a big in-the-streets, winner-take-all battle that culminates with regime change, but in the past half century it has far more often involved a trillion tiny acts of resistance that sometimes cumulatively change a society so much that the laws have no choice but to follow after. Certainly, American society has changed profoundly over the past half century for those among us who are not male, or straight, or white, or Christian, becoming far less discriminatory and exclusionary.

Radicals often speak as though we live in a bleak landscape in which the good has yet to be born, the revolution yet to begin. As Constantino points out, both of them are here, right now, and they always have been. They are represented in countless acts of solidarity and resistance, and sometimes they even triumph. When they don't—and that's often enough—they still do a great deal to counterbalance the official organization of our country and economy. That organization ensures oil spills, while the revolutionaries, if you want to call them that, head for the birds and the beaches, and maybe, while they're at it, change the official order a little, too.

Of course, nothing's quite as simple as that. After all, there are saints in government and monsters in the progressive movement; there's petroleum in my gas tank and money in my name in banks. To suggest that the world is so easily divided into one hand and the other, selfish and altruistic, is impossibly reductive, but talking in binaries has an advantage: it lets you focus on what is seldom acknowledged.

To say there is no alternative dismisses both the desire for and the possibility of alternative arrangements of power. For example, how do you square a Republican Party hell-bent on preserving tax cuts for the wealthiest 2 percent of Americans with a new poll by two university economists suggesting that nearly all of us want something quite different? A cross-section of Americans were shown pie charts depicting three degrees of wealth distribution in three societies, and pollsters asked them what their ideal distribution of wealth might be. The unidentified charts ranged from our colossal disparity to absolute equality, with Swedish moderation in between.

Most chose Sweden as the closest to their ideal. According to the pollsters, the choice suggested that "Americans prefer some inequality to perfect equality, but not to the degree currently present in the United States."

It might help to remember how close we had come to Sweden by the late 1970s, when income disparity was at its low ebb and the Reagan revolution was yet to launch. Of course, these days we in the United States aren't offered Swedish wealth distribution, since the system set up to represent us actually spends much of its time representing self-interest and moneyed interests instead. The Republicans are now being offered even larger bribes than the Democrats to vote in the interests of the ultra-affluent, whether corporate or individual. Both parties, however, helped produce the Supreme Court that, with the *Citizens United* decision in January, gave corporations and the wealthy unprecedented power in our political system, power that it will take all our energy to counteract and maybe, someday, force into retreat.

By the way, in searching for that Thatcher no-alternative quote, I found myself on a page at Wikipedia that included the following fund-raising plea from a Russian woman scientist: "Almost every day I come home from work and spend several hours improving Wikipedia! Why would I donate so much of my free time? Because I believe that by giving my time and effort—along with thousands of other people of different nationalities, religion, ages—we will one day have shared and free knowledge for all people."

Imperfect as it may be, ad-free, nonprofit Wikipedia's sheer scope—3.5 million entries in English alone, to say nothing of smaller Norwegian, Vietnamese, Persian, and Waray-Waray versions with more than 100,000 articles each—is an astonishing testimony to a human urge to work without recompense when the cause matters.

BUTTERFLY SPOTTING

The novelist and avid lepidopterist Vladimir Nabokov once asked someone coming down a trail in the Rockies whether he'd seen any butterflies. The answer was negative—there were no butterflies. Nabokov, of course, went up that same trail and saw butterflies galore.

You see what you're looking for. Most of us are constantly urged to see the world as, at best, a competitive place and, at worst, a constant war of each against each, and you can see just that without even bothering to look too hard. But that's not all you can see.

Writing my recent book about disasters, *A Paradise Built in Hell*, led me to look at the extraordinary way people behave when faced with catastrophes and crises. From news coverage to Hollywood movies, the media suggest that, in these moments of turbulence when institutions often cease to function, we revert to our original nature in a Hobbesian wilderness where people take care of themselves alone.

Here's the surprise, though: in such situations, most of us take care of each other most of the time—and beautifully at that. Perhaps this, rather than (human) nature red in tooth and claw, is our original nature. At least, the evidence is clear that people not only behave well but take deep pleasure in doing so, a pleasure so intense it suggests that an unspoken, unmet, enormous appetite for meaningful work and vibrant solidarities lives within us. Those appetites can be found reflected almost nowhere in the mainstream media, and we are normally told that the world in which such appetites might be satisfied is "utopian," impossible to reach because of our savage competitiveness, and so should be left to the most impractical of dreamers.

Even reports meant to be sympathetic to the possibility that another better world could exist in us right now accept our social-Darwinian essence as a given. Consider a November *New York Times* piece on empathy and bullying in which David Bornstein wrote,

> We know that humans are hardwired to be aggressive and selfish. But a growing body of research is demonstrating that there is also a biological basis for human compassion. Brain scans reveal that when we contemplate violence done to others we activate the same regions in our brains that fire up when mothers gaze at their children, suggesting that caring for strangers may be instinctual. When we help others, areas of the brain associated with pleasure also light up. Research by Felix Warneken and Michael Tomasello indicates that toddlers as young as 18 months behave altruistically.

Are we really hardwired to be aggressive and selfish, as Bornstein says at the outset? Are you? No evidence for such a statement need be given, even in an essay that provides plenty of evidence to the contrary, as it's supposed to be a fact universally acknowledged, rather than an opinion.

THE COMPASSION BOOM

If I were to use the normal language of the marketplace right now, I'd say that compassion and altruism are hot. It might, however, be more useful to say that the question of the nature of human nature is being reconsidered at the moment by scientists, economists, and social theorists in all sorts of curious combinations and coalitions. Take, for example, the University of California's Greater Good Science Center, which describes itself as studying "the psychology, sociology, and neuroscience of well-being, and teaches skills that foster a thriving, resilient, and compassionate society." Founding director Dacher Keltner writes, "Recent studies of compassion argue persuasively for a different take on human nature, one that rejects the preeminence of self-interest."

A few dozen miles away is Stanford's Center for Compassion and Altruism Research and Education, which likewise draws on researchers in disciplines ranging from neuroscience to Buddhist ethics. Bornstein's essay mentions another organization, Roots of Empathy in Toronto, that reduces violence and increases empathy among children. Experiments, programs, and activities like this proliferate.

Independent scholars and writers are looking at the same underlying question, and stories in the news this year—such as those on school bullying—address questions of how our society gets organized, and for whose benefit. The suicides of several queer young people generated a groundswell of anti-bullying organizing and soul-searching, notably the largely online "It Gets Better" attempt to reach out to queer youth.

In a very different arena, neoliberalism—the economic system that lets the invisible hand throttle what it might—has finally come into question in the mainstream (whereas if you questioned it in 1999, you were a troglodyte and a flat-Earther). Hillary Clinton lied her way through the 2008 primary, claiming she never supported NAFTA, and her husband, who brought it to us, publicly apologized for the way his policies eliminated Haiti's rice tariffs. "It was a mistake," Bill Clinton told the Senate Foreign Relations Committee on March 10. "I had to live every day with the consequences of the loss of capacity to produce a rice crop in Haiti to feed those people because of what I did."

Think of those doing the research on altruism and compassion as a radical scholarly movement, one that could undermine the philosophical and political assumptions behind our current economic system, which is also our political system. These individuals and organizations are putting together the proof that not only is another world possible, but it's been here all along, as visible, should we care to look, as Nabokov's butterflies.

Do not underestimate the power of this force. The world could be much better if more of us were more active on behalf of what we believe in and love; it would be much worse if countless activists weren't already at work, from Aung San Suu Kyi in Burma and the climate activists in Tuvalu to the homeless activists around the corner from me. When I studied disasters past, what amazed me was not just that people behaved so beautifully but that, in doing so, they found such joy. It seems that something in their natures, starved in ordinary times, was fed by the opportunity, under the worst of conditions, to be generous, brave, idealistic, and connected; and when this appetite was fulfilled, the joy shone out, even amid the ruins.

Don't think of this as simply a description of my hopes for the future, but of what was going on right under our noses; it's a force we would do well to name, recognize, celebrate, and enlarge upon now. It is who we are, if only we knew it.

December 2010

INSIDE OUT, OR INTERIOR SPACE

(and Interior Decoration)

MUDDING AND TAPING

There are times when it's clear to me that by getting and spending, we lay waste our powers, and times when, say, the apricot velvet headboard against the lavender wall of a room in an old hotel fills me with a mysterious satisfied pleasure in harmonies of color, texture, atmospheres of comfort, domesticity and a desire to go on living among such color and texture and space and general real estate. There are times when I believe in spiritual detachment, though there was a recent occasion when I bothered to go take a picture of my old reading armchair to the upholsterer's around the corner to see if can be made beautiful again and worry about whether charcoal velveteen would go with my next decor. There are times when I enjoy the weightlessness of traveling and wish to own nothing and afternoons when I want to claim every farmhouse I drive by as my own, especially those with porches and dormers, those spaces so elegantly negotiating inside and out, as though building itself could direct and support an ideal life, the life we dream of when we look at houses.

For admiring houses from the outside is often about imagining entering them, living in them, having a calmer, more harmonious, deeper life. Buildings become theaters and fortresses for private life and inward thought, and buying and decorating is so much easier than living or thinking according to those ideals. Thus the dream of a house can be the eternally postponed preliminary step to taking up the lives we wish we were living. Houses are cluttered with wishes, the invisible furniture on which we keep bruising our shins. Until they become an end in themselves, as a new mansion did for the wealthy woman I watched fret over the right color for the infinity edge tiles of her new pool on the edge of the sea, as though this shade of blue could provide the serenity that would be dashed by that slightly more turquoise version, as though it could all come from the ceramic tile suppliers, as though it all lay in the colors and the getting. And yet . . .

I met a prodigal leftist at his house, where the infinitely intricate old Victorian sofa reupholstered in Indonesian ikat fabric amazed me, because it was so thoughtfully exquisite and because I didn't know that revolutionaries were allowed to have such things—one of the dictates of the 1970s was that we would hold off on pleasure until after the revolution, and, as all the finger-smudged light switches, tattered posters and crusty kitchens of the collective households bore witness, at least some pleasures, notably the aesthetic ones, were being forestalled. There was another revolutionary, this one with a fugitive era behind her, whose apartment was an exquisite symphony of colors and nicely appointed forms, heavy Mexican goblets, shining floors, wide white-painted blinds set the expensive way inside the window frame. Even the cat that wandered across all the furniture, including the writing desk and the dining table, was Abyssinian, tawny with a pumpkin-colored underside that harmonized with the rest in this sanctuary from which to continue staging insurrections. Then there were the antinuclear radicals living outside the usual networks and inside an adapted school bus I remember best for including a sewing machine, a windowsill of potted plants, and a rack of preserves in pretty jars, held on during travel by a wooden bar across each row. Home sneaks in everywhere, even the gardens the interned Japanese Americans built in their doubly hostile desert camps, or in the way the endlessly displaced might tack up a calendar from home whose images continue to matter long after the months and days are past, even the newspaper and magazine clippings pasted on the walls of old prospector sheds abandoned in the desert long ago.

You feel it too, you who hold this book that is both a bundle of ideas and another twig to lay on the future fire of your home, though whether your lust lies in Eames chairs or old Doric pillars remains unknown to the writer who herself is sitting facing a white west wall with three panels of molding; has to her right a shelf with antlers, dolls, and books; and to her left, a bay window; and tilted on that wall before her, a bulletin board of pictures of horses, dead swans, phantom girls, a full-page magazine reproduction of Rosa Parks in her booking photograph, an old map of the world in which California is still an island, a few letters to answer, and some ancient African iron-bar money made to resemble fishes and birds, with fins and wings to keep it moving, all tacked up together; then to the right, on the desk, a little egg cup filled with soft oval gray beach stones flecked with a lighter, more translucent stone; and on the desk itself, a preserves jar used as a pencil cup, a brooch and a turquoise necklace waiting to be put away, an article on the ravaged landscape of Baghdad, a calculator, and an old sewing machine parts tin labeled Brother, filled with the cards of an endless wave of meetings and encounters, and a sea of papers.

WALNUT VENEER

Maybe it's important to make a distinction between what gets called materialism and what real materialism might be. By *materialistic* we usually mean one who engages in craving, hoarding, collecting, accumulating with an eye to stockpiling wealth or status. There might be another kind of materialism that is simply a deep pleasure in materials, in the gleam of water as well as silver, the sparkle of dew as well as diamonds, an enthusiasm for the peonies that will crumple in a week as well as the painting of peonies that will last. This passion for the tangible might not be so possessive, since the pleasure is so widely available; much of it is ephemeral, and some of it is cheap or free as clouds. Then too, the hoarding removes the objects—the Degas drawing, the diamond necklace—to the vault where they are suppressed from feeding anyone's senses.

One of the top ninety-nine peculiarities about houses and homes is that they are both: real-estate speculation and sanctuary. Artists have a different relation to the material, since, after all, the main animosity toward the realm of substances and solid objects is that they distract from the life of the mind or spirit; but it's the job of artists to find out how materials and images speak, to make the mute material world come to life, and this too undoes the divide. Words of gold, of paint, of velvet, of steel, the speaking shapes and signs that we learn to read, the intelligence of objects set free to communicate and to teach us that all things communicate, that a spoon has something to say about values, as does a shoe rack or a nice ornamental border of tulips and freesias. But just as passion can become whoredom, as home becomes real estate, so the speaking possibility of the material world can degenerate into chatter and pitches: the latest catalogue in my mailbox proclaims, "BLUSH: pales beyond comparison. These edgier new pinks are a lot less about yesterday's innocence and a lot more about today's soft modern. Just a blush quietly steals the scene in key moments. Like these sheer glass dessert plates. Or exaggerated shirt-striped bed linens." And the pink is a very nice pink too, in the photographs, even without the coconut-covered cake atop the pink cake platter. Desire is easy. And everywhere.

DRAINBOARD

Maybe a house is a machine to slow down time, a barrier against history, a hope that nothing will happen, though something always does. But the materials themselves are sometimes hedges against time, the objects that change and decay so much more slowly than we do, the empire bed in which were conceived children who died a century ago, the old silverware from weddings several wars before that you can buy at the better garage sales, the ones held by people who seldom moved so that objects could drift down on them like muffling snow over the decades until death or dissolution obliged them to dig out. Those estate sales in the houses where an old person has died—I went to one recently near UCLA. The vast accumulation of what must have been a marriage begun in the 1940s or 1950s—a prosperous conventional life with side tables, fake pearls, Persian rugs, silver ewers, china vases, dollhouse dishes, old-fashioned luggage, and more—was all laid out for strangers to browse, the equipment of a particular life turned back into commodities the way that a stricken body is broken down into organ donations.

CONSTRUCTION SITE

The best piece of furniture in classical literature is Penelope and Odysseus's marriage bed, which has as one bedpost an olive tree growing out of the ground of the bedroom, a bed that Odysseus in some pre-Homeric moment of home improvement made himself. But the rooted bed seems to belong most truly to Penelope, who remains homebound, while another piece of carpentry, a wooden ship, belongs to Odysseus, who moves endlessly, restlessly in the book that bears his name before arriving back in the territory that is synonymous with Penelope. Twenty years later he returns, and she tests him by offering to have their bed moved to another room. His knowledge that it's immovable confirms his true identity: furniture reaffirms the marriage.

It often seems that the house is an extension of the female body, and the car, of the male body, for thus go the finicky and exacting arenas of self-improvement, the space that represents the eroticized self; and in these female interiors and male rockets lies the old literary division of labor, of travelers and keepers of the flame, of the female as a fixture in the landscape the male traverses and conquers. Certainly historically, men had far more mobility than women. Until Odysseus comes home, but then the story stops. And the legend has him restless, leaving again, to sail beyond the Gates of Hercules and into the unknown, a gate Virginia Woolf sailed past from within her house and by leaving it on foot to prowl London. She wrote in annoyance at the limits of life in the living room, "For there we sit surrounded by objects which perpetually express the oddity of our own temperaments and enforce the memories of our own experience." Inside, it's harder to be someone else; houses are anchors and even dead weights on the transmigratory drift of souls, dog tags that are as much bigger than their owner as the dogs are to the tags. We want both, to burn it down and be no one and to be recognized by the dog on the daily walk up the drive from work, and we get both but never exactly when and how we imagined it.

Athenian women, writes Richard Sennett, "were confined to houses because of their supposed physiological defects." Another architectural historian, Mark Wigley, writes,

> In Greek thought women lack the internal self-control credited to men as the very mark of their masculinity. This self-control is no more than the

maintenance of secure boundaries. These internal boundaries . . . cannot be maintained by a woman because her fluid sexuality endlessly overflows and disrupts them. And more than this she endlessly disrupts the boundaries of others, that is, men. . . . In these terms the role of architecture is explicitly the control of sexuality, or more precisely, women's sexuality, the chastity of the girl, the fidelity of the wife. . . . While the house protects the children from the elements, its primary role is to protect the father's genealogical claims by isolating women from other men.

The house was a container for the uncontained, a prison for those who might—not in their linear trajectories but their social mores—go out of bounds, and thus it is that Odysseus sleeps around with various princesses and nymphs on his sea voyage while Penelope wards off her suitors and waits, settled into the stasis that domestic space is meant to embody anyway. You can imagine a modern version in which they live on a houseboat or a motor home so that motion and stasis, discovery and comfort are not divided and dispatched along opposite directions.

KITCHEN ISLAND

Martha Stewart was both Penelope and Odysseus, a trickster building an empire by playing a homemaker. She sold paradise, or the path to it, and it made her and the major stockholders in Martha Stewart Omnimedia rich, even if Omnimedia sounded kind of like Ozymandias. For several years her food-and-home magazine triumphantly presented a vision of idealized life and instructions on the journey toward it. In the absolute paradise—Eden before the fall, Virgil's Golden Age—work is unnecessary. "Ripe fruit," as Andrew Marvell remarked, "doth drop about my head," and the trees that drop it don't need pruning or fertilizing either. But this vision has faded away. In its place is the silver age, in which leisure and labor are combined into a harmonious whole, a pastoral, or rather, a georgic. In recent years, a whole genre of literature of restoring the country home, usually in some fabulous part of Europe, has arisen as the modern version, a *This Old House* in the Peaceable Kingdom—part catalogue, part travelogue, part instruction manual—in this era when executives all seem to wish they were chefs.

Stewart's great contribution was to make the setting of the stage into the drama itself.

Her empire's putative subject is pleasurable leisure but its subtext is always labor, a labor redeemed or at least redecorated as pleasure, an interminable journey disguised as arrival. There are considerable pleasures in pruning the roses, as there are in pumping iron, but they are not leisure in the old sense of the word. The moment of arrival is always delayed, for that is the moment of true idleness. Being present in the sphere of friendship, of love, of amiable society does not quite happen in her world. In Stewart's world the bride is always getting dressed, the hostess is always setting the table for the guests who have not yet arrived, like Penelope weaving and unweaving at her loom to forever delay the moment when she must choose a suitor to marry, only this Penelope seems to have skipped the suitors or forgotten them in favor of the loom. It recalls Jorge Luis Borges's essay on Achilles and the tortoise, playing with an old paradox of Zeno's—that if time can be divided infinitely, then Achilles racing a tortoise will never catch up because both will move through an infinite number of increments that eternally delay arrival. The repainting of the window frames, the arranging of the wreaths, the crafting of the candlesticks, the growing of the sage for the scones for the basket for the breakfast table for the Easter whose resurrection always remains on the horizon.

On the one hand we can imagine Martha running a house in which needlepointed cushions say *Arbeit Macht Frei*; on the other, we can summon up William Morris and John Ruskin trying to locate the meaning in labor in the face of the Industrial Revolution. One of the great ironies of her empire is that she was supposed to be teaching people to make a home, but her kinship network seemed to consist largely of dogs, cats, pet birds, Auracana chickens laying colorful eggs, and other purchasable members of a menagerie. The guests in Stewart's world never seem to arrive, and she herself seemed to live in a series of mansions with animals and servants as her only companions. In the *Odyssey*, island-dwelling Circe turned unwary visitors into the meek pigs, lions, and wolves that roamed around her stone mansion, and Stewart in her domesticity seems more Circe than Odysseus or Penelope. A big loom and a surpassingly beautiful bed are the furnishings Homer describes, along with Circe's golden cup whose contents turn men into beasts.

The house is the stage set for the drama we hope our lives will be or become. And it's much easier to decorate the set than to control the drama or even find the right actors or even any actors at all. Thus the hankering for houses is often desire for a life, and the fervency with which we pursue them is the hope that everything will be all right, that we will be loved, that we will not be alone, that we will stop quarreling or needing to run away, that our lives will be measured, gracious, ordered, coherent, safe. Houses are vessels of desire, but so much of that desire is not for the physical artifact itself.

And then there is that ominous phrase, *behind closed doors*, for good décor doesn't solve all these questions of conduct and discord and even violence and death. Think of the blood of her rapist/lover dripping through the nice carpeting to the elegant ceiling of the apartment below in Thomas Hardy's novel *Tess of the d'Urbervilles*, while Tess in her fashionable clothes breaks into a shuttered country mansion with her belatedly returned husband before going to jail and being hanged. Or of the domesticity of domestic violence in the United States, where women are encouraged to be afraid to leave the house but statistics suggest danger really lies inside with the known rather than outside with the unknown.

CRESCENT WRENCH

There is a flipside to this division of labor and desire, the huge population of men who might better than anyone earn the term *homemaker*, the carpenters, framers, cabinetmakers, plumbers, electricians, painters, plasterers, and other craftspeople, still overwhelmingly male, who actually make and remake and change houses, these independent contractors who show up in domestic space to cut it open, tear it up, make a mess, and then make it something else, make it approximate the dream of the homeowner. One builder I knew spoke of all the wealthy women he worked for whose beds were too full of pillows, another of the loneliness the repairmen were called upon to assuage: work they had not contracted for. These men in their canvas clothes and tool belts embody the role traditionally ascribed to women in another respect: they spend a great deal of time shopping—for half-inch copper pipe, for flathead ⅜" screws, for tongue-and-groove oak flooring, for Navajo white paint, for polished slate tiles—and every construction project is in part a little flurry of comings and goings from the supply stores that inhabit their own zone in almost every town and city, the resource pile from which each house arises with its own trails stretching back to brick factories and slate quarries and forests filtered through lumber mills. But it is the nature of American imagination to think largely of the consumer rather than the producer, and so homes belong to their owners, not to their makers in most representations. Thus domesticity has a secret masculinity, the empire of labor that built every realm of leisure. Martha Stewart, on the other hand, was punished for turning homemaking into empire building, and all her domestic arts were lost on the prison she was sentenced to for five months.

BUTCHER BLOCK

All these pictures in all the magazines and books and catalogues depict the home before life begins, the house with the flowers on the table and the pillows on the sofa and no one yet arrived, unrumpled sheets, uneaten cakes. Crime photographs show the aftermath of a drama, evidence that may include the lifeless corpse among the furniture and other trappings of everyday life that is no longer everyday or life, the domesticity of gone forever. Maybe all those magazines full of unpopulated pictures of granite and chrome kitchens and austerely elegant dining rooms and beautiful window treatments are crime scenes as God sees them, before anything happens, before our fate is known even to ourselves, before our time—as measured by alarm clocks or retro kitchen clocks or wood-encased mantelpiece clocks or the blinking red eye of the DVD player's built-in digital clock shining out in the darkness or even an heirloom grandfather clock with sun and moon on its face—has run out.

Here in old police photographs are the scenes of the murder of Marie-Oliva LePrince on the Rue Saint Denis in Paris in 1898, strangled at the age of fifty by her twenty-one-year-old delivery boy Xavier Schneider. We learn from the photographs that her parlor had a hardwood floor of wide dark planks with an interesting grain, a gilt clock under glass on a side table, a wallpaper that in black and white is startling in the boldness of its contrast. A landscape painting of a body of water surrounded by two dark coulisses of land and trees tilted forward from the wall on the left, the painting hovering above a frilly lampshade like a cloud above the sun. A pattern of beautiful botanical prints, each plant enclosed in a sort of double-pointed oval of wallpaper, adorned the room she used as the shop for her small business of making artificial flowers, which she sold along with feathers; and a little table is visible beyond, draped in a heavy fringed brocade, the doors paneled and painted dark, the chairs dark too. Here is her body sprawled in a dazzling cloud of natural light on another wide plank floor, half underneath a nice oval table whose surface, also caught in the blinding light from the window, seems to be spread with papers; behind her, the same cameos of botanical specimens, climbing up the wall just as calmly as though no one had been violently killed within a few feet of them. The candlestick on the chest of drawers is very nice too, tall with a twisting trunk. And the cloth on the oval table is thin this time, falling in ripples from the edge. Though Madame LePrince is still half under the table, lifeless as a piece of furniture but not nearly as stable, except in the photograph, which holds the threat of becoming itself in all its weirdness someone else's home ornament, as the furniture no doubt became, and the tables may yet be in the living world, holding the burdens of another who knows nothing of the sad end of the feather dealer and flower maker.

A book of color pictures of Swedish houses I picked up recently shows a historic house with the same wide planks and dramatic wallpaper in one of the rooms, and they are what we are supposed to look at in the absence of drama, though drama there must have been in a place so old. But the bodies are nowhere.

DEEP FREEZE

Maybe the problem is pictures, that we think in pictures, and we want to: the point of a wedding may be to reduce the weather-like volatility of a relationship into an authoritative picture of cake, happiness, lace, and rented tuxedo. Homes too are imagined as they should be—the Platonic version—before the mail begins to pile up on the table, before the collaps-ible pool dominating the yard leaves a round ring of brown on the grass, before our bodies leave their imprints in the furniture and their smudges on the walls, before the apple tree took on that strange lopsided shape, before the floor lost its sheen, before the last 117 purchases buried the ar-chitecture altogether. Dream homes are dreamt in pictures, and again and again, well-off people move to the country because the picture is so great: there are the mountains, here are the ten acres with wall or split-rail gir-dled round, in the middle is the rustic cabin or the rugged adobe or the ranch house with the stone fireplace. And like children in fantasy books, the buyers step into the picture only to find out that there is still the prob-lem of time: the mountains are uplifting, but they want to do things, they want to talk to people, they want access to the comforts of civilization, and these may not be included with the elk or the woodpeckers or the aspen grove, let alone the blizzard, the snowed-out roads, the broken well pump; and so they move, and someone else comes along and tries out living in pictures. Or maybe we want to be still as pictures, keep inserting ourselves into them, but find we are too restless and active to stay in them. As though we wanted to be pressed flowers, but went on blooming and going to seed, decaying and regenerating.

NU BLINDS

In James Joyce's *Ulysses*, Leopold and Molly Bloom live, famously, at 7 Eccles Street in Dublin, in a house big enough to allow two lives to pursue wildly different directions; we see him in the weak light of his kitchen pouring milk for the cat, "dark eyeslits narrowing with greed till her eyes were green stones," hear her upstairs turning over and causing "the loose brass quoits of the bedstead" to jingle; we accompany him with some reading material to the jakes, the outhouse, in the back garden. Joyce's real-life wife, Nora Barnacle, had grown up with her six siblings and parents in a tiny two-room house in Galway that seems hardly big enough to have accommodated a couple in love, a house in which every sneeze and scratch and mood must have been shared or at least widely known. What was absent in that house is individualism, the space for independent action and private choice.

On the other hand, a friend who is a high-end housepainter told me once of the new homes of the wealthy he was often hired to repaint, of the cathedral-ceilinged living rooms used only to impress the rare visitor, the bedrooms and suites so well appointed with private bathrooms and home entertainment systems that not only did the house provide a retreat from society but also an isolation of each from each, a sort of minimum security—for breaking out, not for breaking in—solitary confinement system. There were lonely trails, he told me, worn into the carpet by the walks from bedroom to refrigerator or microwave, as though each dweller had become furtive, an animal in its den, coming out only to feed, and not at the dinner table.

Imagine what was once the family space becoming a kind of terra incognita, the swampy wilderness to be traversed by each fugitive from communion, the deep carpet sprung up into grasslands and forests, the hundreds of miles of trackless waste between each bedroom, the bear traps laid for the unwary by some other wanderer who may be kin or killer or both, the roofs crumbling in, the blizzards whose snowfall makes it impossible to trace your own footprints backward to where you began to venture out, the blinding shafts of light, the wildlife arriving as it has in ruinous cities such as Rome then and Detroit now, the crumbling decay of old artifacts that may never be deciphered by anyone even before the jungle grows over them, the house as it is in our dream lives, where old fears and new rooms are constantly discovered, where every house contains, like our own heads, everything. Though it's hard to know whether these families in suburban McMansions treading the plush carpets at separate times or the Barnacle crew had more room inside.

TALL HEDGE

I knew an artist once who had a beautiful home that kept growing, being improved, with garden, ornament, plastered walls, a kitchen wide enough to waltz across and more, a private paradise, but one that cost so much that the more it grew the more she was forced to work her job in another state to pay for it, a conundrum as good as that of Achilles and the Tortoise: would she have been better off settling for a pretty-good home and more time to spend in it? She was only an extreme version of an ordinary story: the family that moves to the outskirts in order to have a larger home, but in so doing, gives up not only the public amenities that cities have and suburbs don't but also surrenders much of the time that might otherwise have been spent with the kids, time that will now be spent commuting alone in a car. The house is the picture of pleasure, while the amount of time it takes to earn it or make it or maintain it or even reach it from the office is just an idea correlated to clocks. It's partly in pursuit of ever-larger homes—the average American home has doubled in the last half century—that Americans got so frantic.

In other times and places, privacy wasn't even a luxury: the duc de Saint-Simone reports that in Versailles, Louis XIV would hold audiences while he was on the toilet, and his dressing was a state ceremony with many privileged to participate in drawing the bed curtains and handing in the holy water and dressing gown. Of course the sacred body of the king was mystically one with the body of the nation, but even ordinary people relied on communal sites for many of their personal needs: the great bathhouses of Eastern Europe, the baker's oven where you took your loaves or roast in times and places without home ovens, the town swimming pool, and the movie theaters all of us old enough to remember life before home video attended like temples of darkness. More of our lives used to be in public, among strangers and acquaintances; that desire to hide out is recent, and expensive.

The other day, a *New York Times* article reported on the objections of the neighbors in Greenwich, Connecticut, to a proposed 39,000-square-foot home with a "3,600-square-foot indoor gym, complete with its own squash court, golf simulator, massage room, beauty parlor and indoor pool, with views of a sunken garden." Penelope's home in Ithaca must have been huge too, since she keeps, among other staff, fifty female servants, but old palaces were like the White House, a place where the business of dominating a region, eating big dinners, and procreating the heirs to power were all transacted, and public and private flowed into each other through open doors. Privacy was for peasants. Gymnasium in Greece was a public place, and in Germany it is the high school.

DOUBLE BOLT

The scholar of religion Mircea Eliade was born in Bucharest, studied in India, returned home in 1937 to run for election as a member of the Everything for the Fatherland party that was an extension of Romania's Iron Guard, was jailed under the king, fled to France when his country fell under communism, and ended up an honored professor at the University of Chicago, where he wrote many books. I went into the hall where most of my bookcases are, looking in my old broken-spined undergraduate paperback copy of his *The Sacred and the Profane* for something about the world pole that seminomadic peoples would set up, a sort of tent pole that symbolically connected heaven and earth and became the center of the world, giving those gathered around it a sense of location, position, place in the world, as home does for each of us. I found instead a passage that announces,

> One of the outstanding characteristics of traditional societies is the opposition that they assume between their inhabited territory and the unknown and indeterminate space that surrounds it. The former is the world (more precisely, our world), the cosmos: everything outside it is no longer a cosmos but a sort of "other world," a foreign, chaotic space, peopled by ghosts, demons, "foreigners" (who are assimilated to demons and the souls of the dead).

This is the old language of anthropology, the discourse on *them*, but it might as well be about us. The "unknown and indeterminate space" is implied to be an old or primitive perception, but it is enormously like the suspicious anxiety of most of the people in my country today. Something very peculiar has taken place during the last quarter century as the social contract has been dismantled and the public arena abandoned; and gone along with it, the sense of existing in a shared realm where your gain and your loss are also mine, where we are tied together in a common fellowship that might be a civilization or a community or a nation. What began as tax revolts a quarter century or so ago dismantled the recently built shelters for the poor, the young, the mad, the damaged, shelters that were economic or social services, were provided as an expression of solidarity and of security, for if we could provide for anyone to whom the worst had happened then none of us need fear that worst so much as before.

But the great overarching roof of social programs was dismantled, the mad were let go into the streets, and the armies of the homeless, who pushed their shopping carts through the 1980s and the 1990s and continue drifting through the inhospitable asphalt wildernesses of the new millennium, appeared as almost everyone quickly forgot that life had been otherwise not so long ago. In this brutal new world of unmitigated market forces, nothing remained yours but the space that you paid for, a realm shrunken back to the bounds of private property, with phantasmagorical fears chewing at the edges, whether criminals (the nice statistic being that the more you stayed home and watched local TV news, the more you were afraid to leave the house) or immigrants or germs, a host of others to be kept out. This is why each house had to be set up at least imaginatively as completely autonomous, with its home entertainment center replacing the old communal movie houses, with a set of weights in the garage for many and a private gym for a few, for isolation (even though these houses in their reliance on electricity, gas, water, and other services remained in fact a part of a shared network; this withdrawal from the community is an ideology and an imaginary space more than an actuality, except in the case of the few survivalists in the backwoods who aren't living entirely off canned goods and trucked-in propane). The world, in Eliade's sense, was no larger than the suburban house lot, a quarter acre of coherence in a sea of savagery and strangeness.

The philosophy behind this retreat from public life was capitalism red in tooth and claw, and it argued like Protestant Christianity that wealth came as a result of virtue, and poverty as a result of vice; that those who suffered, earned it; and indeed the suffering, particularly the legions of the homeless, served as reminders of how a pitiless economy would grind anyone underfoot who faltered. And so, faltering became far more terrifying, and dissent—even dedicating your life to something more altruistic or adventurous than getting and spending—faded a little from everyday life. The argument against the public good was buttressed by private good: Who needed good tap water when it was buyable in bottles? Who needed public schools when there were private academies? Who needed to undermine the causes of crime and provide public protection for the victims when private security forces were mushrooming so spectacularly, with gates, closed-circuit cameras, handguns, and more? All this was the backdrop to the rising obsession with home ownership and home improvement.

It was as though all that realm of citizenry and public life had shrunk back and no one dared hope for a better society or desired membership in some continental sense of possibility; they just tended lawns or refinished the kitchen cabinets, as though the nation-state in this otherwise globalized age had shrunk to the size of a single-family house, as though everyone was living in a country of one or two or maybe six, including four minors, plus a dog and a cat, a microscopic empire ruled by fiat. Thus the people sleeping under cardboard in doorways and the people having a more expansive master suite built shared a common fate not in material goods but in this atomization, of one against the world. For the non-homeless, this retreat was into a house that was once again a fortress as it had been in various perilous pasts, but this time the world had been made unstable for the sake of tax cuts and more cuts. The old modernist dream of a better world had become the dream of a better home and garden, and a massive industry of television programs, magazines, books, tax deductions, Home Depot warehouses, and more specialized stores fed this appetite or this distraction.

The twenty-first-century American housing boom was globalized anyway, critics argued, because it was fed by artificially low interest rates held down by the Republican administration and backed by massive investment from China, situated as purchases of extremely low-yield or even negative-yield treasury bonds. China did this to keep its own economy from booming into a rising yuan and living standard that would undermine its status as the world's great discount manufactory; the United States did this to keep its own economy from sliding into recession or even depression. A cheap yuan kept their economy going, as a booming housing market kept the U.S. market going, though going as a house of cards ready to tumble. Which is to say that a withdrawal from public life and national ideals can have consequences in those spheres anyway. "A nation," says Leopold

Bloom, "is people living in the same place," a lackluster answer that annoys his nationalist interrogators even before he adds, "or also in different places." But not necessarily at home in the world. Just in the home.

CLOSING COSTS

Making and controlling a world is much of what child's play once consisted of, when it consisted of toy soldiers, dolls, blocks, train sets, Noah's arks, Lincoln Logs, Erector Sets, dollhouses, and other devices that before Gameboys let children be engineers, builders, and designers. The tiny scale lets children be giants, Iron Guards, kings or queens of Ithaca, prime ministers, in charge of their world as they are not in the world. Maybe we all dream of being God, the god who breaches dams, moves houses suddenly, erects bridges, decides where forests will be and who will die; and we graduate from the dollhouse to our own house if we are lucky, where we assume a role somewhere between God the Creator and the chambermaid, choosing but carrying out more painfully the clean floor, the dinner for six, the potted plants, the framed prints. The execution is difficult. The dreaming is easy and unending.

2006

NOTES FROM NOWHERE

Iceland's Polite Dystopia

In late 2007, an Icelandic teenager named Vífill Atlason created a minor international incident when he phoned the White House, told the operator he was the president of Iceland, and managed to set up an appointment to speak with George W. Bush. When the White House figured out what was going on, Atlason was taken away by Icelandic police and questioned for several hours, then told that he would be placed on an American no-fly list. No conversation took place. I, on the other hand, managed to make a lunch date with President Ólafur Ragnar Grímsson not long after I arrived in Iceland, simply by bumping into him at an art exhibit and asking. Iceland is a nation of just over 300,000 citizens, a scale at which everything should be and can be accessible to the ordinary citizen as well as the crashing writer. In fact, I was picked up for my date by Dorrit Moussaieff, the president's Israeli-born second wife, who happened to be heading off with another American to another lunch. This other American, an extremely wealthy New Yorker in well-ironed jeans, liked Iceland so much that he was thinking about settling here, and as we crossed downtown Reykjavík in the chauffeured presidential Land Cruiser, he listed his reasons: clean air, clean water, no crime, and no immigrants. He liked Iceland, apparently, for being a gated community with the whole North Atlantic as its gates, but he still had his concerns. The graffiti lightly spattered over the city bothered him enough to mention it twice.

And then they went to their lunch, and the chauffeur and I rolled onward to Bessastaðir, the suburban presidential residence. Built as a school in the eighteenth century, Bessastaðir is one of the few old buildings left on this long-deforested island, where for a millennium most structures were made from driftwood and sod. Bessastaðir's cluster of immaculate red-roofed white buildings looks like a small country estate, and though it is set apart from the other houses in the neighborhood by a wide grassy lawn, it has no apparent defense against interlopers, not even a serious fence. The president travels without visible security everywhere in Iceland, showing up at art openings and ribbon cuttings to mingle and shake hands when he's not overseas—as he often is—pitching Iceland to investors, talking up the democratic virtues of small states, and organizing climate-change initiatives. Grímsson had lived at Bessastaðir for three four-year terms, and the question of his fourth was up in the air when I arrived. The president is by no means as powerful as Iceland's parliament or its prime minister, Geir Haarde. But he does have real authority in some areas, notably the ability to veto legislation, and—more to the point—he is recognized by most as the nation's symbolic leader, which is why I wanted to talk to him.

Iceland's population is one thousandth that of the United States, and I wanted to know if the problems we faced at home were a function of size. An encouraging domestic development during the long years of the Bush administration had been the tendency of U.S. cities and states to set their own policies, particularly on the environment and climate change—to withdraw from the unaccountable federation to a more responsive, more localized scale. And so I looked toward Iceland with optimism. I was in a country with no army and little crime, where children are free to run outdoors unsupervised. Most of the people in Iceland are related to one another, and few of them seem to feel that American anxiety of being adrift without an anchor of stable identity or community. Iceland is one of the most literate countries on earth, with the world's highest per-capita book sales. Not only does it have a long tradition of writer-politicians but, as a returning émigrée explained it to me (though her sense of things might have been a little out of date), "Here the garbageman has read Cicero." Certain democratic measures are built into the culture: for instance, the way everyone's surname is just his or her father's first name with the suffix *-son* or *-dóttir* appended; a wife doesn't take her husband's name, and even the most distinguished names are rarely passed from one generation to the next. Iceland is the only part of Europe that never begat monarchs or a hereditary aristocracy, and I hoped to find here a kind of perfection of the democratic ideal, or at least a hopeful indication of what could be.

✧

Grímsson himself is an imposing man, exceedingly proper and courteous. He speaks formal English in full paragraphs. When I said to a friend of his that he seemed a bit wooden, she laughed at my caution and said, "He's wooden all the way through!"

At sixty-five, Grímsson is a year older than his republic (until World War II, Iceland was a possession of Denmark), and his hair is brushed over in an orderly white-blond wave. He grew up in a fishing village on the wild and remote Westfjords peninsula, received a Ph.D. in political science in England, from the University of Manchester, and taught for several years at the University of Iceland before venturing into politics. When we met, he was wearing huge cuff links and a tie patterned with tiny feathers, and he showed me to a small study. The president sat in a high-backed arm-chair, upholstered in worn tapestry. I sat in an armless version, and for the next ninety minutes we spoke at cross purposes.

"I think the twenty-first century will be a fascinating period," he said, a period in which we will "see the relevance as well as the renaissance of small states." But the vision he described as we ate our catfish and salmon seemed decidedly mainstream, even American. He celebrates small states mostly for how they function economically and in the international society of states. Small states move in a more flexible way, he said, which makes it easier for them to solve problems. He gave me an example. He had just come from the tiny, oil-rich nation of Qatar, whose government had hosted a conference, involving diplomats from such similarly tiny neighbors as the United Arab Emirates, that had put a temporary stop to the escalating violence in Lebanon. "They said to me very openly, 'The reason why we could do it is that we were small Arab countries, we were friends with everybody—we didn't have any vested interest, we didn't have any ulterior motives, we did not have any long-term military strategy—so we could talk to everybody on a faithful basis.'" Of course, Qatar is ruled by a hered-itary emir. Small may give leaders the flexibility they need to make deals, but it is not necessarily democratic.

Such contradictions left Grímsson unfazed. He began his first presi-dential campaign, he said, by traveling to every town and village in Iceland, "except two or three very small and remote ones," to meet with the electorate, and this journey had more profoundly informed his thinking on participatory democracy than even his years as a professor of political science. "Constitutions and formal democratic rules—of course they are necessary and they are essential," he continued, "but the great force of democracy, especially in modern times, is what we have called the will of the people." This will, he said, was not always expressed through such traditional means as voting. "There are strong democratic pressures almost in the air without them necessarily having to be organized in a systematic way."

Indeed, Grímsson may well be a principal beneficiary of the unsystematic way. He stood unopposed in the upcoming election—Icelanders, as one small-town librarian told me disapprovingly, have come to believe that it is "impolite" to run against a sitting president, and it has become customary to let them stay in office as long as they like. And so while Americans were absorbed in another electoral horse race, Iceland had no race at all.

The exquisite rhubarb crisp that ended my meal at Bessastaðir reminded the president of boyhood days helping his grandmother put up jars of rhubarb preserves. Nearly every autumn saw a flurry of activity to dry enough fish and salt enough lamb to avoid starvation during the dark and isolated winter, he said, and people who come here now, "who see this ultramodern society," fail to understand that it has been only a very short time since Iceland was a poor country, "almost a developing country."

Iceland is marked, maybe even scarred, by several hundred years of such poverty. It began to lessen only after 1902, when Iceland got its first motorized boats, bringing a wave of modest prosperity to the country's fishermen, who still produce more than half of its exports. World War II brought the next and larger wave: as the Nazis occupied Denmark, Iceland fell under the protection of Allied troops, thereby allowing the nation to liberate itself from centuries of colonial rule and become an independent republic, although the American military continued to maintain a base there from which to monitor the Soviet Union. In 2006, the United States discovered that it had other priorities, recalled its fighter jets and military personnel, and closed the base.

Long before the U.S. military presence ended, the ruling Independence Party began to cast around for something new to pump up Iceland's economy. The nation had for decades harnessed the turbulent landscape to produce "clean" energy, though geothermal power and hydropower are not quite as green as we would like to think. They take a toll in the form of toxic emissions and the destruction of wild places, though most of Iceland's postwar energy developments were small in scale and impact. In the mid-1990s, however, the government decided to offer up Iceland's vast natural resources to energy-intensive industries such as aluminum production, which also generates significant pollution, in a scheme that involved damming virtually every major river in the country. This willingness to sacrifice Iceland's wilderness to foreign corporations reflected Iceland's image of itself as a new player on the world stage, as "modern" (even if giant dams are rather old-fashioned icons of progress) and "high-tech" (even though it still exports more fish than aluminum). One popular claim was that Iceland would become "the Kuwait of the north."

Many Icelanders have been troubled by the decision to sell off the landscape. The signature such debate took place over the Kárahnjúkar Hydropower Project, which involved building several dams along two major glacial rivers, a series of deep tunnels to carry water to hydropower stations, and a new electrical infrastructure to connect those stations to a coastal smelter. The measure became increasingly unpopular as Icelanders got to know something about the massive amount of remote wilderness that would be—and now has been—drowned; about the reindeer that calved there and the pink-footed geese that nested there; about the serious pollution the hydropower smelters would emit, even if the electricity itself was emissions-free; and about the scandalous economics of the deal, whereby the citizens would pay billions for the infrastructure and the U.S.-based aluminum manufacturer Alcoa, which would most benefit from Iceland's increased smelting capacity, would provide only a few hundred jobs to locals in return. In a country the size of Iceland, a few hundred jobs outside the capital count, and there has been a ripple effect on the declining eastern economy and population—but at a cost many think is too high.

To hear ordinary citizens speak about the dams, you'd think they lived under a vast tyranny; they speak of powerlessness, secrecy, intimidation, and loss. And yet little in the way of actual political protest has emerged. Icelandic presidents are barred from party membership, but before he took office, Grímsson was a member of the Peoples' Alliance Party, which in 2000 joined Iceland's three other center-left parties to become the Social Democratic Alliance. The hope was that the coalition could gather enough seats in parliament to defeat the ruling Independence Party, whose website announces its principles as "the freedom to work and freedom of the individual, abolition of any kind of restraints," and "a dynamic and open economy." Despite offering a fairly tepid version of Clintonian moderation, the Peoples' Alliance effort thus far has not succeeded. Kolbrún Halldórsdóttir, a member of parliament who co-directs the Left Green Party—founded in 1999, in part to oppose the dam projects—suggested that this conservative streak was just a part of the national character. "It is difficult to get people to join political parties. It is difficult to get people to join the associations and ad hoc groups that are working on these issues," she said. "We would be much stronger if we had more people. But they are not willing to come."

There have been few petition drives and no national referendums on the dams. Indeed, the only concerted campaign has come from a small organization named Saving Iceland, which is run, according to its website, not by Icelanders but by "a network of people of different nationalities." The most dogged and potent local opposition has come from artists, who began protesting outside the parliament building almost as soon as the proposals were aired. For a 2003 TV documentary about a site soon to be submerged by a dam, the photographer-naturalist Guðmundur Páll Ólafsson tore out the pages of his book on the region to demonstrate what was being done to the landscape itself. At an exhibition in downtown Reykjavík this summer, the artist Rúrí mounted a video installation, called *Flooding/Nature Lost,* that featured footage of geese and other birds sitting on their eggs until the rising waters of Kárahnjúkar's reservoir dissolved the nests and washed away the eggs. The birds walked away, puzzled and pathetic. Rúrí, a kind, spiky-haired woman in her fifties, has devoted much of the past decade to creating a mournful video catalogue of Icelandic waterfalls, particularly those already or potentially lost. Of the dam projects, she said, "This is sad and ridiculous in a democratic society, especially one that claims to be the oldest in the world."

Iceland's national parliament, or Althing—the word for "assembly" being, in Icelandic, *thing*—was formed in 930 AD, about sixty years after the first settlers came over from Norway. They met at a site whose name, Thingvellir, "the plain of the *thing*," still commemorates this ancient annual gathering, which was a combined parliamentary session, court review, and country fair. I visited it on a pleasant May day when a down jacket and lined gloves were the right attire, and wild ducks and geese called overhead. I was driving in my rented car across a high plain strewn with volcanic debris—big, twisting, dark boulders upholstered in pale, thick moss that disguised jagged edges and crevices—when suddenly half the landscape dropped away and I began a descent into the wide valley created by the meeting of the Eurasian and North American tectonic plates. A long ledge of dark gray stone eighty or a hundred feet high ran along the far end, and the Axe River dropped off this ledge (in a foaming waterfall that in another country might itself be a big tourist attraction) and into the grassy valley below, where other streams braided together to create a web of estuaries and tiny islands. On the far side of this riparian oasis was a series of long stony fissures, from a few feet to perhaps twenty feet wide, filled with astonishingly clear deep-blue water, a canyonland in miniature with its own flora of mosses, grasses, and stunted trees. The Thingvellir region, like much of Iceland, is as lush as Ireland and as harshly grand as Utah.

The old Icelanders gathered here in the uninterrupted light at midsummer every year, and the *lögsögumadr*, or law speaker, recited one-third of the nation's laws, so that the whole code would be declaimed every three years. Courts met to deliberate transgressions, and new laws were made. Informal lawyers negotiated, and judges settled the penalties for unlawful violence, theft, and other crimes—fines were levied for most offenses and exile imposed for the worst. No one was imprisoned.

I was reading *Njal's Saga* when I visited, which chronicles several generations of feuds that were occasionally resolved by the lawyerly Njal's visits to the Althing. The sagas written down in the twelfth and thirteenth centuries are the great literary patrimony of Iceland, where the language has changed so little that modern Icelanders can still more or less read them. Njal's careful legal deliberation, though, was an odd contrast to much of the saga's grisly violence, as though *Black's Law Dictionary* had been spliced into Grand Theft Auto. At one point, Njal notes the importance of the rule of law—"With laws shall our land be built up but with lawlessness laid waste"—and not many pages later, his eldest son catches sight of his enemies on an ice sheet beside the river and, in a celebrated passage, decides to make the most of the opportunity:

> Skarp-Hedin made a leap and cleared the channel between the ice-banks, steadied himself, and at once went into a slide: the ice was glassy-smooth, and he skimmed along as fast as a bird. Thrain was then about to put on his helmet. Skarp-Hedin came swooping down on him and swung at him with his axe. The axe crashed down on his head and split it down to the jaw-bone, spilling the back-teeth on to the ice.

These mostly Norse settlers were land-hungry but also monarch-weary, and they wanted to do what had not been done in Europe since the time of the Roman republic: maintain order without overlords. This sounds like a remarkable concept, but if you consider the early Icelanders as a people akin to, say, the Algonquins or the Mohicans, who governed themselves quite nicely without crowned heads and tax collectors, the achievement finds its place in a long history of small self-governing societies that didn't generate fixed hierarchies or bureaucracies. Farmers allied themselves with chieftains who had decision-making power at the Althing, but the farmers could switch their allegiance: they were not vassals bound to a lord, and the chieftains were themselves farmers. The family unit was important. It still is.

Jared Diamond has written that these self-governing Icelanders were "too poor to afford a government," and they did indeed struggle to survive in the country's harsh climate—they cherished the right of "driftage," or the right to collect all the driftwood and debris on a given stretch of coastline. But they also had splendid horses, much land, herds of cattle and sheep, all the fish they could catch, a voice in their own affairs, and a great deal of freedom. It wasn't a feminist paradise, but women retained meaningful rights and roles, a big difference from the celebrated democracy of ancient Athens, where women were largely housebound and hushed up. In *Iceland: The First New Society,* the historian Richard F. Tomasson grumbles that Iceland "suffered from the fatal flaw of the old Germanic polity," which was "an inability to develop any ordered and regular hierarchy of authority." This "flaw" was hardly fatal, though. The old Icelandic society lasted more than three hundred years, until internal feuding made it vulnerable to a takeover by the king of Norway in 1262. Not a bad run.

William Morris, the great Victorian artisan, writer, and revolutionary, derived such inspiration from the Icelandic sagas that he traveled through the country by pony for several weeks in 1871. His taste for the old stories was partly romantic enthusiasm for a world of fierce, fearless characters and partly an appreciation for lean prose. But the firsthand experience of the visit—"Awful looking are these Icelandic wastes," he wrote, "yet beautiful to a man with eyes and heart"—occasioned a far more specific epiphany, which was that "the most grinding poverty is a trifling evil compared with the inequality of classes." The trip was a turning point in his life.

Iceland past and present confirmed in Morris his own radically democratic desires, and he afterward devoted much of his life to bringing about his vision of utopian anarchism. In Morris's novel *News from Nowhere,* a protagonist much like the author falls asleep after a rancorous meeting of various left-wing activists: "There were six persons present, and consequently six sections of the party were represented, four of which had strong but divergent Anarchist opinions." They have been talking about what would constitute the ideal society after the revolution, and the protagonist wakes up the next morning in twenty-first-century London, a world that is Morris's own vision of what a postrevolutionary nation could become. One of Morris's guides shows him the Houses of Parliament, now used to store manure. "'Now, dear guest, let me tell you that our present parliament would be hard to house in one place, because the whole people is our parliament,'" he explains. "'I must now shock you by telling you that we no longer have anything which you, a native of another planet, would call a government.'" The guide then jokes that what can be said of politics in this country is what was once famously (and truly) said of snakes in Iceland in the very short chapter of an eighteenth-century natural history: "There are no snakes in Iceland."

In Morris's utopia everyone participates in governance and no one is a politician; it is direct rather than representative democracy—and a fantastic vision only in that it requires the existence of a passionately engaged civil society. Such direct democracy has been deployed by the loyalists during the Spanish Civil War; by the Zapatistas, who withdrew from the Mexican government in 1994 and have governed themselves ever since in the state of Chiapas; by traditional peasant cultures, such as the Regantes of Bolivia; and by much of the direct-action movement against corporate globalization at least since the Seattle World Trade Organization shutdown in 1999. I bring up Morris's vision not to argue that Iceland—or, for that matter, the United States—is ready to become a direct democracy but only to remind us that, as the chant goes, this is what democracy looks like. The sign at a Zapatista village I visited late last year declares, "Here the people govern and the government obeys." In Iceland, as in most representative democracies, neither claim is true, at least most of the time.

Like Ólafur Grímsson before him, Svanur Kristjánsson is a political science professor at the University of Iceland. Whereas Grímsson's focus was on theories of power, however, Kristjánsson has specialized in the theory of democracy, which means that he notices the practice is not ideal in most places, including his own country. Kristjánsson is rumpled and fair-haired, with sad eyes and English polished at the University of Illinois at Urbana-Champaign, in the 1970s. When I met him at his book-filled office in an ugly modern campus building, he told me that being small hadn't done much for Iceland. Indeed, he noted as much in a 2004 paper in the journal *Scandinavian Political Studies*:

> The positive aspects of the Icelandic political tradition still reflect the
> assumption, often unspoken, that democracy means citizen control. In
> the republic of Iceland, tradition has it that the people alone should hold
> sovereign power. This golden past stands in sharp contrast to the present state
> of affairs, which can best be described as muddling through in the search
> for democracy. . . . The Icelandic system of governance has become a rather
> messy and complicated political arrangement, resembling the situation in
> other modern democracies.

I asked him what had happened. "You can run into your prime minister at the store," he said. "You know the minister, the president—you
can make an *appointment* with the president." But at the same time, there
is "an incredible lack of civic courage" within the governing class, "a lack
of people standing up and telling the truth," and this vacuum was quickly
filled by action from others—from aluminum companies, from international investors, from Iceland's new class of the super-rich. Which is to say
that representative democracy fails wherever its citizens let it fail, even on a
charming island with a thousand-year democratic tradition.

Kristjánsson gave two cases in point. The first took place a quarter century ago, when the government devised a fishing-quota system, ostensi-
bly to protect Icelandic waters from overfishing. This seemed like a good
idea—the fish stock really was being depleted—but the government had
also come under the sway of fashionable ideas about privatization. Owners of fishing vessels were given quotas based on their current catch, but
those quotas could be sold and compounded, and so the big trawlers soon
began to amass permits, and the small fishermen began to go extinct. The
fish, Iceland's patrimony and its richest asset for centuries, became private property, and the villages themselves faced extinction. Now dozens
of boats sit ashore in old fishing towns like Stykkishólmur, the rows of
permits in their windows not renewed since the 1990s. "Those who owned
the quota, they sold it and then they moved away," Kristjánsson said, his

voice catching at the memory. His father was a fisherman too, he said, and he saw that sell-off as a betrayal.

Then Kristjánsson told me about an older, less acquiescent approach to dealing with change. In 1970, the government decided to dam the Laxá River. "It's one of the most beautiful places in the world," he said, alight again with the passion many Icelanders have for their countryside. Farmers in the valley behind the dam, threatened with the loss of their land and their livelihood, tried every legal means to stop construction, with no success, and so they decided to take another, more direct approach. On the appointed night, more than two hundred citizens gathered at the construction site. Some of them manned tractors to dig a hole in the earthen dam, others placed dynamite in that hole, and a third group set off the dynamite. "The people went there and they blew it up," Kristjánsson said. "They *blew it up.*"

When I later read about the incident, I saw that the outcome was even more surprising. "It is evident from the documents from the hearings that everyone was proud of his act," reports Haraldur Olafsson in a 1981 article in *Environmental Review,* "and through interviews and other sources I find that many more than were prosecuted would have liked to have been in the group that was judged." Only sixty-five were convicted and fined, and the Supreme Court ultimately overturned even the fine itself. One of the participants remarked to another reporter, "We ought to earn the Nobel Peace Prize, since we actually used Nobel's invention to re-establish peace between man and nature."

Listening to Icelanders, I felt like I was hearing a fairy tale told backward, a tale in which they had been dispossessed of their great gifts and birthrights. First the right to fish was privatized, the fish were made into an alienable commodity, and the small coastal villages began to wither. Then, in 1998, the medical data and extraordinarily extensive genealogical records of everyone in the country were—famously, absurdly—sold to a private corporation, which retained the exclusive right to benefit from discoveries made from studying this homogeneous population's most intimate genetic secrets. Simultaneously, the wilderness, or at least a major chunk of it, was sacrificed to produce cheap power for Alcoa's smelter, and the other rivers were offered up soon thereafter. It was a tragedy of privatization and of acquiescence.

Icelanders are aware of the problem and yet seem unable to fix it. In *Dreamland: A Self-Help Manual for a Frightened Nation*, Iceland's best-selling book in 2006, Andri Snær Magnason writes, "It is not overstating the case to say that Iceland's greatest natural treasures have been on clearance sale for the last thirty years, without the nation ever having had it explained to them what was on sale." This sentence, with the people it mentions sounding so strangely passive, could be rewritten to say that Icelanders had not demanded explanation with sufficient force. Iceland had been, Magnason remarked to me in an anarchist-collective café in downtown Reykjavík, living in "an end-of-history era" until the dam and smelter plans shattered the contentment. In the late Eighties and early Nineties, Björk was becoming Iceland's first major celebrity export, everyone was planting trees, the fisheries seemed well-managed, and the country had the world's first democratically elected female president, Vigdís Finnbogadóttir. But this paradisiacal state didn't last. Iceland's deep attachment to place is clashing with its fantasies about becoming rich, and fighting back is not easy for everyone to do. Magnason joked, "We talk about our Viking heritage, but we always skip the fact that 50 percent of the settlers were slaves. We talk about our businessmen and their Viking mentality, but we also have a slave mentality."

The day that Ólafur Ragnar Grímsson gained his fourth term as president of Iceland, the sun rose over Reykjavík as it usually does on June 28, less than three hours after the official sunset at midnight and after another night without real darkness. There had been no media circus, no polls, no fund-raising, no competing claims, no placards, no debates, no scandals, and, of course, no campaign and no election. No one had bothered to run in token opposition, even as a single-issue nut.

There was no election, but there was, coincidentally, a free public concert featuring Björk and Iceland's new international superstars, Sigur Rós, the stated purpose of which was to "raise awareness for environmental issues in Iceland." I had hoped that the "eco-concert," as its organizers had called it, might engender some sort of upsurge of passion and engagement, a sort of latter-day Althing, or at least launch grassroots dissident activity with consequences. And, in fact, nearly 30,000 people—about a tenth of the population of Iceland—gathered in a Reykjavík park on a golden summer evening when the temperature was in the mid-forties. The music, particularly Sigur Rós's majestic, fey meandering, was spectacular. Images of those distressed birds on nests lapped by floodwater were projected on the giant video screen, but no one said anything about the environment until the very end, when Björk, after shouting out her anthem, "Declare Independence," chanted, "Náttúra, náttúra, náttúra, náttúra!" (Nature, nature, nature, nature!) And that was that. The next morning I ran into Magnason, who had helped organize the event, and asked him why at a concert for the environment no one had said anything about the environment, or politics, or democracy, or dams, or actions people could take to make a difference. "They didn't want to preach," he said firmly, as though it were the most reasonable thing in the world.

2008

THE VOLCANO ERUPTS

Iceland in Upheaval

In December, reports surfaced that Treasury Secretary Henry Paulson pushed his Wall Street bailout package by suggesting that, without it, civil unrest in the United States might grow so dangerous that martial law would have to be declared. Dominique Strauss-Kahn, managing director of the International Monetary Fund (IMF), warned of the same risk of riots, wherever the global economy was hurting. What really worried them wasn't, I suspect, the possibility of a lot of people thronging the streets with demands for social and political change, but that some of those demands might actually be achieved. Take the example of Iceland, the first—but surely not the last—country to go bankrupt in the current global crash.

While the United States was inaugurating its first African-American president, Icelanders were besieging their parliament. The YouTube video of the scene—drummers pounding out a tribal beat, the flare and boom of teargas canisters, scores of helmeted police behind transparent plastic shields, a bonfire in front of the stone building that resembles a country house more than a seat of government—was dramatic, particularly the figures silhouetted against a blaze whose hot light flickered on the gray walls during much of the eighteen-hour-long midwinter night. People beat pots and pans in what was dubbed the Saucepan Revolution. Five days later, the government, dominated by the neoliberal Independent Party, collapsed, as many Icelanders had hoped and demanded it would since the country's economy suddenly melted down in October.

The interim government, built from a coalition of the Left-Green Party and the Social Democrats, is at least as different from the old one as the Obama administration is from the Bush administration. The latest prime minister, Jóhanna Sigurðardóttir, broke new ground in the midst of the crisis: she is now the world's first out lesbian head of state. In power only until elections on April 25, 2009, this caretaker government takes on the formidable task of stabilizing and steering a country that has the dubious honor of being the first to drop in the current global meltdown. (In fact, Sigurðardóttir and her party were in power until May of 2013.) Last week, Sigurðardóttir said that the new government would try to change the constitution to "enshrine national ownership of the country's natural resources" and to "open a new chapter in public participation in shaping the structure of government," a 180-degree turn from the neoliberal policies of Iceland's fallen masters.

Iceland is now a country whose currency, the króna, has collapsed, whose debt incurred by banks deregulated in the mid-1990s is ten times larger than the country's gross domestic product, and whose people have lost most of their savings and face debts and mortgages that can't be paid off. Meanwhile, inflation and unemployment are skyrocketing, and potential solutions to the crisis only pose new problems.

The present government may differ from the old, but not as much as the Icelandic people differ from their pre-October selves. They are now furious and engaged, where they were once acquiescent and uninvolved.

Before the crash, Ólafur Ragnar Grímsson, the figurehead president of Iceland, liked to compare his tiny society—the island nation has 320,000 people—to Athens. One of my Icelandic friends jokes darkly that, yes, it's Athens, but not in the age of Socrates and Sophocles; it's Athens *now* in the age of anti-governmental insurrection. The Iceland of last summer—I was there for nearly three months—seemed socially poor but materially rich; the Iceland I read and hear about now seems to be socially rich at last, but terrifyingly poor materially.

Iceland is a harsh, beautiful rock dangling like a jewel on a pendant from the Arctic Circle. Bereft of mineral resources, too far north for much in the way of agriculture, it had some fish, some sheep, and, of late, some geothermal and hydropower energy and a few small industries, along with a highly literate human population whose fierceness was apparently only temporarily dormant during the brief era of borrowing to spend. The people I've talked to since are exultant to have reclaimed their country and a little terrified about the stark poverty facing them.

After going hat in hand for bailout funds to Washington, the Bank of England, and the European Central Bank, Iceland turned to Russia and, reluctantly, to the global lender of last resort, the International Monetary Fund (IMF), that temple of privatization and globalization. Usually along with money, the IMF imposes its own notions of what makes an economy work—as it did in Argentina until that country's economy collapsed eight years ago, leading to an extraordinary rebirth of civil society and social upheaval. In Iceland, the process was reversed: first upheaval, then the IMF. Now, you have an insurrectionary public *and* a new incursion of the forces of neoliberalism that helped topple the country in the first place.

As economic hard times have spread, so have a spate of protests and insurgencies across Europe—of which Iceland's has only been the most effective so far—suggesting that a new era of popular power in the streets may be arriving. Iceland's upheaval poses the question of what the collapse of capitalism will bring the rest of us. Last fall, major financial newspapers were already headlining "the end of American capitalism as we knew it," "capitalism in convulsion," "the collapse of finance," and "capitalism at bay." The implication was that something as sweeping as the "collapse of communism" nineteen years earlier had taken place.

Since then, the media and others seem to have forgotten that the body in question was declared terminally ill and have focused instead on how to provide very expensive first aid for it. This avoids the question of what the alternatives might be, which this time around are not anything as one-size-fits-all and doctrinaire as old-school socialism but a host of existing localized, grassroots, and mostly small-scale modes of making goods, providing services, and serving communities—and remaining accountable.

SOD HOUSES TO PRIVATE JETS AND BEYOND

Iceland is a strange country, as I found out. Situated on the volcanically and seismically active seam between the North American and European tectonic plates, the place seems to belong to both continents, and neither. Usually regarded as part of Scandinavia, it was controlled by Norway, and then Denmark, from the collapse of its proudly independent parliamentary system in the thirteenth century to 1944. That year, while Denmark was occupied by the Nazis, it officially became an independent republic.

But the United States military had arrived three years earlier and would stay on another sixty-two years, until 2006, at its huge air base in Keflavik. Before the collapse last fall, some of the biggest protests in the republic's history were about the occupying army, which broadcast its own television shows and brought a host of Americanizations and some prosperity to the island. More recently, Iceland became a place of wild neoliberal ambitions and Scandinavian welfare-state underpinnings. Ordinary people worked too many hours, like Americans, and took on too much debt to buy big cars, new condos, and suburban houses.

Poverty was not very far behind just about everyone in Iceland: person after person told me that his or her grandparents or parents had lived in a sod house, built out of the most available material in a country with scarce small trees, and that they themselves or their parents had worked in the fish-processing factories. The country's best-known artist showed me, with a deft flick of his wrist, how his grandmother could fillet a cod "like that," and added that most of the island's fish are processed offshore now. Until recently Reykjavík, the capital, was just a small town, and Iceland a rural society of coastal farms and fishermen.

The boom in this once fairly egalitarian nation created a new class of the super-wealthy whose private jets landed in the airport in downtown Reykjavik and whose yachts, mansions, and other excesses sometimes made the news, as did charges of corruption in business and in the government that countenanced that business. It wasn't corruption, however, that did in the Icelandic economy. It was government-led recklessness and deregulation. I had expected to find that, in such a small country, democracy would work beautifully, that the people would be able to hold their government accountable, and that its workings would be transparent. None of those things were faintly true.

A lot of people muttered then, in hapless dismay, about what the government was doing—notably destroying the country's extraordinary wilderness to create hydropower to run the energy-intensive aluminum smelters of transnational corporations. A small group of dedicated people protested, but their sparks never seemed to catch public fire or do much to slow down the destruction. Icelanders generally seemed to tolerate privatizations and giveaways of everything from their medical histories and DNA to their fishing industry and wilderness, and a host of subsidiary indignities that went with this process.

Take, for example, the transnational retail empire of the Baugur Group (as of last week essentially bankrupt and owing Icelandic banks about $2 billion), run by father-and-son team Jón Ásgeir Jóhannesson and Jóhannes Jónsson. Their Bónus stores, with a distinctive hot-pink piggybank logo, had managed to create a near-monopoly on supermarkets in Iceland. They provided cheap avocados from South Africa and mangos from Brazil, but they'd apparently decided that selling fresh fish was impractical; so, in the fishing capital of the Atlantic, most people outside the center of the capital had no choice but to eat frozen fish.

Icelanders also ate a lot of American-style arguments in favor of deregulation and privatization, or looked the other way while their leaders did. Kolbrún Halldórsdóttir, then an opposition Left-Green parliamentarian, now Minister of the Environment in the new government, didn't. She told me last summer, "The nation was not asked if the nation wanted to privatize the banks." They were not asked, but they did not ask enough either.

Fortune magazine blamed one man, David Oddsson, prime minister from 1991 to 2004, for much of this privatization:

> It was Oddsson who engineered Iceland's biggest move since [joining]
> NATO: its 1994 membership in a free-trade zone called the European
> Economic Area. Oddsson then put in place a comprehensive economic-
> transformation program that included tax cuts, large-scale privatization, and
> a big leap into international finance. He deregulated the state-dominated
> banking sector in the mid-1990s, and in 2001 he changed currency policy
> to allow the krona to float freely rather than have it fixed against a basket of
> currencies including the dollar. In 2002 he privatized the banks.

In 2004, he was replaced as prime minister, but in 2005 he took over the Central Bank. By the mid-1990s Iceland had, through dicey financing and lots of debt, launched itself on a journey to become one of the world's most affluent societies. *Fortune* continues: "But the principal fuel for Iceland's boom was finance and, above all, leverage. The country became a giant hedge fund, and once-restrained Icelandic households amassed debts exceeding 220 percent of disposable income—almost twice the proportion of American consumers."

THROWING EGGS AT THE BANK

The first of the hedge-fund-cum-nation's three main banks, Glitnir, collapsed on September 29, 2008. A week later, the value of the króna fell by nearly a third. Landsbanki and Kaupthing, the other two banking giants, collapsed later that week. Britain snarled when Landsbanki froze the massive Internet savings accounts of British citizens and turned to anti-terrorism laws to seize the Icelandic bank's assets, incidentally reclassifying the island as a terrorist nation and pushing its economy into a faster tailspin.

Not so surprisingly, Icelanders began to get angry—at Britain, but even more at their own government. The crashing country, however, developed one growth industry: bodyguards for politicians in a country where every pop star and prime minister had once roamed freely in public. An Icelandic friend wrote me, "Eggs were being thrown at the Central Bank. Such emotional protests have not been seen since the early part of the twentieth century, although then people were too poor to throw eggs." Soon eggs were also being heaved at Prime Minister Geir Haarde, whose policies were an extension of Oddsson's.

A dormant civil society erupted into weekly protests that didn't stop even when the government collapsed, since Icelanders were also demanding that the board of governors at the Central Bank be suspended. One of Prime Minister Jóhanna Sigurðardóttir's first acts was to ask for their resignations. So far they have not cooperated.

Andri Snaer Magnason, author of the scathingly funny critique of his country's politics and society, *Dreamland: A Self-Help Guide for a Frightened Nation,* told me this week:

In economics, they talk about the invisible hand that regulates the market. In Iceland, the free market became so wild that it was not fixed by an invisible hand, but an invisible guillotine. So, in one weekend, the whole class of our newly rich masters of the universe lost their heads (reputation, power, and money), and all the power and debt of the newly privatized companies fell into the hands of the people again. So we have a very uncertain feeling about the future. At the same time, there is power in all the political debate and lots of political and social energy—endless [political] parties popping up, Facebook groups, cells and idealists, and possibly a new constitution (not that we have read the old one), and people are speaking up. So, economic fear, political courage, shaking economy, and search for new values—we need profound change. Now, businesspeople are losing their jobs, and they are scratching their heads and thinking that maybe politics do affect one's life. We need less professional politics and more participation of the people. I hope people will not give up now just because one government fell.

The economic fate of Iceland is uncertain and troubling. One friend there tells me that the already bankrupted banks may go bankrupt again, because their debt is so colossal. The billions in new loans from abroad are terrifyingly large for a country whose population is a thousandth the size of ours, and the Icelandic currency, the króna, is probably doomed.

The obvious solution is for Iceland to join the European Union (EU), and the April elections include a referendum on that question. Doing so, however, would involve letting the EU manage the country's fishing waters, its traditional and genuine source of wealth. That, in turn, would presumably open those waters up to all European fishermen and to a bureaucracy whose interests and ability to manage Icelandic fisheries are dubious. Iceland fought the Cod Wars with England in the 1970s to protect just those waters from outside fishing, and even in the years when everyone seemed focused on technology and finance, fish still accounted for about 40 percent of the country's exports.

ARGENTINA AND ICELAND

A recent headline in the British *Guardian* read: "Governments across Europe tremble as angry people take to the streets." From the perspective of those governments, a fully engaged citizenry is a terrifying prospect. From my perspective, it's what disasters often bring on, and it's civil society at its best. I'm hoping Iceland's going the way of Argentina.

In mid-December 2001, the Argentine economy collapsed. In its day, Argentina had been the poster child for neoliberalism, with its privatized economy guided by International Monetary Fund policy. The economy's managers, foreign and domestic, were proud of what they'd done, until it turned out that it didn't work. Then, the government tried to freeze its citizens' bank accounts to keep them from turning their plummeting pesos into foreign currency and breaking the banks.

The poor had already been politically engaged, and the unions had called a one-day general strike (just as French unions last week called more than 1 million people into the streets to protest job losses in the latest economic crisis). When the banks were frozen, however, middle-class Argentines woke up broke—and angry.

On December 19, 20, and 21 of 2001, they took to the streets of Buenos Aires in record numbers, banging pots and pans and shouting "all of them out." In the next few weeks, they forced a series of governments to collapse. For many people, those insurrectionary days were not just a revolt against the disaster that unfettered capitalism had brought them, but the time when they recovered from the years of silence and withdrawal imposed on the country in the 1980s by a military dictatorship via terror and torture.

After the crash of 2001, Argentines found their voice, found each other, found a new sense of power and possibility, and began to engage in political experiments so new they required a new vocabulary. One of the most important of these experiments would be neighborhood assemblies throughout Buenos Aires, which provided for some of the practical needs of a now-cashless community, and also became lively forums where strangers became *compañeros*.

Such incandescent moments when people find their voices and power as part of civil society are epiphanies, not solutions, but Argentina was never the same country again, even after its economy recovered. Like much of the rest of Latin America in this decade, it swung left in its political leadership, but far more important, Argentines developed social alternatives and found a new boldness that had previously been lacking. Some of what arose from the crisis, including workplaces taken over by workers and run as collectives, still exists.

Argentina is big in land, resources, and population, with a very different culture and history than Iceland. Where Iceland goes from here is hard to foresee. But as Icelandic writer Haukar Már Helgason put it in the *London Review of Books* last November:

> There is an enormous sense of relief. After a claustrophobic decade, anger and resentment are possible again. It's official: capitalism is monstrous. Try talking about the benefits of free markets and you will be treated like someone promoting the benefits of rape. Honest resentment opens a space for the hope that one day language might regain some of its critical capacity, that it could even begin to describe social realities again.

The big question may be whether the rest of us, in our own potential Argentinas and Icelands, picking up the check for decades of recklessness by the captains of industry, will be resentful enough and hopeful enough to say that unfettered capitalism has been monstrous, not just when it failed but when it succeeded. Let's hope that we're imaginative enough to concoct real alternatives. Iceland has no choice but to lead the way.

2009

THE GREAT TŌHOKU EARTHQUAKE AND TSUNAMI

Aftermaths in Japan

When I met him, Otsuchi city administrator Kozo Hirani, a substantial, balding man in a brown pinstripe suit, was on the upper floor of a warren of small-scale temporary buildings that now house the town's administration. To reach him I had flown to Tokyo, taken a train more than three hundred miles north to Morioka, the capital of Iwate Prefecture, then got into a van with seven people from Tokyo's International University who'd decided to see the disaster zone for themselves and help me while they were at it. Two were continental Europeans, five were Japanese, including one young man with the face of a warrior in a nineteenth-century Japanese print. His only job was to hand over exquisitely wrapped boxes—almost certainly containing some kind of sweet—in pretty shopping bags to everyone we visited, starting with Hirani. A huge cardboard carton of these items had been loaded into the van in which we traveled through the disaster zone.

When the city administrator first saw the wall of black water coming at him, it was so vast and incongruous that he didn't recognize it for what it was. Hirani survived the tsunami that swept the mayor and most of the small town's higher-ranking officials away in the middle of the afternoon on March 11, 2011, leaving him with the burden of responsibility for the recovery of his town. "I lost five of my subordinates. One sank in front of me. It was twenty-four hours before the helicopters came," he told me through an interpreter. "I was rescued by helicopter and when I saw the city from the sky I thought everything was at an end. It is very tough. My subordinates were in their twenties and thirties—I am fifty-five. Why did I survive?" Almost 10 percent of the town's population of about 15,000 died in the tsunami, one of the highest per capita death tolls in the affected area along the northeast coastal prefectures of Iwate, Miyagi, and Fukushima (which is the name of the prefecture as well as the inland city).

As we approached Otsuchi through mountainous countryside, we saw heavy equipment dismantling wrecked buildings, their twisted steel girders exposed. I thought we must be near the coast, but we kept going for a long time through wreckage and neat hills of debris; in the flatlands nearer the sea not much was left besides foundations. Some buildings were standing here and there, but they didn't look as though they would be rehabilitated. A few brightly illuminated drink vending machines stood like crazily cheerful sentinels in the ruins. There and elsewhere along the coast, I saw many buildings whose first stories were utterly destroyed, their second stories damaged, and the rest increasingly intact the higher they went. I had been to New Orleans six months after Katrina, before the real cleanup began in many neighborhoods, but the deluge there now seems gentle by comparison. Lined up in the dirt of Otsuchi—in Japan even wreckage is made neat—was a long double row of hundreds of cars, twisted and crushed by the extraordinary force of the sea. In one of the houses, still standing but torn open, I saw a family's pretty blue and white china dishes, a stack of five-sided bowls, flowered side plates, and a little oval dish, un-broken and unclaimed.

I hadn't understood that the tsunami, at its height, was 140 feet—40 meters—high. It had been about 33 meters high on the peninsula that pro-tects Otsuchi to the south, and so the wall of water that hit the town, according to a map published in the *Asahi Shimbun* on the anniversary, may have been only about 22 meters high. I say *only*, but that's a wall of water the height of a seven-story building, and because of the narrowness of the valley and the steepness of its walls, it ran far inland, scouring everything it touched, turning a fishing town into splinters strewn with corpses.

As the tsunami approached, Hirani took refuge in the city hall, which was surrounded by water and out of contact with the rest of the world. "So our biggest worry was what happened to our families." His wife and father, who lived locally, were okay, though they feared he was dead, as did his children further away. He added with a faint smile, "They now appreciate me much more." But he lost a lot of his friends. "This loss is so big. We can rebuild—but the heart, the sorrow." There were practical things to deal with—cases of burnout among emergency service workers, trauma with all the survivors. One government employee killed himself, and many were in counseling. A friend of Hirani's had examined 450 waterlogged bodies in the course of looking for his mother. He found her, but it didn't end there. "In his dreams his mother comes with this changed body and the other bodies come and ask for help." He took indefinite leave and died in a traffic accident.

From a practical standpoint Hirani thought they should adopt an approach whereby family members don't look at a body until there is a DNA match. Bodies were still showing up. The previous day they had found two in a car, and officially 470 locals were still missing. Japanese officials are reluctant to classify all the missing as dead, and so the statistics still name thousands of missing along with the nearly 20,000 dead. "We live near the ocean," Hirani said to me, "and our joy is the ocean. The ocean might get very harsh once in a hundred years, but usually people have respect but not fear."

Some Sea Shepherd activists trying to document porpoise slaughter in the region were also in Otsuchi on March 11. One of them wrote soon afterward:

> The police, who had taken up a post at the only place we could pass, were frantically motioning for everyone to get through the gates in the tsunami wall. We got through. These walls and gates are massive structures that appear to be built to withstand military bombardment. They extend high up into the air and rim the entire harbor area of the town. It was not long before the water drained from the harbor and then refilled. We learned from the firemen to expect to see several cycles of this draining and refilling. The water then rapidly refilled the harbor and rose right up to inundate all of the areas on the water side of the wall. It happened very quickly. It drained again, this time almost down to the mud. Then the returning water pushed past and over the draining water creating a wall of black howling water. This time the water rose even faster and topped the wall. It kept rising up on the hillsides and filling the valleys and crevices beyond. Several times this happened and

all the while aftershocks were happening. Then it started to snow. Mixing in with the snow was ash from the many fires burning in the hills and damaged buildings. The smoke was choking.

They tried to rescue a woman stranded on floating debris and then to direct a boat to get her. But darkness shut them in and they didn't succeed. Power was out in most of the disaster region and they spent the night in blackness, with the fires gleaming in the hills.

I heard a similar story from a carnation grower in Miyagi Prefecture to the south, who was trying to find his way back to his farm in the darkness that night and heard the cries of trapped people all around him. The roads were blocked with debris, so he walked, through water so cold he went numb, past rubble, past the sounds of the desperate and the dying. He eventually responded to one woman who was pinned against a wall with water up to her neck. He managed to get her to a safer place but ignored many of the others, convinced he could do nothing, torn and consumed with worry about his farm. In the light of day on the 12th he saw "many fires and dead bodies lying on the roadside." It takes time to get carnations going, and so he had no income last year, but he did at least start growing them again. He complained that those who remained in their own homes, however shattered, did not receive the assistance that the displaced did.

An earthquake can be a great social leveler at first, but policy and prejudice will decide who gets aid and recompense and compassion later, and it will never be equitable, as this farmer knew well. Disaster solidarity often fractures along these lines. But it is important to keep the generosity in mind: Hirani estimated that between 10,000 and 20,000 volunteers had come to his small town alone. Last year young Japanese people were volunteering in large numbers and, at least in some cases, rethinking their ambitions and purpose in life. Every disaster leaves a small percentage of people committed to ideals they might not have found otherwise.

There is no such thing as a natural disaster, the disaster sociologists say. In other words, no matter what the origins of a disaster, human systems— physical, cultural, political—can amplify, channel, or mitigate what happens. In an earthquake it's not the shaking of the earth but the collapse of buildings that's responsible for nearly all loss of human life. Japan may be the best country in the world when it comes to seismic safety codes, and its tsunami alert system worked fine too. They even have an earthquake early-warning system that responds to the P-waves which precede the more damaging S-waves, giving people several seconds to prepare—not much, but maybe time enough to get under a table or into a doorway, pull over to the side of the road, turn off power or gas, take stock.

Later I met Yoshiteru Murosaki, the director of the National Research Institute of Fire and Disaster, who told me that one of the reasons for the many tsunami deaths was that a lot of people sought refuge in places that would have been safe in the last several tsunamis. But this one was much higher, as high as the 1896 tsunami, if not quite as high as the monster waves of 869 are said to have been. Others trusted the seawalls to protect them, but the water overtopped them and kept coming. Roughly two-thirds of the dead were over sixty, people less able or willing to evacuate. (In Hurricane Katrina the elderly made up a disproportionate percentage of the dead for similar reasons, and the same is true of many disasters.) Murosaki told me that the way to deal with tsunamis is to have good evacuation procedures rather than to avoid building on the seacoast. Twenty thousand died here, but in countries without building codes, without sirens and evacuation drills and awareness, the number of dead might have been many times higher. Nevertheless, many communities are retreating from the tsunami zone and rebuilding on higher ground.

That much can be said for the foresight and prudence of the Japanese government. Then there's Fukushima Daiichi, the six nuclear reactors that were also battered by the tsunami: not by the highest waves, but by waves high enough to overtop the little protection that existed and to flood the basement where the emergency generators were fecklessly located—the generators that instantly became useless. Thus the nuclear power plant was completely disabled as no such plant had been before. As Arnie Gundersen, an energy consultant, put it,

There were numerous red flags indicating potential problems for anyone following Tepco [the Tokyo Electric Power Company] during the past decade. Crucial vulnerabilities in the Fukushima Daiichi reactor design; substantial governance issues and weak management characterized by major frauds and cover-ups; collusion and loose regulatory supervision; as well as understanding but ignoring earthquake and tsunami warnings, were key ingredients of the March 2011 disaster. Moreover, all these crucial vulnerabilities had been publicly highlighted years before the disaster occurred.

One of the casualties of the disaster was the relationship between the people and the government. Almost everyone I spoke to, even the most mild-mannered, said they no longer trusted the government, and they said it bluntly, or angrily, or with a deep sense of betrayal. Activists and radicals—with whom I also spoke—didn't have a lot of trust to lose. But for many people, recognition of the initial failures and cover-ups—the secrecy, lies, and tolerance of contamination, the prioritization of business over protection of the vulnerable—has meant a great and terrible rupture. "We have to fear properly," Murosaki said. "Not too much, but enough. What is proper fear?"

Governments fear their people. They fear we will exercise our power to change them, and they fear we will panic. The first is a realistic if undemocratic fear, since changing them is our right; the second is a self-aggrandizing fantasy in which attempts to alter the status quo are seen as madness, hysteria, mob rule. They often assume that we can't handle the data in a crisis and so prefer to withhold crucial information, as the Pennsylvania government did in 1979 at the time of the Three Mile Island partial nuclear meltdown and the Soviet government did during the Chernobyl meltdown in 1986. Panic is what you see in disaster movies, where people run about doing foolish things, impeding evacuation and rescue, behaving like sheep. But governments and officials are not very good shepherds. During the massacre at Virginia Tech in 2007, the university authorities locked down the administrative offices and warned their own families, while withholding information from the campus community. The Bush administration lied about the toxicity of the air near Ground Zero in New York after 9/11, putting hundreds of thousands of people at risk for the sake of a good PR front and a brisk return to business as usual. Disasters often crack open fissures between government and civil society.

Around the time of the anniversary it emerged that, early on, the prime minister had looked at the possibility of evacuating Tokyo. But you cannot evacuate a city of 35 million densely packed people. Where would they go? It would have been a crisis on the scale of the Second World War for Japan and a huge blow to the international economy. A couple of weeks after the anniversary it was revealed that the most damaged Fukushima reactor had nothing like the water-cooling levels it was thought to have and was in fact hotter at that point than it had been at the time of the accident. This is the worst disaster the country has faced since the end of the war, and it occasioned the first public speech by a Japanese emperor since Hirohito announced defeat on August 15, 1945, less than a week after the second American nuclear bomb exploded over Nagasaki.

Emperor Akihito, Hirohito's son, made his first public broadcast on March 16, 2011. At age seventy-eight and recovering from heart surgery, he made his second broadcast in Tokyo for the anniversary. Along with an audience of media personnel and local officials, with bereaved families in the front rows, I watched the feed in the huge theater of the International Center in Sendai, the capital of Miyagi Prefecture and the largest city in the disaster region. The stage held an enormous triple bier of white flowers, before which a huge screen dropped down to show the stage in Tokyo, with its own elaborate array of white flowers. The empress was dressed in a traditional kimono, her eyebrows raised into a single line of perpetual distress, next to the emperor in an elegant dark suit. They bowed deeply before the flowers and the inscription—"spirit of the victims"—and the emperor spoke. "As this earthquake and tsunami caused the nuclear power plant accident," he said, "those living in the designated danger zone lost their homes and livelihoods and had to leave the places where they used to live. In order for them to live there again safely, we have to overcome the problem of radioactive contamination, which is a formidable task." This passage was censored by the networks when the speech was broadcast.

Overcoming the problem of contamination remains a formidable task. The government's preferred approach has been to play down the problem and call for team spirit. With radiation present in the vicinity of the nuclear reactors, the official exposure safety limit was at first raised to twenty times its previous level. When no one wanted vegetables from Fukushima, the Ministry of Education decided to buy them up and put them in school lunches. This put the burden on parents and children to opt out, not an easy thing to do in a society that values harmony and conformity. Nicely dressed mothers in Tokyo met with the heads of their municipalities to demand that school meals be tested; they were assured that everything was fine. In Fukushima just over half of the fifty-nine municipalities test for radiation in school lunches, some before the children sit down to eat, some afterward. Whether or not they change the menu when the levels are too high is not clear. Several municipalities complained that they didn't have the measuring equipment, and citizens have sometimes obtained the equipment themselves. People often find that the government is obstructive or useless in disasters and do much of the crucial work themselves as members of ad hoc or nongovernmental organizations. In Japan measuring radiation is now one of those activities.

An old man in Tokyo proposed that the elderly should volunteer to consume the rice from Fukushima, since they are less susceptible to the effects of radiation, but in November it was still being prepared for school lunches in Fukushima Prefecture. There, notices to evacuate were given late or not at all, and, by stopping short of declaring many contaminated areas unsafe, the government has avoided the burden of compensation for residents, who of course have no buyers for their homes. Even so, more than 63,000 people have evacuated the vicinity of the plant. Like the people who fled Hiroshima and Nagasaki after the nuclear bombs were dropped in 1945, Fukushima evacuees feel they must conceal their origins when they move elsewhere. I also heard about a teacher who was ostracized by his colleagues for expressing a desire to leave. Fear of ostracism sometimes outweighs fear of radiation.

Disasters in the West are often compounded by the belief that human beings instantly revert to savagery in a calamity, with the result that the focus shifts from rescue to law enforcement and the protection of property, as it did recently in Haiti and New Orleans, and in San Francisco after the

1906 earthquake. In Japan the greater problem seems to be conformity. In Fukushima, children who refused to drink the milk in their school lunches were called to the front of their classes and humiliated by their teachers. "They were treated like traitors during the war," a woman said in a video clip I saw on television. (She was telling the story to the chief cabinet minister and the trade and industry minister, who chuckled in response.) A mother I met in Sendai was told by the in-laws she lived with that she could leave if she wanted to, but her husband and child were not going anywhere. Leaving meant leaving the group.

Seigo Kinoshita, a sixty-seven-year-old evacuee in Iwate Prefecture, told me in the small parlor of his temporary housing that he was tired of people saying *ganbare*, an exhortation that roughly translates as "do your best." Even the milk box next to his front door had a sticker on it that said "ganbare" and, in English, "Never give up!" It's hard to be lectured by your milk box. There were four calendars on the walls of the tiny room in which we talked, maybe because they were the only decorations he had, maybe to make time pass faster or express how greatly it weighed on him in the little terraced house on a roadside high above the wiped-out town of Rikuzentakata. He had initially taken refuge in a chilly Buddhist temple with three hundred others, including eighty children from a daycare facility, not all of whom had parents to claim them when the roads opened three days later. Now he was a displaced person.

Some of the most powerful antinuclear demonstrations since March 2011 have been orchestrated and dominated by mothers. Many disaster-zone families are emotionally or physically divided, since women tend to be more concerned about the radiation, and often it is the women and children who have fled, leaving the husband/father behind because his job ties him down or because he worries less about his health. On November 1, 1961, women in more than sixty American cities demonstrated against nuclear weapons, and for years Women Strike for Peace remained one of the most extraordinary activist organizations in the United States. The

atmospheric nuclear detonations—dozens a year between 1945 and 1963, mostly in Nevada—were contaminating breast milk and leading to fears about children's health. Women Strike for Peace played an important role in bringing about the end of above-ground testing and, later, in the creation of the anti–Vietnam War movement. After Fukushima, too, breast milk was contaminated, meaning the most elemental act of nurture could be deadly. You can clean up after an earthquake or hurricane but you can't see what may be inside you, ready to harm the children you may one day have—that is terrifying at first, then demoralizing. Often in disasters people feel tremendous solidarity with all the others who have undergone the same upheaval and loss, but in a situation like this, it isn't clear who has sustained what damage and when, if ever, it will be over.

I met a graduate student in Sendai who told me that one of the major problems survivors reported was the presence of restless ghosts: the spirits of the dead that were still hanging around in need of comfort and propitiation. Right after the disaster and on Obon, the day of the dead in Japan, huge bonfires were lit on the beaches for the ghosts to find their way to shore. In the Tōhoku region, my friend Ramona Handel-Bajema co-directs large-scale relief with AmeriCares, an independent humanitarian relief organization, and I drove out with her to see a small garden project that was not yet planted—mid-March is still wintry in northern Japan. Gardens are one way of restoring people's lives, particularly those of the elderly with time on their hands. Ramona told me about people tending gardens in the foundations of their destroyed houses. To see "cabbages growing where their bedroom once was" represented a consolation and rebirth of sorts. She also told me about a community she works with where the schoolteachers fell into an argument about evacuating the elementary school. One teacher took a handful of students to safety and the rest were drowned. Another of Ramona's projects is taking care of the older siblings of these drowned children, whose parents are lost in mourning, and helping them to enjoy the natural world again.

The priest in charge of a Buddhist temple in Sendai showed me how the stands of tall, thin pine trees that had been planted along the coast had been shattered into spears by the tsunami. He was now working on a scheme to turn the huge mountains of rubble into levees of sorts on which mixed forests of native trees might be planted. While many were preoccupied with the suffering in the present, he was thinking about preventing the next calamity, and pressed on me DVDs of a tree-planting cartoon superhero's adventures in English and in Japanese. In Sendai I met other Buddhist priests and—a rarity there—a Christian priest, all working as counselors and social organizers dealing with the trauma: one with the Philosophy Café, where people could come and talk about their experiences; another with Café du Monk (*monku* means "complaint" in Japanese). "The only thing I can do is stand beside people in grief—focus on listening," one of them said, but the ecumenical group was also working on more practical projects to do with displacement and housing, and with measuring radiation in food and breast milk.

Before I left Japan I went to Hiroshima and met two *hibakusha*, survivors of the atomic explosion. Both men are now in their eighties. They had been at middle school in that era when students were taken out of school to do manual labor for the war effort; neither had been ready to talk about what had happened to them until a couple of years ago, when their sense of posterity's need to have this information finally outweighed their desire to leave the horror behind. It can take a very long time to come to terms with catastrophe—a year isn't very long when it comes to knowing how a society will remember, regenerate, and transform itself.

For me, Hiroshima was a stunning place. Throughout Japan, the old buildings, the bamboo groves, the Buddhist temples, all familiar from imitations and representations in the West, were startling at first hand. I had first seen Hiroshima's Atomic Bomb Dome in my teens in the film *Hiroshima mon amour*; as an antinuclear activist in the 1980s and 1990s I saw photographs of it all the time. It was the icon of the destroyed city, the symbol of why we were against these weapons. A long train ride from Tokyo and a taxi ride to my high-rise Hiroshima hotel, and I was looking out of a nineteenth-floor window in the cold drizzly dusk at the skeletal steel frame of what, before the bomb fell, was the dome of the Prefectural Industrial Promotion Hall. As one of the few surviving structures near the hypocenter of the explosion, it became a symbol of the bombing—and perhaps of the survival of some bit of the city even in the face of the most powerful weapon ever made. Walking there the next day I saw, directly in front of the dome, a sort of shrine with water bottles on it, as though the thirst of the survivors—or their ghosts—was still in need of slaking.

The word *shima* means "island": Fukushima, meaning "fortunate island," is now an ironic name. Hiroshima means "big island," perhaps because it is situated in the delta of a river whose several tributaries divide the city into several long narrow islands that stretch to the coast. In the basement of the Peace Memorial Museum, where I met the *hibakusha*, there was a map of the impact of the American bomb, with the hypocenter colored red, making the city resemble an unfamiliar internal organ with veins flowing through it. The old men pointed at it as they described walking home through the burning, blackened, deadly urban heart on the morning of August 6, 1945, and spoke of how the dying walked with their hands outstretched, the skin hanging off them. One of them rolled up his sleeve to expose the burn scars from the fallout that descended on him and described a lifetime of wearing long-sleeved shirts even on hot days when everyone else was in short sleeves. The other talked about the varieties of cancer he'd developed. Children in utero in the summer of 1945 who were born with severe birth defects are now sixty-seven, and the caregivers they've lived with all their lives are dying off.

The northern tip of the central island in Hiroshima is a memorial space. On both banks of the rivers are shrines and sculptures; the Peace Memorial Museum includes dioramas, photographs, and relics of the first nuclear bomb dropped on human beings. The walls near the diorama showing the city before and after the blast are papered with letters that the mayors of Hiroshima began writing in the 1960s, objecting to all nuclear testing, whether Soviet, American, British, or French. Hiroshima has recovered in part by redefining its identity. Once a military garrison town, it considers itself a "city of peace." And prosperity: it has elegant cafés, a vast mall where expensive European designer products are on sale along with more quotidian furnishings, clothes, and snacks. Hiroshima has a major Mazda auto plant. What it means to be a city of peace is defined fairly narrowly, as being against nuclear weapons and nuclear war.

Japan is in crisis about nuclear power. While I was there, the mayor of Kyoto told Kepko, the regional electrical power company, to close down its nuclear power plant and seek renewable alternatives. Fifty-two of Japan's fifty-four nuclear power plants have been shut down, and local governors are refusing contractors permission to continue with the building of new plants. On the face of it, the country is fine without them, but the long-term problems are serious. If Japan doesn't return to nuclear power, the world's third largest economy will have to step up its scramble for fossil fuels to keep its manufacturing and its cities running. It would have to backtrack on its carbon-emissions commitments, which would throw the delicate process of global carbon reductions even further off track. Japan can continue with nuclear power, which has proven so dangerous and mis-managed; it can abandon nuclear power and increase its reliance on oil and coal; or it can opt for decline. Add an aging population and a low birth rate, and the tsunami begins to seem like the least of Japan's problems. It's possible to imagine a fourth option in which Japan embraces renewable energy and takes pride in building a new green identity, as Hiroshima built a new identity on its charred remains. But nothing suggests that this future is likely to be realized.

Disasters are often like revolutions, moments when people and gov-ernment move far apart; and if government doesn't seem criminal at such times, it may seem superfluous, out of touch, or incompetent. In Mexico City in 1985, an earthquake with casualties comparable to those of the tsu-nami in Japan changed the face of grassroots and national electoral poli-tics. The authorities have reason to fear the aftermath of disaster. Mikhail Gorbachev regards the mishandling of the Chernobyl meltdown as the beginning of the end of the Soviet Union. Perhaps Japan's disaster will come to seem like an integral part of an extraordinary year of upheaval—from Tunisia, Egypt, and the Arab Spring to Chile, Spain, and Greece, as well as everywhere that Occupy has reached. As in these other places, the relationship between people and government in Japan has been ruptured, but in Japan there is no insurrection as yet.

I met antinuclear activists who were proud of a demonstration in Tokyo, in which 10,000 people had participated, raucously: impressive for Japan, but in a city of 35 million, not so huge. Demonstrations and protests do not yet seem to be a force that catalyzes change in civil society, though the shift away from nuclear power may be happening anyway (and the impact of Fukushima Daiichi on the global future of nuclear power should not be underestimated). The alienation and distrust that is everywhere has yet to find an adequate outlet. Perhaps change here will be subtle and slow. But it's clear that Japan will never be the same.

2012

ARRIVAL GATES

The Inari Shrine in Kyoto, Japan

After the long flight across the Pacific, after the night in the tiny hotel room selected so that I could walk to the world's busiest train station in the morning, after the train north to the area most impacted by the tsunami in the Great Tōhoku earthquake of March 11, 2011, after the meetings among the wreckage with people who had seen their villages and neighbors washed away, after seeing the foundations of what had once been a neighborhood so flattened it looked like a chessboard full of shards, after hearing from so many people with grief and rage in their voices talking about walls of water and drownings and displacement and refuge but also about betrayal by the government in myriad ways, after the Christian minister pontificated forever while the Buddhist priests held their peace in the meeting my hosts secretly scheduled at the end of the twelve-hour workday, after I told people I was getting sick but the meeting went on, after I left the meeting in the hopes of getting to the hotel and stood outside in the cold northern night for a long time as a few snowflakes fell—or was it raindrops? I forget—after the sickness turned into a cough so fierce I thought I might choke or come up with blood or run out of air, after the tour continued regardless, after the speaking tour at the universities, after the conferences where I talked about disaster and utopia, after the trip to the conference in Hiroshima where I walked and saw with my own eyes the bombed places I had seen in pictures so often and met with the octogenarians who told me, with the freshness of people who had only recently begun to tell, the story of what they had seen and been and done and suffered and lost on August 6, 1945, after the sight of the keloid scars from the fallout that had drifted onto the arm of a schoolboy sixty-seven years before, so that he grew into a man who always wore long sleeves even in summer, after the long walks along the beautiful river distributaries of Hiroshima and among its willows and monuments to the vaporized and poisoned dead, draped in garlands of paper cranes amid plum trees in bloom but not yet cherries, after the one glorious day in Kyoto when I was neither at work nor overwhelmed and alone but accompanied by a pair of kind graduate students, after a day of wandering through old Buddhist temples with them and seeing the dim hall of the thousand golden Buddhas lined up in long rows, I arrived at the orange gates.

You get off the local train from the city of Kyoto and walk through a little tourist town of shops with doorways like wide-open mouths disgorging low tables of food and crafts and souvenirs and then walk uphill, then up stairs, under a great Torii gate, one of those structures with a wide horizontal beam extending beyond the pillars that hold it up, like the Greek letter π, and then a plaza of temples and buildings and vendors, and then you keep going up. There are multiple routes up the mountain, and the routes take you through thousands of further Torii gates, each with a black base and a black roof-like structure atop the crosspiece, each lacquered pure, intense orange on the cylindrical pillars and crosspiece. The new ones are gleaming and glossy. Some of the old ones are dull, their lacquer cracked, or even rotting away so that the wood is visible underneath.

The orange is so vivid it is as though you have at last gone beyond things that are colored orange to the color itself, particularly in the passages where the Torii gates are just a few feet apart—or, in one extraordinary sequence, many paces long of gates only inches apart—a tunnel of total immersion in orange. (Vermilion, say some of the accounts, but I saw pure intense orange.) Nearly every gate bears black inscriptions on one side, and if I could read Japanese I might've read individual businesspeople and corporations expressing their gratitude, because rice and prosperity and business are all tied up together in the realm of the god Inari, but I couldn't. The place was something else to me.

I later read that the Fushimi Inari-taisha is the head shrine of 30,000 or so Shinto shrines in Japan devoted to Inari. It is said to have been founded in 711 and burned down in 1468, during a civil war, but much of it seems to have been replaced in overlapping waves, so that the whole is ancient and the age of the parts varied, some of them very new. The gates seem designed to pass through, and the altars—platforms and enclosures of stone slabs and obelisks and stone foxes—for stillness, so that the landscape is a sort of musical score of moving and pausing. The altars looked funereal to a Western eye, with the stone slabs like tombstones, but they were something altogether different.

The foxes were everywhere, particularly at these altar zones. Moss and lichen grow on their stone or cement backs, so some are more green than gray and others are spotted with lighter gray. They often have red cloth tied around their necks, the fabric faded to dusty pink, and there at the altar sites are rope garlands and stones with inscriptions carved into them. The foxes, hundreds of them, a few at a time, sit up, often in pairs, sometimes with smaller Torii gates that were offerings arrayed around them, and then sometimes even smaller foxes with the gates, as though this might continue on beyond the visible into tinier and tinier foxes and gates. You could buy the small gates and foxes at the entrance and some places on the mountainside.

Foxes, I knew, are *kitsune* in Japan, the magical shapeshifters in folktales and woodblock prints—and manga and anime now—who pass as human for months or for years, becoming beautiful brides who run away or courtiers who serve aristocrats but serve another, unknown purpose as well. The foxes at the Inari shrine are the god's messengers, a website later told me, more beneficent than some of the foxes in the stories. Elusive, beautiful, unpredictable, *kitsune* in this cosmology represent the unexpected and mysterious and wild aspects of nature. Rain during sunshine is called a fox's wedding in Japanese.

Gates, foxes, foxes, gates. The gates lead you to gates and to foxes, the trails wind all over the slope of the steep, forested hill. Most of the literature speaks as though there is a trail you take, but there are many. If you keep going you might come to a dense bamboo forest with trunks as thick as the poles of streetlights, and a pond beyond that, or you might just keep mounting forest paths that wind and tangle, with every now and again a little pavilion selling soft drinks and snacks, notably tofu pockets—*inarizushi*—said to be the foxes' favorite food. And more gates, unpainted stone as well as lacquered wood.

Arrival implies a journey, and almost all the visitors that day arrived out of a lifetime in Japan, seeing a different place than I did, traveling mostly in small groups, seeming to know why they were there and what to expect. I came directly from the grueling tour of disaster, but with a long-time interest in how moving through space takes on meaning and how meaning can be made spatially, with church and temple designs, landscape architecture and paths, roads, stairs, ladders, bridges, labyrinths, thresholds, triumphal arches, all the grammar that inflects the meanings of our movement.

I had been invited to Japan for the one-year anniversary of the triple disaster, reporting on the aftermath and talking about my book *A Paradise Built in Hell*, which had been translated into Japanese and published just before one of the five largest recorded earthquakes hit the country, and the ocean rose up to, in places, 140 feet and scoured the shore, and the six Fukushima nuclear reactors fell apart and began to spread radiation by air and by sea. But that's another story. The Inari shrine was not part of it. My encounter there wasn't the culmination of that journey but perhaps a reprieve from it, and an extension of other journeys and questions I have carried for a long time.

Arrival is the culmination of the sequence of events, the last in the list, the terminal station, the end of the line. And the idea of arrival begets questions about the journey and how long it took. Did it take the dancer two hours to dance the ballet, or two hours plus six months of rehearsals, or two hours plus six months plus a life given over to becoming the instrument that could, over and over, draw lines and circles in the air with precision and grace? Sumi-e painters painted with famous speed, but it took decades to become someone who could manage a brush that way, who had that feel for turning leaves or water into a monochromatic image. You fall in love with someone and the story might be of how you met, courted, consummated, but it might also be of how before all that, time and trouble shaped you both over the years, sanded your rough spots and wore away your vices until your scars and needs and hopes came together like halves of a broken whole.

Culminations are at least lifelong, and sometimes longer when you look at the natural and social forces that shape you, the acts of the ancestors, of illness or economics, immigration and education. We are constantly arriving; the innumerable circumstances are forever culminating in this glance, this meeting, this collision, this conversation, like the pieces in a kaleidoscope forever coming into new focus, new flowerings. But to me the gates made visible not the complicated ingredients of the journey but the triumph of arrival.

I knew I was missing things. I remember the first European cathedral I ever entered—Durham Cathedral, when I was fifteen, never a Christian, not yet taught that most churches are cruciform, or in the shape of a human body with outstretched arms, so that the altar is at what in French is called the chevet, or head, that there was a coherent organization to the place. I saw other things then and I missed a lot. You come to every place with your own equipment.

I came to Japan with wonder at seeing the originals of things I had seen in imitation often, growing up in California: Japanese gardens and Buddhist temples, Mount Fuji, tea plantations and bamboo groves.

But it wasn't really what I knew about Japan but what I knew about the representation of time that seemed to matter there. I knew well the motion studies of Eadweard Muybridge in which a crane flying or a woman sweeping is captured in a series of photographs, time itself measured in intervals, as intervals, as moments of arrival. The motion studies were the first crucial step on the road to cinema, to those strips of celluloid in which time had been broken down into twenty-four frames per second that could reconstitute a kiss, a duel, a walk across the room, a plume of smoke.

Time seemed to me, as I walked all over the mountain, more and more enraptured and depleted, a series of moments of arrival, like film frames, if film frames with their sprockets were gateways—and maybe they are: they turn by the projector, but as they go, each frame briefly becomes an opening through which light travels. I was exalted by a landscape that made tangible that elusive sense of arrival, that palpable sense of time that so often eludes us. Or, rather, the sense that we are arriving all the time, that the present is a house in which we always have one foot, an apple we are just biting, a face we are just glimpsing for the first time. In Zen Buddhism you talk a lot about being in the present and being present. That present is an infinitely narrow space between the past and future, the zone in which the senses experience the world, in which you act, however much your mind may be mired in the past or racing into the future, whatever the consequences of your action.

I had the impression, midway through the hours I spent wandering, that time itself had become visible, that every moment of my life as I was passing through orange gates always had been and always would be passing through magnificent gates that only in this one place are visible. Their uneven spacing seemed to underscore this perception; sometimes time grows dense and seems to both slow down and speed up—when you fall in love, when you are in the thick of an emergency or a discovery; other times it flows by limpid as a stream across a meadow, each day calm and like the one before, not much to remember; or time runs dry and you're stuck, hoping for change that finally arrives in a trickle or a rush. All these metaphors of flow can be traded in for solid ground: time is a stroll through orange gates. Blue mountains are constantly walking, said Dōgen Zenji, the monk who brought Sōtō Zen to Japan, and we are also constantly walking, through these particular Shinto pathways of orange gates. Or so it seemed to me on that day of exhaustion and epiphany.

What does it mean to arrive? The fruits of our labor, we say, the reward. The harvest, the home, the achievement, the completion, the satisfaction, the joy, the recognition, the consummation. Arrival is the reward, it's the time you aspire to on the journey, it's the end, but on the mountain south of Kyoto on a day just barely spring, on long paths whose only English guidance was a few plaques about not feeding the monkeys I never saw anyway, arrival seemed to be constant. Maybe it is.

I wandered far over the mountain that day, until I was outside the realm of the pretty little reproduction of an antique map I had purchased, and gone beyond the realm of the gates. I was getting tired after four hours or so of steady walking. The paths continued, the trees continued, the ferns and mosses under them continued, and I continued but there were no more Torii gates. I came out in a manicured suburb with few people on the streets, and walked out to the valley floor and then back into the next valley over and up again through the shops to the entrance to the shrine all over again. But I could not arrive again, though I walked through a few more gates and went to see the tunnel of orange again. It was like trying to go back to before the earthquake, to before knowledge. An epiphany can be as indelible a transformation as a trauma. Once I was through those gates and through that day, I would never enter them for the first time and understand what they taught me for the first time.

All you really need to know is that there is a hillside in Japan in which time is measured in irregular intervals and every moment is an orange gate, and foxes watch over it, and people wander it, and the whole is maintained by priests and by donors, so that gates crumble and gates are erected, time passes and does not, as elsewhere nuclear products decay and cultures change and people come and go, and that the place might be one at which you will arrive someday, to go through the flickering tunnels of orange, up the mountainside, into this elegant machine not for controlling or replicating time but maybe for realizing it, or blessing it. Or maybe you have your own means of being present, your own for seeing that at this very minute you are passing through an orange gate.

2014

JOURNEY TO THE CENTER

(on Elín Hansdóttir's Labyrinth Path)

The
journey
is
always
into
the
dark,
the darkness that is the unknown,
for the future is always unknown.
The journey is always into the dark
except for those who run away,
the breech births,
and those who stall
and
the
unknown
catches up with them
anyway.

A vast artillery of techniques, from divination in the entrails of animals
and in the dark sky of stars to the polls and studies of our own age,
has been deployed as though they could be a torch, a flashlight in
that dark journey, but the future always surprises, and no quantity of
predictions makes it predictable. Darkness is a pejorative in English,

This was the text for an artist's book about the labyrinth; the original formatting is
preserved but flows differently here.

the darkness that is supposed to be bad times and moral failure, and the term has often carried emotional, moral and religious overtones, as has its opposite: the children of light, snowy angels, fair maidens, and all those knights in shining armor and cowboys in white hats. "Darkness cannot drive out darkness; only light can do that. Hate cannot drive out hate; only love can do that," said the dark-skinned Martin Luther King Jr., but sometimes love is darkness; sometimes the glare of light is what needs to be extinguished. Turn off the lights and come to bed.

Darkness has its uses, its virtues, and its spirit, the spirit of embracing— of embracing the unknown I was going to write, and then thought that might be too narrow, and *embracing* might be a way to describe this nocturnal atmosphere in which things are not so separate. In the deepest dark, in the velvet of blackness, what is there can only be distinguished by touch. John Berger wrote, "In war the dark is on nobody's side, in love the dark confirms that we are together."

Darkness is amorous, the darkness of passion, of your own unknowns rising to the surface, the darkness of interiors, and perhaps part of what makes pornography so pornographic is the glaring light in which it transpires, that and the lack of actual touch, the substitution of eyes for skin, of seeing for touching
that is the difference between distance and closeness,
warmth and coldness.
In the dark there is no distance,
and perhaps that's what some fear in it.
In darkness things merge,
which might be how passion becomes love
and how making love begets progeny
of all natures and forms.
Merging is dangerous.
Darkness is generative,
and generation, biological and artistic both,
requires this amorous engagement with the unknown,
this entry into the realm where you

do

not

quite

know

what you are doing

and what will happen next.

To embrace the future, the dark, you make. Making is a letting go of your own stuff into the world, of the ideas and offspring that the breeze of time takes away as though you were a dry dandelion, a thistle, a milkweed, a poplar whose seeds travel on the winds of time, in this way that wind makes love to flowers and seeds, in this way that time tears them apart and carries them onward. The white ghosts of those seeds travel forward in time and land when the wind ceases to bear them up and then only maybe to take root and start the story over again, or another story.

When you spend time in the desert, you come to love shadow, shade, and darkness, the respite they give to the menacing glare of day that burns you out and dries you up. The light is beautiful but too powerful, and at midday it flattens everything into a bland harshness, but early and late in the day the light is more golden and the shadows are longer. So long that every bump has a long shade streaming from it across the land. Bushes have the shadows of trees, and boulders, the shadows of giants; every crevice and fold and protrusion of the landscape is thrown into the high relief of light and shadow, and your own shadow is twice, seven, ten times your height, licking like a cool tongue of darkness across the landscape. At those times day and night are intermingled.

Too much whiteness and you go snow-blind.

You can see in the dark,

but brightness blinds you to the subtleties of the night world, so that if you make a fire in that desert or walk by flashlight your eyes adjust, and everything outside the illuminated area

sinks into indistinguishable blackness. Turn away from the
fire, turn off the light, and the darkness ceases to be solid
black and turns into visible terrain, even on starry nights
without the moon's blue shadows and cool watery light.

So it is in the labyrinth called *Path,* where you enter, the door shuts
behind you, and you pause while your eyes adjust and what at first
seemed like pure blackness begins to sort itself out into angles and
facets. One of the uncanny aspects of Elín's *Path* is that the traveler—
viewer we usually say about works of art, but this art is more and other
than visual, and the person who visits it is first of all a traveler—is
that the travelers who enter it one by one bump up against their own
ideas about light and darkness. It's the most natural thing in the
world to interpret the darknesses within *Path* as solids and the subtly
luminous planes and zones, illuminated with a faint lavender light
from narrow cracks in the structure, as openings, but often it's the
opposite: pale are the hard walls, inviting is the endless darkness.

Path has been erected in four places now, but I saw it or rather traveled
it in its second incarnation—entered it seven times in the late spring
and midsummer in Iceland a few years ago. When I first entered it
early that May, darkness was already growing rare and late in Iceland,
disorienting for a person from near the Horse Latitudes, and by mid-June
there was no real darkness, no night, no respite from the rational light
of day and wakefulness, it seemed, anywhere on that island, except for
Elín's *Path.* The labyrinth seemed like a burrow, a refuge, an island of
night in that country of day. The piece was as welcoming and uncanny as
sleep in that bright relentless summer when I was thirsty for darkness.

You dove into the structure's darkness—dove, because like a diver,
you had people standing by to pull you out if you got too lost or
too frightened, as people become even in illuminated labyrinths.
And when you went as far as you could go the walls began to
press together and there was no way forward; you turned back
and wandered through the luminous and darker darknesses to the
light and were done with the exploring, at least bodily, for the

mind

lingered.

The piece stripped you of certainties, of confidence, disoriented you
and rendered your sight unreliable, put you in a cloud of unknowing
and set you on a path whose twists and turns and distance were
unknown. This is perhaps closer to our real condition in many ways
than the assuredness with which we meet the world even when it
turns out we don't know what we're doing or what to expect, even
when the world surprises us and expectations don't map possibilities.
Which is to say it did what darkness and labyrinths do,
both get us lost literally
and let us know who we really are,
metaphysically.

Labyrinth in Luce Irigaray's feminist etymology has to do with
labia, the lips, but the more commonly accepted interpretation is
that the word somehow has to do with the labrys, the two-headed
axe of ancient Greece that nevertheless became a lesbian icon some
decades ago, perhaps because it has to do with fierce goddesses and
matriarchs—a labrys hacked open the route for Athena's birth out of
Zeus's head. What is an axe doing in a labyrinth? They cut through
things, straighten the way. English *axes* is the plural both of the tool or
weapon and of the straight line of a trajectory, the axis of a boulevard
through a city, of the Champs Élysées or of Broadway or Laugavegur
in Reykjavík, the long boulevards that are also sight lines through
cities, incisions in them, since a street is only the void defined by the
volumes of buildings. But in a labyrinth the axes are broken, or rather
coiled—lines wound like the spool of thread Ariadne gave Theseus so
that he might find his way out of the labyrinth in Crete, the labyrinth
made to hide the monster. In some of the ancient drawings of Ariadne,
the spool of thread she holds looks like a spiral labyrinth itself. The
thread Theseus unwinds is a reminder that the labyrinth is also a
line, an axis, wound up so that vast distance fits into small space.

"I know of one labyrinth which is a single straight line," says one of Borges's characters. "Along that line so many philosophers have lost themselves that a mere detective might well do so, too." Borges was labyrinthine; he loved innumerable quantity, visions of the infinite and uncountable, tangles, riddles, complexities, and within them an Argentine sense of inexorable fate. Borges is now the name of a tree-lined boulevard in Buenos Aires, so that you can now walk the straight route of his commemoration, if not the circuitous routes of his imagination; but I digress, I wander, though my subject is wandering itself.

In a labyrinth that is not the straight line of Borges, the only way forward is digressive, a constant turning and twisting that is both a means of disorientation and of compressing considerable distance.

A labyrinth winds the axis of a journey into a small space, embodies as a metaphor the journey into the unknown or makes the metaphor concrete so that you bodily enter the metaphor and, for once, the metaphysical journey of your life and your actual movements are one and the same. "Their paths are linear," writes Penelope Reed Doob, but "their pattern may be circular, cyclical; they describe both the linearity and architecture of space and time." And describe the way time is space, space is time, when you travel—a metaphor for life itself, with the proviso that *metaphor* itself is a Greek word that means "to carry over," and in Athens, the transit system is still called the Metaphor. A metaphor carries the abstract into the concrete, the tangible into the conceptual, and vice versa.

A labyrinth is a metaphor in both senses, carrying you on a brief journey that reminds you that you are always on a journey. You are always in the labyrinth, always a little lost and always feeling your way forward, there is always an unexpected turn ahead, in fact you were born into the labyrinth out of the darkness of the womb and you will only exit in that other darkness of tombs.

The two paths, literal and metaphorical, become one path on which you know at last that you are a traveler in darkness. But in the labyrinth, you arrive before that finale, and one of the great spiritual uses of a labyrinth is to compress the journey of pilgrimage into a local space, so that you may wander, may know that in order to get to your destination, you must turn away from it, become lost, spin about, and then only after the way has become overwhelming and absorbing, arrive, without having gone far.

In this way it is the opposite of a maze, which has not one convoluted way but many ways and often no center, so that wandering has no cease or at least not a definitive conclusion. In a labyrinth you're lost; you arrive nevertheless; and then you reverse your journey. Maybe the journey outward is what all the writers on labyrinths have neglected: what happens after you arrive is always a complicated question and an overlooked challenge. It is like time going backward, like rewinding thread or film, but you never quite return to where you began because the person who had truly arrived at the center is by that time subtly someone else.

The end of the journey through the labyrinth is not at the center but at the threshold where it began. Or maybe home is where one returns from the pilgrimage, the adventure; maybe it's the unpraised edges and margins that also matter. It's not immersion but emergence.

In this folding up of great distance into small space, the labyrinth is like two other manmade things, like the spool of thread and like the words and lines and pages of a book.
It turns a road into a spool of thread and a story.
Imagine all the sentences in this small book
as lengths
of a single thread
that we have wound up into pages;
imagine that they could be unwound;
that you could walk the line
they make;
and try
to
imagine
how long that line might be.

Reading is also traveling, with the eyes along the length of an idea, which can be folded up into the compressed space of a book and unfolded within your imagination and your understanding. Knowing that, you also know that we read the landscape as we go and that we travel in stories and by stories, that our life is a story being written by feet and imagination, a story that we ourselves are, in part, the author of, even though we have little idea how it will turn out, what the next winding of the labyrinth is. E. L. Doctorow once said that writing was like driving home in the dark; you can only see as far ahead as the headlights' beam, but it gets you there. So is everything else. Journeys, labyrinths, threads are the powerful metaphors that contain and carry everything forward.

When you enter the literal labyrinth, its maker has assumed the high power and responsibility of narrating your journey for a little while. In her labyrinth you are the story, but she is the storyteller. This can be a respite, a passage of life with a guide, like Dante led along by Virgil, and it can also be frightening, a reminder that you are not in control. The one thread of your own life tangled up with countless other threads in the usual tapestry of heartbreaks, doubts, joys, epiphanies, and routines. You are not entirely the storyteller but neither is the artist; in her labyrinth, what transpires as your journey unwinds is, in part, of your making, whether darkness and the unknown bring fear or wonder into being, whatever longer thread you spin this passage into. Path maker and path walker are collaborators of a sort, in that dark.

And the same goes for reading, but, reader, remember that the thread you unspool here will not get you through the labyrinth. To read or think about it is no substitute for that plunge into the dark. You must go. Or if you read this far away from *Path* or long after, you have to ask about the other labyrinths upon which you might be embarking or avoiding, about your own darknesses and interiors.

Whether or not you enter labyrinths through the labia, there is another labyrinth in the human body: in the windings of the inner ear, whose channels provide both hearing and balance. Anatomists long ago termed this passage the labyrinth, which suggests that if the labyrinth is the channel through which sound enters the mind, then we ourselves bodily enter this dark labyrinth like sounds on the way to being heard by some great unknown presence. To walk this path is to be heard, and to be heard is a great desire of the majority of us, but to be heard by whom, by what, and how? To be a sound traveling toward the mind—is that another way to imagine this path, this journey, the unwinding of this thread? Who hears?

Christians walking church labyrinths imagine they are traveling a pilgrimage to Jerusalem, and Muslims face Mecca and make the hajj once in their life to that black stone, the Kaaba, in the white glare of desert, and they both might say that the sound is being heard by God. A thread, a story, a sound, a song along a path, and the journey is always inward. But maybe here God is only another name for the unknown, for that embracing darkness that is space and silence and the unwinding openings of possibility.

In some versions, the Virgin Mary conceived through the ear, so that the labyrinth within was the path that the divine spark took into her being, so that she conceived by hearing and brought forth a man who was in some sense the Word and still is a story and words.
"Just as from the small womb of Eve's ear
Death entered in and was poured out,
So through a new ear, that was Mary's,
Life entered and was poured out.
Or so said St. Ephraim."
Which is to say that there is an eros of hearing, as well as a labyrinth in the ear, and you enter the labyrinth named *Path* as a sound heard by darkness. The labyrinth that might be the lips that speak is also the ear that hears.

In Greece there were gods, not God, and in the center of the labyrinth was the Minotaur, that beast born of the queen of Crete who conceived a passion for the great snow-white bull who is to that story what the white whale might be to *Moby-Dick*; he sets calamity in motion; the Minotaur is calamity itself, and Daedalus built the labyrinth to hide

it from the world. The queen's name means "shining," and she was a
daughter of the sun. But who and what the bull was is all confused,
for in some other myths Zeus himself assumes the form of a bull; and
in Crete the real name of the Minotaur (which translates as "bull of
Minos") was Asterion, ruler of the stars. Which is the name Borges used
in his story "House of Asterion." And the bullheaded man wrapped in
tatters of divinity was betrayed by his half-sister, Ariadne, who gave the
spool of thread to Theseus so that he might find his way back out of the
labyrinth after he slayed the hybrid creature with a labrys, the two-headed
axe that shows up in his hands in many Roman mosaic labyrinths on
floors. In Ovid's Latin version of this old Greek tale, Ariadne fled with
Theseus, but he abandoned her on Naxos, and like her brother, the ruler
of the stars, she suffered and then went up into the sky as Corona, the
constellation of the northern crown. The stars, a labyrinth in darkness;
the constellations, threads we stretch between them.

But I meander, for all I meant to say about the labyrinth of the inner ear
was that in *Path*
there is a soundtrack by the artist's brother Úlfur—
whose name means Wolf, not bull—
that is an almost subliminal throbbing,
rather like the heartbeat a baby must hear in utero.
Or maybe when you are a word heard by the god
who is the god of the lost, of unknowns and unknowables,
you in turn hear his heartbeat.

Moving inward like sound, moving outward like thought.

2012

LETTER TO A DEAD MAN

ON THE OCCUPATION OF HOPE

Dear young man who died on the fourth day of this turbulent 2011, dear
Mohammed Bouazizi,

I want to write to you about an astonishing year—with three months
yet to run. I want to tell you about the power of despair and the margins of
hope and the bonds of civil society. I wish you could see the way that your
small life and large death became a catalyst for the fall of so many dictators
in what is known as the Arab Spring.

We are now in some sort of an American Fall. Civil society here has
suddenly hit the ground running, and we are all headed toward a future no
one imagined when you—a young Tunisian vegetable seller capable of giving so much, who instead had so much taken from you—burned yourself to
death to protest your impoverished and humiliated state.

You lit yourself on fire on December 17, 2010, exactly nine months before Occupy Wall Street began. Your death two weeks later would be the
beginning of so much. You lit yourself on fire because you were voiceless,
powerless, and evidently without hope. And yet you must have had one
small hope left: that your death would have an impact, that you, who had
so few powers—even the power to make a decent living or protect your
modest possessions or be treated fairly and decently by the police—had
the power to protest. As it turned out, you had that power beyond your
wildest dreams, and you had it because your hope, however diminished,
was the dream of the many, the dream of what we now have started calling
the 99%.

And so Tunisia erupted and overthrew its government, and Egypt
caught fire, as did Bahrain, Syria, Yemen, and Libya. Where the nonviolent protests elsewhere turned into a civil war, the rebels have almost

won after several bloody months. Who could have imagined a Middle East without Ben Ali of Tunisia, without Mubarak, without Gaddafi? And yet here we are, in the unimaginable world. Again. And almost everywhere.

Japan was literally shaken loose from its plans and arrangements by the March 11 earthquake and tsunami, and that country has undergone profound soul-searching about values and priorities. China is turbulent, and no one knows how much longer the discontent of the repressed middle class and the hungry poor there will remain containable. India: who knows? The Saudi government is so frightened it even gave women a few new rights. Syrians wouldn't go home even when their army began to shoot them down. Crowds of up to a million Italians have been protesting austerity measures in recent months. The Greeks, well, if you've been following events, you know about the Greeks. Have I forgotten Israel? Huge demonstrations against the economic status quo there lasted all summer and into this fall.

As you knew at the outset, it's all about economics. This wild year, Greece boiled over again into crisis with colossal protests, demonstrations, blockades, and outright street warfare. Icelanders continued their fight against bailing out the banks that sank their country's economy in 2008 and continue pelting politicians with eggs. Their former prime minister may become the first head of state to face legal charges in connection with the global financial collapse. Spanish youth began to rise up on May 15.

Distinctively, in so many of these uprisings, the participants were not advocating not for one party or a simple position, but for a better world, for dignity, for respect, for real democracy, for belonging, for hope and possibility—and their economic underpinnings. The Spanish young whose future had been sold out to benefit corporations and their 1% were nicknamed the *Indignados*, and they lived in the plazas of Spain this summer. Occupied Madrid, like Occupied Tahrir Square, preceded Occupy Wall Street.

In Chile, students outraged by the cost of an education and the profound inequities of their society have been demonstrating since May—with everything from kiss-ins to school occupations to marches of 150,000 or more. Forty thousand students marched against "education reform" in Colombia last week. And in August in Britain the young went on a rampage that tore up London, Birmingham, and dozens of other communities, an event that began when the police shot Mark Duggan, a dark-skinned twenty-nine-year-old Londoner. Young Britons had risen up more peaceably over tuition hikes the winter before. There, too, things are bleak and volatile—something I know you would understand. In Mexico, a beautiful movement involving mass demonstrations against the drug war has arisen, triggered by the death of another young man and by the grief and vision of his father, left-wing poet Javier Sicilia.

The United States had one great eruption in Wisconsin this winter, when the citizens occupied their state capitol building in Madison for weeks. Egyptians and others elsewhere on the planet called a local pizza parlor and sent pies to the occupiers. We all know the links. We're all watching. So the Occupy movement has spilled over from Wall Street. Hundreds of occupations are happening all over North America: in Oklahoma City and Tijuana, in Victoria and Fort Lauderdale.

THE 99%

"We are the 99%" is the cry of the Occupy movement. This summer one of the flyers that helped launch the Occupy Wall Street protest read: "We, the 99%, call for an open general assembly Aug 9, 7:30 pm at the Potato Famine Memorial NYC." It was an assembly to discuss the September 17 occupation-to-come.

The Irish Hunger Memorial, so close to Wall Street, commemorates the million Irish peasants who starved in the 1840s, while Ireland remained a food-exporting country and the landed gentry continued to profit. It's a monument to the exploitation of the many by the few, to the forces that turned some of our ancestors—including my mother's four Irish grandparents—into immigrants, forces that are still pushing people out of farms, homes, nations, regions.

The Irish famine was one of the great examples of those disasters of the modern era that are crises not of scarcity, but of distribution. The United States is now the wealthiest country the world has ever known and has an abundance of natural resources, as well as of nurses, doctors, universities, teachers, housing, and food—so ours, too, is a crisis of distribution. Everyone could have everything they need and the rich would still be rich enough, but you know that *enough* isn't a concept for them. They're greedy, and their thirty-year grab for yet more has carved away at what's minimally necessary for the survival and dignity of the rest of us. So the Famine Memorial couldn't have been a more appropriate place for Occupy Wall Street to begin.

The 99%, those who starve during famines and lose their livelihoods and homes during crashes, were going to respond to the 1% who had been served so well by the Bush administration and by the era of extreme privatization it ushered in. As my friend Andy Kroll reported at TomDispatch of the first ten years of the millennium, "The top 1% of earners enjoyed 65% of all income growth in America for much of the decade." He added, "In 2010, 20.5 million people, or 6.7% of all Americans, scraped by with less than $11,157 for a family of four—that is, less than half of the poverty line." You can't get by on less than $1,000 a month in this country where a single visit to an emergency room can cost your annual income, a car, twice that, and a year at a private college, more than four times that.

Later in August came the website started by a twenty-eight-year-old New York City activist, *we are the 99 percent*, to which hundreds daily now submit photographs of themselves. Each of them also testifies to the bleak conditions they find themselves in, despite their hard work and educations which often left them in debt, despite the promises dangled before them that (if they played the game right) they'd be safe, housed, and living a part of that oversold dream.

It's a website of unremitting waking nightmares, economic bad dreams that a little wealth redistribution and policy changes would eliminate (even without eliminating the wealthy). The people contributing aren't asking for luxuries. They would simply prefer not to be worked to death like so many nineteenth-century millworkers, nor to have their whole world come crashing down if they get sick. They want to survive with dignity, and their testimony will break your heart.

Mohammed Bouazizi, dead at twenty-six, you to whom I'm writing, here is one of the recent posts at that site:

> I am 26 years old. I am $134,000 in debt. I started working at 14 years old, and have worked Full-Time since I turned 20. I work in I.T. and got laid off in July 2011. I was LUCKY, and found a job RIGHT AWAY: with a Pay Cut and MORE HOURS? Now, I just found out that my Dad got laid off last week—after 18 YEARS with the same employer. I have debilitating (SP! Sorry!) O.C.D. and can't take time away from work to get treatment because I can't afford my mortgage payments if I don't go to work, and I'm afraid I'll lose my NEW job if I take time off!!! WE ARE THE 99%.

Some of the people at *we are the 99%* offer at least partial views of their faces, but the young IT worker quoted above holds a handwritten letter so long that it obscures his face. Poverty obscures your face too. It obscures your talents, potential, even your distinctive voice; and if it goes deep enough, it eradicates you by degrees of hunger and degradation. Poverty is a creation of the systems against which people all over the planet are revolting this wild year of 2011. The Arab Spring, after all, was also an economic revolt. What were all those dictatorships and autocracies for, if not to squeeze as much profit as possible out of subjugated populations—profit for rulers, profit for multinational corporations, profit for that 1%.

"We are not goods in the hands of politicians and bankers" was the slogan of the first student protest called in Spain this year. Your beautiful generation, Mohammed Bouazizi, has arisen and is bringing the rest of us along, even here in the United States.

THE PEOPLE'S MICROPHONE

Its earliest critics seemed to think that Occupy Wall Street was a lobbying group whose chosen task on this planet should be to create a package of realistic demands. In other words, they were convinced that the occupiers should become supplicants, asking the powerful for some kind of handout like college debt forgiveness. They were suggesting that a dream as wide as the sky be stuffed into little bottles and put up for sale. Or simply smashed.

In the same way, they wanted this movement to hurry up and appoint leaders, so that there would be someone to single out and investigate, pick off, or corrupt. At heart, however, this is a leaderless movement, an anarchist movement, catalyzed by the grace of civil society and the hard work of the collective. The Occupy movement—like so many movements around the world now—is using general assemblies as its form of protest and process. Its members are not facing the authorities, but each other, coming to know themselves, trying to give rise to the democracy they desire on a small scale rather than merely railing against its absence on a large scale.

These are the famous Occupy general assemblies in which decisions are made by consensus and, in the absence of amplification (by order of the New York City police), the people's mike is used: those assembled repeat what is said as it's said, creating a human megaphone effect. This is accompanied by a small vocabulary of hand gestures, which help people participate in the complex process of a huge group having a conversation.

In other words, the process is also the goal: direct democracy. No one can hand that down to you. You live direct democracy in that moment when you find yourself participating in civil society as a citizen with an equal voice. Put another way, the Occupiers are not demanding that something be given to them but formulating something new. That it involves no technology, not even bullhorns, is itself remarkable in this wired era. It's just passionate people together—and then Facebook, YouTube, Twitter, text messages, emails, and online sites like this one spread the word, along with some print media, notably the *Occupied Wall Street Journal*.

The beauty and the genius of this movement in this moment is that it has found a way to define its needs and desires without putting limits on them that would exclude many. In doing so, it has spoken to nearly all of us.

There is the terrible rage at economic injustice shared by college students looking at a future of debt and overwork, as well as those who couldn't afford college in the first place, by working people struggling ever harder for less, by the many who have no jobs and few prospects, by people forced out of their homes by the games banks play with mortgages and profits, and by everyone affected by the catastrophe that is health care in this country. And by the rest of us, furious on their behalf (and on our own).

And then there is the joyous hope that things could actually be different. That hope has been fulfilled a little in the way that an open-ended occupation has survived four weeks and more and turned into hundreds of Occupy actions around the country and marches in almost 1,000 cities around the world last Sunday, from Sydney to Tokyo to Santa Rosa. It speaks for so many; it speaks for the 99%; and it speaks clearly, so clearly that an ex-Marine showed up with a hand-lettered sign that said, "2nd time I've fought for my country, 1st time I've known my enemy."

The climate change movement showed up at Occupy Wall Street, too. What's blocking action on climate change is what's blocking action on all the other issues that matter: it would cut into profits. Never mind the deep future, not when what's at stake is quarterly earnings.

In a YouTube video of the New York occupation, I watched an old woman in a straw hat say, "We're fighting for a society in which everyone is important." What a beautiful summation! Could any demand be clearer than that? And could the ways in which people have no value under our current economic regime be more obvious?

WHAT IS YOUR OCCUPATION?

Occupy Wall Street. Occupy together. Occupy New Orleans, Portland, Stockton, Boston, Las Cruces, Minneapolis. *Occupy.* The very word is a manifesto, a position statement, and a position as well. For so many people, particularly men, their occupation is their identity, and when a job is lost, they become not just unemployed but no one. The Occupy movement offers them a new occupation, work that won't pay the bills, but a job worth doing. "Lost my job, found an occupation," said one sign in the crowd of witty signs.

There is, of course, a bleaker meaning for the word *occupation*, as in the U.S. occupation of Iraq. National Public Radio gives the Dow Jones report several times a day, as though the rise and fall of the stock market had not long ago been decoupled from the rise and fall of genuine measures of well-being for the 99%. Wall Street has long occupied us as if it were a foreign power.

Wall Street *is* a foreign country—and maybe an enemy country as well.

And now it's occupied. The way that Native Americans occupied Alcatraz Island in San Francisco Bay for eighteen months four decades ago and galvanized a national Native American rights movement. You pick some place to stand, and when you stand there, you find your other occupation—as a member of civil society.

In Ohio this May, a group of activists dressed as Robin Hood literally lowered a drawbridge they made so they could cross an actual moat around Chase Bank's headquarters and invade its shareholders' meeting. Forty Robin Hoods also showed up en masse last week in kayaks for a national mortgage bankers' meeting in Chicago. Houses facing foreclosure are being occupied. Foreclosure is, of course, a way of turning people into non-occupants.

At this moment in history, occupation should be everyone's occupation.

BABY PICTURES OF A REVOLT

Young man whose despair gave birth to hope, no one knows what the future holds. When you set yourself afire almost ten months ago, you certainly didn't know, nor do any of us know now, what the long-term outcome of the Arab Spring will be, let alone this American Fall. Such a movement arrives in the world like a newborn. Who knows its fate, or even whether it will survive to grow up?

It may be suppressed like the Prague Spring of 1968. It may go through a crazy adolescence like the French Revolution of 1789 and yet grow beyond its parents' dreams. Radiant at birth, wreathed in smiles, it may become a stolid bourgeois citizen as did such movements in Czechoslovakia, Hungary, and the reunited Germany after civil society freed those countries from totalitarianism in 1989.

It may grow up into turbulence as has the Philippines since its 1986 revolution ousted the kleptocracy of the Marcos family. Revolution may be assassinated young, the way the democratic government of Mohammed Mossadegh was in Iran in 1953, that of President Jacobo Arbenz in Guatemala in 1954, and President Salvador Allende's Chilean experiment on September 11, 1973—all three in CIA-backed military coups. On behalf of the 1%.

Whether it's a human child or a child of history, we can't know who or what it will become, but it's still possible to grasp something about it by asking who or what it resembles. What does Occupy Wall Street look like? Well, it's similar to its siblings born around the world this year, of course, and perhaps in some way to the American civil rights movement that began in the 1950s.

There was a national uprising in the United States no less spontaneous in its formation during the Long Depression of the 1870s, but the Great Railroad Strike of 1877 was violent, while the Occupy movement is deeply imbued with the spirit and tactics of nonviolence. The Great Depression, the one that began in 1929, created a host of radical movements, as well as the Hoovervilles of homeless people. There are family resemblances. The marches and actions against the coming invasion of Iraq on February 15, 2003, on all seven continents (yes, including Antarctica) are clearly kin. The anti-corporate globalization movement is a godmother. And then there's a sibling just a decade older.

COUSIN 9/11

Zuccotti Park is just two blocks from Wall Street and also just a block from Ground Zero, the site of the 9/11 attack. On that day, it was badly damaged. This September 21, my dear friend Marina Sitrin wrote me from Occupy Wall Street: "There are people from more diverse backgrounds racially, more diverse age groups, including not just a few children here with their parents, and a number of working people from the area. In particular, some of the security guards from the 9.11 memorial, a block away have been coming by for lunch and chatting with people, as has a local group of construction workers."

If the Arab Spring was the decade-later antithesis of 9/11, a largely non-violent, publicly inclusive revolt that forced the Western world to get over its fearful fantasy that all young Muslims are terrorists, jihadis, and suicide bombers, then Occupy Wall Street, which began six days after the tenth anniversary of that nightmarish day in September, is the other half of 9/11 in New York. What was remarkable about that day ten years ago is how calmly and beautifully everyone behaved. New Yorkers helped each other down those dozens of floors of stairs in the Twin Towers and away from the catastrophe, while others lined up to give blood, desperate to do something, anything, to participate, to be part of a newfound sense of community that arose in the city that day.

There was, for example, a huge commissary organized on Chelsea Piers that provided free food, medical supplies, and work equipment for the people at Ground Zero and also helped find housing for the displaced. It was not an official effort, but one that arose even more spontaneously than Occupy Wall Street, without leaders or institutions—and it was forcibly disbanded when the official organizations got their act together a few days later. Those who participated experienced a sense of democracy amid all the distress and sorrow, a tremendous joy in finding meaningful work and deep social connections, and a little temporary joy, as they often do in disaster.

When I began to study the history of urban disaster years ago, I found such unexpected exhibitions of that kind of joy again and again, uniting the generative moments of protests, demonstrations, revolts, and revolutions with the aftermath of some disasters. Even when the losses were terrible, the ways that people came together to meet the occasion were almost always remarkable.

Since I wrote *A Paradise Built in Hell: The Extraordinary Communities That Arise in Disaster*, I have been asked again and again whether economic crisis begets the same kind of community as sudden disasters. It did in Argentina in 2001, when the economy crashed there. And it has now, in the streets of New York and many other cities, in 2011. A sign at Occupy San Francisco said, "IT'S TIME." It is. It's been time for a long time.

NO HOPE BUT IN OURSELVES

The birth of this moment was delayed three years. Argentinians reacted immediately to the 2001 crisis and to long-simmering grievances with an economy that had ground so many of them down even before the government froze all bank accounts and the economy crashed. On the other hand, our economy collapsed three years ago this month to headlines like

"Capitalism is dead" in the business press. There was certainly some fury and outrage at the time, but the real reaction was delayed, or decoyed.

The outrage of the moment did, in fact, result in a powerful grassroots movement that focused on a single political candidate to fix it all for us, as he promised he would. It was a beautiful movement, a hopeful movement, much more so than its candidate. The movement got its lone candidate into the highest office in the land, where he remains today, and then walked away as though the job was done. It had just begun.

That movement could have fought the corporations, given us a real climate-change policy, and more, but it allowed itself to be disbanded as though one elected politician were the equivalent of 10 million citizens, of civil society itself. It was a broad-based movement, of all ages and races, and I think it's back, disillusioned with politicians and electoral politics, determined this time to do it for itself, beyond and outside the corroded arenas of institutional power.

I don't know exactly who this baby looks like, but I know that who you look like is not who you will become. This unanticipated baby has a month behind it and a future ahead of it that none of us can see, but its birth should give you hope.

love,
Rebecca

October 2011

APOLOGIES TO MEXICO

The Drug Trade and GNP (Gross National Pain)

Dear Mexico,

I apologize. There are so many things I could apologize for, from the way the U.S. biotech corporation Monsanto has contaminated your corn to the way Arizona and Alabama are persecuting your citizens, but right now I'd like to apologize for the drug war, the 10,000 waking nightmares that make the news and the rest that don't.

You've heard the stories about the five severed heads rolled onto the floor of a Michoacan nightclub in 2006, the three hundred bodies dissolved in acid by a servant of one drug lord, the forty-nine mutilated bodies found in plastic bags by the side of the road in Monterrey in May, the nine bodies found hanging from an overpass in Nuevo Laredo just last month, the Zeta Cartel's videotaped beheadings just two weeks ago, the carnage that has taken tens of thousands of Mexican lives in the last decade and has terrorized a whole nation. I've read them and so many more. I am sorry 50,000 times over.

The drug war is fueled by many things, and maybe the worst drug of all is money, to which so many are so addicted that they can never get enough. It's a drug for which they will kill, destroying communities and ecologies, even societies, whether for the sake of making drones, Wall Street profits, or massive heroin sales. Then there are the actual drugs, to which so many others turn for numbness.

There is variety in the range of drugs. I know that marijuana mostly just makes you like patio furniture, while heroin renders you ethereally indifferent and a little reptilian, and cocaine pumps you up with your own imaginary fabulousness before throwing you down into your own trashiness. And then there's meth, which seems to have the same general effect as rabies, except that the victims crave it desperately.

Whatever their differences, these drugs, when used consistently, constantly, destructively, are all anesthesia from pain. The Mexican drug cartels crave money, but they make that money from the way Yankees across the border crave numbness. They sell unfeeling. We buy it. We spend tens of billions of dollars a year doing so, and by some estimates about a third to a half of that money goes back to Mexico.

THE PRICE OF NUMBNESS

We want not to feel what's happening to us, and then we do stuff that makes worse things happen—to us and others. We pay for it, too, in a million ways, from outright drug-overdose deaths (which now exceed traffic fatalities, and of which the United States has the highest rate of any nation except tiny Iceland, amounting to more than 37,000 deaths here in 2009 alone) to the violence of drug-dealing on the street, the violence of people on some of those drugs, and the violence inflicted on children who are neglected, abandoned, and abused because of them—and that's just for starters. The stuff people do for money when they're desperate for drugs generates more violence and more crazy greed for the money to buy the next round. And drug use is connected to the spread of HIV and various strains of hepatitis.

Then there's our futile "war on drugs" that has created so much pain of its own. It's done so by locking up mothers and fathers and brothers and sisters and children for insanely long prison sentences and offering no treatment. It does so by costing so much it's warping the economies of states that have huge numbers of nonviolent offenders in prison and not enough money for education or health care. It does so by branding as felons and pariahs those who have done time in the drug-war prison complex. It was always aimed most directly at African Americans, and the toll it's taken would require a week of telling.

No border divides the pain caused by drugs from the pain brought about in Latin America by the drug business and the *narcotraficantes*. It's one big continent of pain—and in the last several years the narcos have begun selling drugs in earnest in their own countries, creating new cultures of addiction and misery. (And yes, Mexico, your extravagantly corrupt government, military, and police have everything to do with the drug war now, but file that under greed, as usual, about which your pretty new president is unlikely to do anything much.)

Imagine that the demand ceased tomorrow; the profitable business of supply would have to wither away as well. Many talk about legalizing drugs, and there's something to be said for changing the economic arrangements. But what about reducing their use by developing and promoting more interesting and productive ways of dealing with suffering? Or even getting directly at the causes of that suffering?

Some drug use is, of course, purely recreational, but even recreational drug use stimulates these economies of carnage. And then there are the overdoses of the famous and the unsung on prescription and drugs. Tragic, but those dismembered and mutilated bodies the drug gangs deposit around Mexico are not just tragic, they're terrifying.

GNP: GROSS NATIONAL PAIN
AND THE PAIN EXPORT ECONOMY

Mexico, my near neighbor, I have been trying to imagine the export economy of pain. What does it look like? I think it might look like air-conditioning. This is how an air conditioner works: it sucks the heat out of the room and pumps it into the air outside. You could say that air conditioners don't really cool things down so much as they relocate the heat. The way the transnational drug economy works is a little like that: people in the United States are not reducing the amount of pain in the world; they're exporting it to Mexico and the rest of Latin America as surely as those places are exporting drugs to us.

In economics, we talk about "externalized costs": this means the way that you and I pick up the real cost of oil production with local and global ecological degradation or wars fought on behalf of the oil corporations. Or the way Walmart turns its employees into paupers, and we pick up the tab for their food stamps and medical care.

226 | With the drug economy, there are externalized traumas. I imagine them moving in a huge circulatory system, like the Gulf Stream, or old trade routes. We give you money and guns, lots and lots of money. You give us drugs. The guns destroy. The money destroys. The drugs destroy. The pain migrates, a phantom presence crossing the border the other way from the crossings we hear so much about.

The drugs are supposed to numb people out, but that momentary numbing effect causes so much pain elsewhere. There's a pain economy, a suffering economy, a fear economy, and drugs fuel all of them rather than making them go away. Think of it as another kind of GNP—gross national pain—though I don't know how you'd quantify it.

A friend of mine who's lived in Latin America for large parts of the last decade says that she's appalled to see people doing cocaine at parties she goes to in this country. I mentioned that to an anthropologist who was even bleaker in describing the cocaine migration routes out of the Andes and all the dead babies and exploited women she'd seen along the way.

We've had movements to get people to stop buying clothes and shoes made in sweatshops, grapes picked by exploited farmworkers, fish species that are endangered, but no one's thought to start a similar movement to get people to stop consuming the drugs that cause so much destruction abroad.

Picture middle-class people here stuffing the blood of *campesinos* up their noses. Picture poor people injecting the tears of other poor people into their veins. Picture them all smoking children's anguish. And imagine if we called it by name.

AMERICA, #1 IN PAIN

I don't know why my country seems to produce so much misery and so much desire to cover it up under a haze of drugs, but I can imagine a million reasons. A lot of us just never put down roots or adapted to a society that's changing fast under us or got downsized or evicted or foreclosed or rejected or just move around a lot. This country is a place where so many people don't have a place, literally or psychologically. When you don't have anywhere to go with your troubles, you can conveniently go nowhere—into, that is, the limbo of drugs and the dead end it represents.

But there's something else front and center to our particular brand of misery. We are a nation of miserable optimists. We believe everything is possible, and if you don't have it all, from the perfect body to profound wealth, the fault is yours. When people suffer in this country—from, say, foreclosures and bankruptcies due to the destruction of our economy by the forces of greed—the shame is overwhelming. It's seen as a personal failure, not the failure of our institutions. Taking drugs to numb your shame also keeps you from connecting the dots and opposing what's taken you down.

So when you're miserable here, you're miserable twice: once because you actually lost your home/job/savings/spouse/girlish figure and all over again because it's not supposed to be like that (and maybe thrice because our mainstream society doesn't suggest any possibility of changing the circumstances that produced your misery or even how arbitrary those circumstances are). I suspect that all those drugs are particularly about numbing a deep American sense of failure or of smashed expectations.

Really, when you think of the rise of crack cocaine during the Reagan era, wasn't it an exact corollary to the fall of African-American opportunity and the disintegration of the social safety net? The government produced failure and insecurity, and crack buffered the results (and proved a boon to a burgeoning prison-industrial complex). Likewise, the drug-taking that exploded in the 1960s helped undermine the radical movements of that era. Drugs aren't a goad to action, but a deadening alternative to it. Maybe all those zombies everywhere in popular culture nowadays are trying to say something about that.

Here in the United States, there's no room for sadness, but there are plenty of drugs for it, and now when people feel sad, even many doctors think they should take drugs. We undergo losses and ordeals and live in circumstances that would make any sane person sad, and then we say if you feel sad, you're crazy or sick and should be medicated. Of course, now ever more Americans are addicted to prescription drugs, and there's always the old anesthetic of choice, alcohol, but there is one difference: the economics of those substances are not causing mass decapitations in Mexico.

ROADS TO DESTRUCTION
AND THE PALACE OF THE DEAD

When I think about the drug wars and the drug culture here, I think about a young man I knew long ago. He was gay, from Texas, disconnected from his family, talented but not so good at finding a place in the world for that talent or for himself. He was also a fan of the Beat novelist and intermittent junkie William Burroughs, and he believed that line about how "the road of excess leads to the palace of wisdom." Maybe it was fine when William Blake said it in the 1790s, since Blake wasn't a crackhead. But my friend got from Burroughs—a man with family money and apparently an iron constitution—the idea that derangement of the senses was a great creative strategy.

This was all part of our youth in a culture that constantly reinforced how cool drugs were, though back then, another Beat writer, the poet David Meltzer, told me methamphetamine was a form of demonic possession. The young man became possessed in this way and lost his mind. He became homeless and deranged, gone to someplace he couldn't find his way back from, and I would see him walking our boulevards barefoot and filthy, ranting to himself.

Then I heard he had jumped off the Golden Gate Bridge. He wasn't yet thirty; he was just a sweet boy. I could tell four or five more stories like his about people I knew who died young of drugs. The meth that helped him down his road of no return was probably a domestic product then, but now vast quantities of it are made in Mexico for us—fifteen tons of it were found earlier this year in Guadalajara, enough for 13 million doses, worth about $4 billion retail.

When I think about the drug wars, I also think about my visit to Santa Muerte (Saint Death) in Mexico City in 2007. My young traveling companion insisted on going there. It was perilous for outsiders like us even to travel through Tepito, the black-marketeers' barrio, let alone go to the shrine where imposing, somber men were praying and lighting candles to the skeleton goddess who is the *narcotraficantes'* patron saint. They worship death; they're intimate with her; they tattoo her on their flesh, and there she was in person—in bones without flesh, surrounded by candles, by gifts, by cigarettes and gold, an Aztec goddess gone commercial.

My companion wanted to take pictures. I wanted to live and managed to convince him that gangsters' devotional moments were not for our cameras. When it came time to leave, the warm patroness of the shrine locked up the stand in which she sold votive candles and medallions, took each of us by an arm—as if nothing less than bodily contact with death's caretaker would keep us safe—and walked us to the subway. We survived that little moment of direct contact with the drug war. So many others have not.

Mexico, I am sorry. I want to see it all change, for your sake and ours. I want to call pain by name and numbness by name and fear by name. I want people to connect the dots from the junk in their brain to the bullet holes in others' heads. I want people to find better strategies for responding to pain and sadness. I want them to rebel against those parts of their unhappiness that are political, not metaphysical, and not run in fear from the metaphysical parts either.

I want the *narcotraficantes* to repent and give their billions to the poor. I want the fear to end. A hundred years ago, your dictatorial president Porfiro Díaz supposedly remarked, "Poor Mexico, so far from God and so close to the United States," which nowadays could be revised to "Painful Mexico, so far from peace and so close to the numbness of the United States."

Yours sincerely,
Rebecca

2012

RECONSTRUCTING THE STORY OF THE STORM

New Orleans Five Years After

Five years later we're still coming to terms with what happened in New Orleans on August 29, 2005, and thereafter, struggling to get the facts straight and to figure out what it said about race, disaster, and even human nature. How we remember Hurricane Katrina is also how we'll prepare for future disasters, so getting the story right matters for survival as well as for justice and history.

In August 2005, 90,000 square miles of the Gulf Coast were devastated; more than 1,800 people died; 182,000 homes were severely damaged in the New Orleans metropolitan area, and 80 percent of the city was flooded. Hundreds of thousands went into an exile from which some will never return. A great and justified bitterness arose in African Americans who were demonized by the media and the government and who felt that they had not been treated as citizens or even as fellow human beings. An African-American woman at an antiwar rally in the nation's capital a month later carried a sign saying, "No Iraqis left me on a roof to die."

The widely told initial version of Hurricane Katrina was a lie and a slander, based on rumors and racism, and it's been falling apart steadily ever since. For the past two years an antithetical version has been overtaking it, one that tells the real story of who went crazy and who was in danger in the days after the hurricane. It has gained more ground than I ever imagined it would, and the history books may yet get this one right.

WHEN THE MEDIA WENT MAD

The story of Hurricane Katrina as originally constructed served authoritarianism, racism, and a generally grim view of human nature. It was first told hysterically, as though New Orleans had been hit by a torrent of poor black people or had become, as Maureen Dowd of the *New York Times* put it then, "a snake pit of anarchy, death, looting, raping, marauding thugs." An overwrought *Huffington Post* columnist even spread rumors of cannibalism, while many major media outlets repeated rumors of snipers firing on helicopters. These rumors were never substantiated, but they interfered with the rescue operations nonetheless.

The gist of these stories was that in the absence of authority, people went berserk. The implied solution was the reimposition of authority—armed, ruthless, and intense. Heavily armed Blackwater mercenaries were dispatched to New Orleans, where, as Jeremy Scahill reported in *The Nation*, they shot at citizens with little fear of repercussion. While the focus was on young men of color as the peril, police and white vigilantes went on a murder spree that was glossed over at the time.

The AP reported on September 1, 2005, "Mayor Ray Nagin ordered 1,500 police officers to leave their search-and-rescue mission Wednesday night and return to the streets of the beleaguered city to stop looting that has turned increasingly hostile." Only two days after the catastrophe struck, while thousands were still stuck on roofs, in attics, on overpasses, on second and third stories, and in isolated buildings on high ground in flooded neighborhoods, the mayor chose protecting property over human life. There was no commerce, no electricity, no way to buy badly needed supplies. Though unnecessary things were taken, much of what got called looting was the stranded foraging for survival by the only means available.

The mainstream media fractured under the pressure of reporting such a huge and complex story. Journalists on the ground often wrote empathic and accurate stories and broke out of their "objective" roles to advocate for the desperate and rail against systemic failures. Meanwhile, further away, credulous television, online, and print reporters spread lurid rumors about baby rapists and mass murders, and they treated minor and sometimes justified thefts as the end of civilization. They used words like "marauding" and "looting" as matches, struck over and over until they got a conflagration of opinion going.

They, along with government officials at all levels, created the overheated atmosphere of fear and hostility that turned the task of rescuing stranded people into an attempt to control a captive population. New Orleans became a prison city; the trapped citizens became prisoners without rights. Those in the Superdome, for example, were prevented from leaving the stinking, scorching zone as people dropped from heat and dehydration. The literal prisoners, adult and juvenile, in the New Orleans jails were abandoned to thirst, hunger, and rising floodwaters. Hospitals packed with the dying were not allowed to evacuate; citizens were not allowed to walk out of New Orleans on the bridge to Gretna because the sheriff on the other side was there with cronies and guns, keeping them out.

The stories of social breakdown were quietly retracted in September and October 2005, but the damage had been done. A great many found new confirmation of the old stereotypes that in times of crisis people— particularly poor and nonwhite people—revert to a Hobbesian war of each against each.

THE CRIMES THAT COUNTED

If you believe what happened after Hurricane Katrina was all about the masses running amok, then the proper response is pretty much the vigilante one: arm yourself, treat your neighbor as your enemy, shoot first, ask questions later. But the evidence suggests that the people running amok were the ones who were supposed to protect the public. They were the sheriff on that bridge to Gretna, the corrupt and overwrought policemen who shot unarmed civilians, and Louisiana governor Kathleen Blanco, who said, "I have one message for these hoodlums: these troops know how to shoot and kill, and they are more than willing to do so if necessary, and I expect they will."

Real people got caught in the crossfire. Take Donnell Herrington, a thirty-three-year-old former Brink's truck driver who stayed behind to help his grandparents and who later rescued many others by boat from their flooded housing project. Herrington was walking to the evacuation site in Algiers Point when a white vigilante with a shotgun attempted to murder him. Herrington was hit so hard the blast lifted him off the ground, and then shot again in the back as he tried to escape. His friend and cousin, who were walking with him, were also injured by the buckshot and then chased down by racists who terrorized them. An African-American couple in the neighborhood drove Herrington to the nearest hospital, where a surgeon stitched him up. According to that surgeon, Herrington nearly bled to death from pellets to his jugular.

His assailants were part of an organized militia that presumed any and all black men were looters and decided that they were justified in administering the ad hoc death penalty for suspected or potential petty theft. No one reported on these vigilante crimes in the first round of coverage.

THE PAST IS EQUIPMENT FOR THE FUTURE

The July 15 federal indictment of Roland Bourgeois Jr. is stamped FEL-ONY, and the charges at the top of the page are "conspiracy, civil rights violations, obstruction of justice, false statements and firearms violations." What that means is that this white man allegedly tried to murder Herrington and his companions because they were black, because they were walking through his neighborhood, and because in the aftermath of Hurricane Katrina there weren't a lot of rules, and those who should've been enforcing them had gone mad.

"It was the plan and purpose of the conspiracy that defendant Roland J. Bourgeois Jr. and others known and unknown to the grand jury would use force and threats of force to keep African-Americans from using the public streets of Algiers Point in the aftermath of Hurricane Katrina," says the indictment. Bourgeois and other vigilantes were situated between the Coast Guard evacuation point and the rest of the city, picking off people who were just trying to get out. "Anything coming up this street darker than a paper bag is getting shot," the indictment charges Bourgeois with saying. He is the first, but may not be the last, of the suburban vigilantes to be indicted.

These indictments are part of a package, along with two sets of indictments of police by Eric Holder's Justice Department, that came down just in time; the five-year anniversary of Hurricane Katrina is also the statute of limitations for some of these charges.

The catastrophe's fifth anniversary is becoming an opportunity for a major re-examination of the colossal disaster. I never thought I'd see the day. Early in 2007, when I started looking into what happened in the aftermath of Hurricane Katrina, it pretty quickly became clear to me that though the city had swarmed with journalists, none of them wanted to touch the crimes Bourgeois and his cronies had committed.

The evidence these journalists overlooked was everywhere. In September 2005, Malik Rahim, the ex–Black Panther who co-founded Common Ground Relief and who lives in the Algiers neighborhood, told Amy Goodman of *Democracy Now!* on camera about vigilante murders of black men. He showed her the body of a dead black man lying under a sheet of corrugated metal, bloated and decaying in the heat. Herrington testified about his near-murder in Spike Lee's documentary *When the Levees Broke*, broadcast in 2006 on the first anniversary of the storm. At the end of the segment, he takes off his shirt so that the buckshot welts on his torso are visible, as is the long scar on his neck.

Some of the evidence I came across wasn't so obvious, but it wasn't hard to find either. I heard from staff at the Common Ground Health Clinic that vigilantes and their associates who came in for care confessed or boasted of crimes. Rahim gave me a DVD of a little-seen documentary in which some of the Algiers Point militia boasted of shooting black men. A few others told me stories that corroborated that the vigilantes had kept a body count. I acquired this evidence without really trying, while pursuing other stories entirely, which made me wonder what was up with the hundreds of reporters who'd come to New Orleans.

On March 1, 2007, I wrote to the best investigative journalist I knew, my friend A. C. Thompson, "Hey, I'm sitting on a kind of wild story, and I'd love to talk to you about it." He'd never been to New Orleans, and it wasn't until *The Nation* and The Nation Institute's Investigative Fund took an interest that A.C. got dispatched to the city. More than three years and dozens of trips to New Orleans later, A.C. has turned the city and the story of Katrina upside down. Without his work, a lot of people would've gotten away with murder and attempted murder.

A.C. uncovered a story no one in the media had touched—the police | 235 killing of Henry Glover, first reported on in *The Nation* on January 5, 2009. He also joined forces with *New Orleans Times-Picayune* reporter Laura

Maggi, who reopened the Danziger Bridge case, in which police shot several unarmed African Americans after the storm, including a middle-aged mother who had her forearm blown off, a mentally disabled man who was shot in the back and killed, and a teenage boy, also killed. (Several others were wounded.)

Justice Department officials have charged eleven policemen for the Danziger Bridge case and five for the Glover case, and most recently sent warning letters to two more for the post-Katrina case in which Danny Brumfield was shot in the back and killed. In total they've opened up six civil rights cases for New Orleans police crimes post-Katrina, and a federal probe of the department is under way. With any luck, it's the foundation of the real story of what went down after the storm, as well as reform of what A.C. tells me is the most corrupt and incompetent police department in the country.

TRUTH EMERGENCIES

Truth may be the first casualty of war; it's certainly the most important equipment to have on hand in a disaster. There's the practical truth about what's going on: Is the city on fire? Is there an evacuation effort on the other side of town? And then there's the larger truth: What goes on in disasters? Who falls apart and who behaves well? Whom should you trust? Most ordinary people behave remarkably well when their city is ripped apart by disaster. They did in San Francisco after the 1906 earthquake; in New Orleans during Hurricane Betsy in 1965; in Mexico City after the 1985 earthquake; in New York City in the aftermath of 9/11; and in most disasters in most times and places.

Those in power, on the other hand, often run amok. They did in San Francisco in 1906, when an obsessive fear that private property would be misappropriated led to the mayor's shoot-to-kill proclamation; a massive military and national guard on the streets; and the death of dozens, perhaps hundreds, of civilians. Much like New Orleans ninety-nine years later, those who claimed to be protecting society were themselves the ones who were terrorizing and shooting. Earlier in 2010, Haitians were subjected to a similar rampage of what the disaster sociologists Lee Clarke and Caron

Chess call "elite panic." For example, fifteen-year-old Fabienne Cherisma was shot to death in late January in Port-au-Prince for taking some small paintings from a shop in ruins, one of many casualties of the institutional obsession with protecting property instead of rescuing the trapped, the suffering, and the needy.

Surviving the new era in which climate change is already causing more, and more intense, disasters means being prepared—with the truth. The truth is that in a disaster, ordinary people behave well overall; your chances of surviving a major disaster depend in part on the health and strength of your society going into it. Even so, countless individuals under corrupt governments—in New Orleans, in Mexico City, in Port-au-Prince—often rise to the occasion with deeply altruistic, creative, and brave responses. These are the norm. The savagery of elite panic is the exception but one that costs lives.

After Hurricane Katrina, neoliberals and Bush provided a near-perfect example of Naomi Klein's theory of disaster capitalism. Everything from supplying buses for evacuation to tarps for torn-up roofs became an opportunity for Bush supporters to reap financial rewards. The city's public housing was torn down; the schools became charter schools, many along military lines. Told this way, what happened was pure loss, for the left as well as for the poor (though the schools before Katrina had been a mess). But that's not all that Katrina triggered.

During the storm and its aftermath, far more people did heroic things, and these, perhaps even more than the crimes Thompson reported on, are the key missing stories of the storm. Before he was shot, Herrington was one of hundreds who got into boats and commenced rescuing people stranded in the floodwater. Some in surrounding communities sneaked past authorities to start rescuing people in the drowned city. Young gang members kept mothers of small children and babies and elderly people provisioned. People banded together in schools and other surviving structures and formed improvisational communities whose members watched out for one another.

As days turned into weeks and then months, volunteers from around the country came to feed the displaced and rebuild the city. Others took evacuees into their homes and helped them start new lives. Middle-aged

Mennonites, young anarchists, musicians, members of the Rainbow Family of hippie communards, environmentalists, Baptists, Catholics, college students on spring break, ex–Black Panthers, movie stars, Habitat for Humanity carpenters, nurses, and nearly every other kind of citizen showed up to save New Orleans. The outpouring of generosity and empathy was extraordinary. New Orleans was saved by love.

I first visited the city post-Katrina six months after the storm, and it looked as though almost nothing had happened since. The place was wrecked. Houses were smashed or shoved by floodwater into the middle of the street; many had the spray-painted markings of search-and-rescue teams, some reporting bodies or pets found inside. Cars were flipped over or propped up on fences and trees. Whole neighborhoods were abandoned and pitch-black at night, because even the streetlights were dead; and in places like the Lower Ninth Ward, returning residents had to make street signs by hand.

The place could have died; its fate was up in the air. It still is—with coastal erosion and rising seas, the petroleum industry's poisons, the troubled economy, and corroded political system that were the city's problems before Katrina hit. Crime has risen, and New Orleans is a violent place. But it's also a vibrant place again. By some estimates more than a million volunteers have come through the city. Some who intended to come for weeks found they couldn't leave: they'd fallen in love with the gregarious sweetness of so many Orleanians and with the chance to make a difference. They've added their commitment to altruism and civil society to the city's mix. New Orleans always had a flourishing public sphere of festivals and street life and a private sphere of social organizations, but there has been a rise in civic engagement, in public meetings, neighborhood groups, and focused organizations dealing with housing, the environment, immigrants' rights, and more. Housing is scarcer and more expensive, but wages have risen since the labor pool shrank. New environmental initiatives are on the table or being realized.

238 | Then there's the catastrophe's impact on national politics. The Bush administration's outrageous incompetence and indifference prompted a hitherto intimidated press and nation to begin criticizing not just the

failed response but the Iraq War and the administration overall. The levees broke and so did the bulwarks that protected the president. As Bush's own pollster put it, "Katrina to me was the tipping point. The president broke his bond with the public. . . . I knew when Katrina—I was like, Man, you know, this is it, man. We're done." The racism and poverty that the catastrophe revealed laid the groundwork for newcomer Barack Obama to ride to victory in 2008. Which is how we got Eric Holder, the attorney general who's taken a direct role in some of the federal indictments in New Orleans this summer.

The very subject of recovery is a complicated one for New Orleans. After 9/11 New York pretty much wanted to get back to where it had been—a thriving, functioning city (albeit one with plenty of poverty and injustice). No one thought New Orleans should get back to what it had been, and the disaster became an opportunity for the city to reinvent itself in various ways. That process continues, and where it goes is anyone's guess. It still depends on the dedication of volunteers and citizens, some of whom are returning, putting their lives back together in what may be, by some intangible measures of joy and belonging, America's richest city, even if it's the poorest by others.

A disaster unfolds a little like a revolution. No one is in charge, and anything is possible. The efforts of elites, often portrayed as rescue or protection, are often geared more toward preserving the status quo or seizing power. Sometimes they win; sometimes they don't. Katrina brought many kinds of destruction and a little rebirth, including the spread of green construction projects, new community organizations, and perhaps soon, thanks to the work of Thompson and others, some long overdue justice for police crimes. It's too soon to tell what it will all mean in a hundred years, but it's high time to start telling the real story of what happened in those terrible first days and weeks.

2010

WE WON'T BOW DOWN

Carnival and Resistance in New Orleans

One day last July I sat next to the musician David Molina on a long bus ride. He showed me his pictures of Carnival in Paucartambo in the Peruvian Andes, and when he was done, I showed him mine of Mardi Gras in New Orleans. The indigenous town at nearly 10,000 feet holds a raucous celebration with fireworks, costumes, people throwing stuff, playing with fire, kidnapping strangers and keeping them hostage at feasts, drinking in quantity, kids staying up into the small hours—the rules are all broken, and the first rule is the one of shyness and separation. New Orleans is about as different from Paucartambo as could be, starting with the fact that parts of it are below sea level, but it too keeps alive the old tradition of Carnival—not just on Mardi Gras, the last day of Carnival season, before Lent begins with Ash Wednesday, but all through the weeks from Twelfth Night, January 5, when it begins. What happens in Carnival is complicated. But let me send another float through this parade of ideas first.

Some years ago I wrote a book about hope. A few years later I went to look at the worst things that happen to people and found some more hope in the resilience, the inventiveness, the bravery, and occasionally the long-term subversion with which people respond. It culminated in another fairly hopeful book, based on the surprising evidence of what actually happens in disaster. Civil society happens, and sometimes joy in that society; institutional failure often also transpires. Sometimes a power struggle to re-establish the status quo follows, and sometimes the status quo wins, sometimes it doesn't. Which is to say, sometimes we win, though that's far from inevitable. This is grounds to be hopeful. Now, being hopeful seems to me like it's preferable to being hopeless, but for six years I've been talking about these books in public. This means I've also been running into people

at readings, talks and interviews who are furiously attached to hopeless-
ness, to narratives of despair and decline, to belief in an omniscient them
who always wins and a feeble us who always loses. To keep hold of this
complex, they have to skew the evidence, and they do. They cherry-pick.
They turn complex facts into simple stories. They constitute a significant
sector of the left.

I don't believe that they represent the whole left; rather, it seems the
self-appointed spokespeople for the left are both more privileged than the
left as such and more attached to defeat. Defeat for the privileged means
cynicism and an excuse for doing little or nothing; defeat for the oppressed
means surrender to hideous or fatal conditions, which might be why hope
has of late come from people like the members of the Coalition of Im-
mokalee Workers, the incredible undocumented-immigrant farmworkers
organization that forced Taco Bell and then McDonald's into negotiations.
Hope, in the myth of Pandora's box, is what is left behind after everything
else has fled; those who hang on to everything else seem to give up or overlook hope. So they often say we always lose.

Always is the key word here, because many leftists are also smitten with
sweeping generalizations—and they are oddly willing to accept generalizations that everything is awful, while if you point out that not everything
is awful they will believe you've said everything is wonderful and try to
shoot that down. Attachment to despair and defeatism is often portrayed
as realism, though it flies in the face of our history, in which, though corporations have continued their T-Rex march, a host of liberations—from
colonialism and age-old discriminations—have proceeded apace, so much
so that our society is pretty unrecognizable from a 1965 perspective, wilder
than anything in the science fiction of the time in terms of changed roles
for women, people of color, and unstraight people; in terms of changed
ideas about nature, religion, power, justice, and more. And corporate
capital has been far from the only force at work in this era that has seen
the World Trade Organization diminished into near irrelevance, the Free
Trade Area of the Americas (FTAA) defeated, and NAFTA almost uni- | *241*
versally reviled.

I think of these naysayers as the Eeyore chorus, after the dismal donkey in *Winnie-the-Pooh*, and I run into them a lot. It may be that for those coming from the mainstream to the left the chance to tell the underside of the official version—that it's corrupt and destructive—seems like the work at hand. I come from the left, and my task is clearly telling the other, overlooked histories of hope, popular power, subversion, and possibility. Which elicits a lot of grumbling from Eeyore's many reps.

I got a dose of one of the really common axioms of defeat from a well-spoken young academic woman early on my book tour. I'd been comparing disaster to Carnival in its disruptiveness and subversion of everyday roles. With some irritation at my invitation to consider a more open world, she raised the old bugbear that Carnival is not subversive because it reconciles people to the status quo. (It's a dimming-down of Mikhail Bakhtin's famous writings on Carnival in his book on Rabelais.) First of all, what is Carnival? I've only been to one, a couple of times, but it was in New Orleans after Hurricane Katrina, and it consisted of a host of phenomena tending in all kinds of political directions.

Mardi Gras and Carnival are not synonymous; the latter is a weeks-long season from Twelfth Night in January to the last day before Lent, during which krewes put on public parades and private balls. Mardi Gras, Fat Tuesday, is that last day. Rex is the central parade of Mardi Gras, led by the business elite of the town, and only grudgingly integrated after being forced to do so by the city (some of the other oligarchical Carnival krewes, Comus and Momus, just stopped parading rather than integrate). The city sponsors and organizes none of Mardi Gras; it just prevents unintegrated krewes from marching, polices a lot, and sweeps up the tons of debris afterward.

So there's Rex, but it has to wait for Zulu, which is a parody of Rex and of stereotypes of African Americans—it features the city's black elite in grass skirts and leopard skin with spears and jungle floats. Zulu's procession goes before Rex and traditionally, I'm told, likes to keep Rex waiting. Louis Armstrong was once the king of Zulu—the Carnival krewes create their own royalty—and once said to the king of England, "This one's for you, Rex," when he sang "(I'll Be Glad When You're Dead) You Rascal You." The spirit of Carnival let a son of the New Orleans streets spit in a king's eye. More recently, a queen of Zulu, Desirée Rogers, became Obama's social secretary.

Zulu, like a lot of the African-American krewes, isn't just an organization that puts on a parade. It's an outgrowth of the social aid and pleasure clubs that were once widespread in the South, and the clubs are a version of the benevolent societies that were once a huge social force for the working class of the United States. My friend Eric Laursen has written about them. He says:

> Fraternal orders (which also included women's organizations) were an enormous social force among American working people in the first half of the 20th Century—nearly as significant as labor unions. Also known as mutual aid societies, their defining features were [what David T. Beito described as] "an autonomous system of lodges, a democratic form of internal government, a ritual, and the provision of mutual aid for members and their families.". . .
>
> The legions who joined the fraternal orders were not anarchists. The orders tended to be organized in a rigidly hierarchical way, and their leaders loved to underscore their Americanism and denounce radicals and revolutionaries. But perhaps they protested a bit too much. Anarchists have always projected mutual aid as the basic organizing principle of a non-hierarchical, non-authoritarian society. And despite their many defects, the fraternal orders carried out perhaps the most ambitious experiment in mutual aid in U.S. history—a project that cut across classes and gave immigrants and people of color a tool for advancing themselves when government and capitalist business structures were both geared to keep them in their place.
>
> The orders provided a powerful demonstration that mutual aid could serve as an alternative method for organizing a complex modern society.

African-American social aid and pleasure clubs grew out of the benevolent societies of the nineteenth century, which, as Laursen points out, provided funerals, medical coverage, and accident and unemployment insurance to their members. Put that way, they sound as dreary as the corporations I write checks to for my health care and other insurances, but they were vibrant organizations that provided a real sense of membership. You weren't giving your money to the faceless bureaucracy and hoping for something back; you were taking care of your brethren, who would take care of you. Put another way, they provided tangible necessities (social aid) when things went wrong but intangible ones (social pleasure) when they went right. Zulu's website proclaims that "during the Christmas season, the organization gives Christmas baskets to needy families, participates in the Adopt-a-School program, contributes to the Southern University Scholarship Fund and donates funds and time to other community organizations."

In one sense Carnival keeps the mutual aid societies of New Orleans alive, but in another sense the societies keep Carnival alive. Mardi Gras is one day, and the big downtown parades are only one aspect of a festival that, like most Carnivals, lasts for weeks. There are a lot of other organizations parading, from Muses, the women's krewe, which is sort of feminist and sort of raunchy, to informal things like Julu, the klezmer-inspired takeoff on Zulu my friend Rebecca Snedeker belongs to. I joined Julu in 2008, and we roamed the streets and stopped off for drinks and ducked out to see other parades. There are about nine gay krewes with their own balls, and there's an AIDS ritual involving cremation ashes on the day of celebration, one day before Ash Wednesday.

The Mardi Gras Indians, who date back to the 1880s, are small bands of African-American men in flamboyant, massive beaded costumes officially modeled after American Indian regalia. They are said to honor the relationship between slaves and American Indians in an earlier time, and their beadwork is really more Yoruba than it is American Indian, part of the mysterious survival in New Orleans of ties to Africa that largely vanished elsewhere. In *The World That Made New Orleans*, music historian Ned Sublette says, "The Indians embody resistance" and "collectively, they're part of what knits New Orleans's black populace together." A common Mardi Gras Indian shout is "We won't bow down." The Mardi Gras Indians head out on their own without announced routes on Mardi Gras and a few other days every year, but making the costumes and maintaining the communities lasts all year.

To say that Carnival reconciles us to the status quo is to say that it affirms the world as it is. Now, for people in Rex, their Mardi Gras probably reinforces their world, but for those in some of the other krewes and rites, the same is true, and the reinforcement of the survival of the mutual aid societies that emerged after slavery is not reaffirmation of capitalism, domination, et cetera. It reinforces, in other words, their ongoing survival of capitalism and racism. Carnival also reinforces joy and ownership of public space and a kind of confidence in coexisting with a wide array of strangers. New Orleans itself is the place where, unlike the rest of the United States, slaves were not so cut off from chances to gather and chances to maintain their traditions. Jazz and jazz funerals, second-line parades, and more derive in many ways from this subversive remnant of a non-European tradition. They didn't bow down. This is something to celebrate, and it is what is celebrated by some of the people in the streets.

In 2006 and 2007 Mardi Gras in New Orleans was also proof to the city that it had survived Katrina, that it had not died. The parades were full of scathing political commentary, even the mainstream ones (and Krewe du Vieux started parade season in 2009 with the theme Fired Up! which brought in a lot of sexy devil costumes and floats depicting local political institutions as flaming hells). To say Carnival of New Orleans is to speak of dozens of disparate traditions and agendas braided together. Which makes the willingness of anyone to generalize about Carnival—which includes the Latin American, Caribbean, European, and New Orleanian versions—troublesome.

Really, I shouldn't even be saying things so obvious except that defeatisms so obviously based on misapprehensions keep getting thrown into my face. Of course our society's dominant culture of media and entertainment serves consumerism and asserts our powerlessness. But if the status quo is the world as it is, it also includes myriad subversions and strategies for survival, and these seem to me to also be reinforced by Carnival. Fifteen years ago a subversive group called Reclaim the Streets (RTS) began turning British political demonstrations into something festive and inventive and even joyous, with a raucous in-your-face joy. "We are about taking back public space from the enclosed private arena. At its simplest it is an attack on cars as a principle agent of enclosure. It's about reclaiming the streets as public inclusive space from the private exclusive use of the car. But we believe in this as a broader principle, taking back those things which have been enclosed within capitalist circulation and returning them to collective use as a commons."

I'd argue that Reclaim the Streets in mostly Protestant Britain reclaimed the street festival, the Carnival spirit, as something deeply subversive. The group even called one of its demonstrations, the famous one on June 18, 1999, the Carnival Against Capital. London's financial district was much disrupted that day by the masked, festive throng. The participants saw taking back public space, making it inclusive, giving it a function other than its everyday one, as radical. This is what Carnival does, and so by RTS's terms, Carnival is radical, not reconciling us to the status quo but subverting it. Carnival is inherently against capital.

From another perspective, the June 18 street party was a bunch of rowdy white kids, but it had sister actions in dozens of countries, including Nigeria, and it prepared the resistant world for the profoundly successful attack on corporate capital at the Seattle WTO meeting later that year, which, with its famed giant puppets, costumes, marching bands and banners, was very Carnivalesque. The Committee for Full Enjoyment faced off the G-8 meeting in Gleneagles, Scotland, with similar tactics. CIRCA, the Clandestine Insurgent Rebel Clown Army, whose tactics were infinitely subversive and never oppositional, threw the police into confusion (but not rage). The performance theorist and activist Larry Bogad calls this "tactical carnival" and notes that in 2001, the FBI listed Carnival Against Capital as a terrorist group (failing to recognize that it was a concept, not an organization, but correctly recognizing that it doesn't really reconcile us to the status quo).

Former RTS organizer John Jordan points out that quite a lot of peasant uprisings began during festivals. In his book *Carnival and Other Christian Festivals*, Max Harris recounts the theological basis for Carnival's inversion of hierarchies, the passage in the Magnificat where Mary says (in Luke 1:52), in celebration of the impending birth of her son, "He hath put down the mighty from their seats and hath exalted the humble." Carnival, he says, is a festival of inversion. Some inversions are symbolic, decorative, recreational, and temporary, but to discount even those is to discount the way that culture can provide us visions, invitations, and tools to make such things more real and enduring, whether a full-fledged revolt, as at the Seattle WTO, or the survival of such things as aid and pleasure and pride and solidarity. Just to disrupt business as usual—as jazz funerals and second-line parades have always done in New Orleans and as Reclaim the Streets did for a few years in a few countries—is subversive.

Carnival doesn't necessarily reconcile us to the status quo. But theories that defeat is inevitable, is our legacy, our history, and our future do. We have arrived in a future that is itself science fiction: we have turned our planet into something far more turbulent and uncertain than anyone anticipated; and to survive it and bring it back to something livable will require a massive subversion of the status quo of corporate production and excess consumption; it will require innovation, imagination, and profound change. The defeatism that says there is nothing we can do or that we have no power sabotages our survival. It is pre-emptive surrender. *Status quo* in Latin means "the state in which," and the state things are usually in includes dominance, acquiescence, and refusal to bow down, in various mixes. More than ever, we need Carnival at its most subversive to survive, and to make resistance a pleasure and an adventure rather than only struggle and grim duty. This is the revolution that Emma Goldman wanted to dance to, the one that draws people in. Don't bow down. To capital. Or to cliché or oversimplification or defeatism. Try rising up instead. It's more interesting.

2009

THE GOOGLE BUS

Silicon Valley Invades

The buses roll up to San Francisco's bus stops in the morning and evening, but they are unmarked, or nearly so, and not for the public. They have no signs or have discreet acronyms on the front windshield, and they ingest and disgorge their passengers slowly, while the brightly lit funky orange public buses wait behind them. The luxury coach passengers ride for free and many take out their laptops and begin their workday on board; there is of course Wi-Fi. Most of them are gleaming white, with dark-tinted windows, like limousines, and some days I think of them as the spaceships on which our alien overlords have landed to rule over us.

Other days I think of them as the company buses by which the coal miners get deposited at the pithead, and the work schedule involved would make a pit owner feel at home. Silicon Valley has long been famous for its endless work hours, for sucking in the young for decades of sixty- or seventy-hour weeks, and the much celebrated perks on many jobsites—nap rooms, chefs, gyms, laundry—are meant to make spending most of your life at work less hideous. The biotech industry is following the same game plan. Hundreds of luxury coaches serve the mega-corporations down the peninsula, but we refer to them in the singular as the Google Bus, and we—by which I mean people I know, people who've lived here a while, and mostly people who don't work in the industry—talk about them a lot. Parisians probably talked about the Prussian army a lot too, in the day.

My brother says that the first time he saw one unload its riders, he thought they were German tourists—neatly dressed, uncool, a little out of place, blinking in the light as they emerged from their pod. The tech workers, many of them new to the region, are mostly white or Asian male nerds in their twenties and thirties; you often hear that to be over fifty in that world is to be a fossil, and the two founders of Google (currently tied for thirteenth richest person on earth) are not yet forty.

Another friend of mine told me a story about the Apple bus from when he worked for Apple Inc. Once, a driver went rogue, dropping off the majority of his passengers, as intended, at the main Apple campus and then rolling on toward San Jose instead of stopping at the satellite location; but the passengers were tech people, so withdrawn from direct, abrupt, interventionary communications that they just sat there as he drove many miles past their worksite and eventually dumped them on the street in a slum south of the new power center of the world. At that point, I think, they called headquarters, and another, more obedient bus driver was dispatched. I told the story to another friend and we joked about whether they then texted headquarters to get the email addresses of the people sitting next to them. This is a culture that has created many new ways for us to contact one another but atrophied most of the old ones, notably speaking to the people around you. All these youngish people are on the Google Bus because they want to live in San Francisco, city of promenading and mingling, but they seem as likely to rub these things out as to participate in them.

The Google Bus means so many things. It means that the minions of the non-petroleum company most bent on world domination can live in San Francisco but work in Silicon Valley without going through a hair-raising commute by car—I overheard someone note recently that the buses shortened her daily commute to 3.5 hours from 4.5. It means that unlike gigantic employers in other times and places, the corporations of Silicon Valley aren't much interested in improving public transport. It means that San Francisco—capital of the west from the Gold Rush to some point in the twentieth century when Los Angeles overshadowed it—is now a bedroom community for the tech capital of the world at the other end of the peninsula.

There are advantages to being an edge, as California long was, but Silicon Valley has made us the center. Five of the six most-visited websites in the world are here, in ranked order: Facebook, Google, YouTube (which Google owns), Yahoo!, and Wikipedia. (Number five is a Chinese-language site.) If corporations founded by Stanford alumni were to form an independent nation, it would be the tenth largest economy in the world, with an annual revenue of $2.7 trillion, some professors at that university recently calculated. Another new report says: "If the Internet was a country, its gross domestic product would eclipse all others but four within four years" (Boston Consulting Group).

That country has a capital that doesn't look like a capital. It looks like beautiful oak-studded hills and flatlands overrun by sprawl: suburban homes (the megamansions are more secluded) and malls and freeways, often jammed with traffic and dotted with clunky campuses, as corporate headquarters of tech firms are always called. Fifty years ago, this was called the "Valley of Heart's Delight," one of the biggest orchard-growing regions in the world. It wasn't to everyone's delight: Cesar Chavez and the United Farmworkers movement started in San Jose because the people who actually picked all those plums and apricots worked long hours for abysmal wages, but the sight and smell of the 125,000 acres of orchard in bloom was supposed to be spectacular.

Where orchards grew, Apple stands. The work hours are still extreme, but now the wages are colossal—you hear tech workers complaining about not having time to spend their money. They eat out often, though, because their work schedules don't include a lot of time for shopping and cooking, and San Francisco's restaurants are booming. Cafés, which proliferated in the 1980s as places to mingle and idle, are now workstations for freelancers, and many of the sleeker locales are routinely populated by silent ranks staring at their Apple-product screens, as though an office had suddenly been stripped of its cubicles. The more than 1,700 tech firms in San Francisco officially employ 44,000 people, and a lot more are independent contractors doing piecework: not everyone rides the bus down south. Young people routinely make six-figure salaries, not necessarily beginning with a 1, and they have enormous clout in the housing market. (The drivers of the Google Bus, on the other hand, make between $17 and $30 an hour.)

I weathered the dot-com boom of the late 1990s as an observer, but
I sold my apartment in mid-2011 and ventured out into both the rental market (for the short term) and home-buying market (for the long term) with confidence that my long standing in this city and respectable finances

would open a path. That confidence got crushed fast. It turned out that the competition for any apartment in San Francisco was so intense that you had to respond to the listings—all on San Francisco–based Craigslist, of course, the classifieds website that whittled away newspaper ad revenue nationally—within a few hours of their posting to receive a reply from the landlord or agency. The listings for both rentals and homes for sale often mentioned their proximity to the Google or Apple bus stops.

At the actual open houses, dozens of people who looked like students would show up with checkbooks and sheaves of résumés and other documents and pack the house, literally: it was like a cross between being at a rock concert without a band and the Hotel Rwanda. There were rumors that these young people were starting bidding wars, offering a year's rent in advance, offering far more than was being asked. These rumors were confirmed. Evictions went back up the way they did during the dot-com bubble. Most renters have considerable protection from both rent hikes and evictions in San Francisco, but there are ways around the latter, ways that often lead to pitched legal battles, and sometimes illegal ones. Owners have the right to evict a tenant to occupy the apartment themselves, a right often abused. (An evicted friend of mine found a new home next door to his former landlord and is watching with an eagle eye to see if the guy really dwells there for the requisite three years.) Statewide, the Ellis Act allows landlords to evict all tenants and remove the property from the rental market, a maneuver often deployed to convert a property to flats for sale. As for rent control, it makes many landlords with stable tenants restless, since you can charge anything you like on a vacant apartment—and they do.

A Latino who has been an important cultural figure for forty years is being evicted while his wife undergoes chemotherapy. One of San Francisco's most distinguished poets, a recent candidate to become the city's poet laureate, is being evicted after thirty-five years in his apartment and his whole adult life here. Whether he will claw his way onto a much humbler perch or be exiled to another town remains to be seen, as does the fate of a city that poets can't afford. His building, full of renters for most or all of the past century, including a notable documentary filmmaker, will be turned into flats for sale. A few miles away, friends of friends were evicted after twenty years in their home by two Google attorneys, a gay couple who moved into two separate units in order to maximize their owner move-in rights. Rental prices rose between 10 and 135 percent over the past year in San Francisco's various neighborhoods, though thanks to rent control, a lot of San Franciscans were paying far below market rates even before the boom—which makes adjusting to the new market rate even harder. Two much-loved bookstores are also being evicted by landlords looking for more money; sixteen restaurants opened last year in their vicinity. On the waterfront, Larry Ellison, the world's sixth richest man and owner of Oracle, was allowed to take control of three city piers for seventy-five years in return for fixing them up in time for the 2013 America's Cup; he evicted dozens of small waterfront businesses as part of the deal.

All this is changing the character of what was once a great city of refuge for dissidents, queers, and experimentalists. Like so many cities that flourished in the post-industrial era, it has become increasingly unaffordable over the past quarter-century but still has a host of writers, artists, activists, environmentalists, eccentrics, and others who don't work sixty-hour weeks for corporations—though we may be a relic population. Boomtowns also drive out people who perform essential services for relatively modest salaries— the teachers, firefighters, mechanics, and carpenters, along with people who might have time for civic engagement. I look in wonder at the store clerks and dishwashers, wondering how they hang on or how long their commute is. Sometimes the tech workers on their buses seem like bees who belong to a great hive, but the hive isn't civil society or a city; it's a corporation.

Last summer, I went to look at a house for sale whose listing hadn't mentioned that the house was inhabited. I looked in dismay at the pretty old house where a family's possessions had settled like silt over the decades: drum set, Bibles, faded framed portraits, furniture grimed with the years, cookware, toys. It was a display of what was about to be lost. The estate agent was on the front steps telling potential clients that they wouldn't even have to evict: just raise the rent far beyond what the residents can afford. Ye who seek homes, come destroy the homes of others more frail.

I saw the same thing happen in the building next door to the rental I eventually found through word of mouth after failing to compete in the open market. These families are not going to live like that again, in pleasant homes in the city center. Other buildings I visited had been emptied of all residents, and every unit was for sale, each furnished with brushed steel appliances, smooth surfaces, and sleek neutral tones to appeal to the tastes of young technocrats.

In the poorer outskirts of the city, foreclosures and short sales go on (an alternative to foreclosure where the house is sold even though the sale won't cover the debts) as they have across much of the country since the crash in 2008, and a group called Occupy Bernal Heights (a neighborhood spin-off of Occupy San Francisco, cofounded by the sex activist Annie Sprinkle) has shown up at the banks and at the houses to defend many owners, one home at a time. Poverty is cruel and destructive. Wealth is cruel and destructive too, or at least booms are.

San Francisco's tech boom has often been compared to the Gold Rush but without much discussion about what the Gold Rush meant beyond the cute images of bearded men in plaid shirts with pickaxes looking a lot like gay men in the Castro in the 1970s. When gold was discovered in 1848, employees left their posts, sailors abandoned their ships, and San Francisco—then a tiny port town called Yerba Buena—was deserted. In the California Mother Lode, some got rich; many died of contagious diseases, the lousy diet, rough life, and violence; some went broke and crawled back to the United States, as the settled eastern half of the country was called when the gold country was an outpost of newcomers mostly arriving by ship and the American West still largely belonged to the indigenous people .

Supplying the miners and giving them places to spend their money became as lucrative as mining and much more secure. Quite a lot of the early fortunes were made by shopkeepers: Levi Strauss got his start that way, and so did Leland Stanford, who founded the university that founded Silicon Valley. The Mexicans who had led a fairly gracious life on vast ranches before the Gold Rush were largely dispossessed. The Native Californians were massacred and driven out of their homes; they watched mining destroy their lands and food sources; many starved or died of disease. The Native population declined by about four-fifths during this jolly spree.

San Francisco exploded in the rush, growing by leaps and bounds, a freewheeling town made up almost exclusively of people from elsewhere, mostly male, often young. In 1850, California had a population of 120,000 according to one survey, 110,000 of them male. By 1852, women made up 10 percent of the population; by 1870, more than a quarter. During this era, prostitution thrived, from the elegant courtesans who played a role in the city's political and cultural life to the Chinese children who were worked to death in cribs, as the cubicles in which they labored were called. Prices for everything skyrocketed: Eggs were a dollar apiece in 1849, and a war broke out later over control of the stony Farallon Islands rookery thirty miles west of San Francisco, where seabirds' eggs were gathered to augment what the chickens could produce. A good pair of boots was a hundred dollars. Land downtown was so valuable that people bought water lots—plots of land in the bay—and filled them in.

Wages were high too, until 1869, when the Central Pacific Railroad (built by Stanford and his three cronies) connected the Bay Area to the East Coast, and the newly unemployed railroad workers and the poor of the East poured in. The *Annals of San Francisco* describes the city twenty years earlier, in 1849:

> As we have said, there were no homes at this period in San Francisco, and time was too precious for anyone to stay within doors to cook victuals. Consequently an immense majority of the people took their meals at restaurants, boarding-houses and hotels—the number of which was naturally therefore very great; while many lodged as well as boarded at such places. Many of these were indeed miserable hovels, which showed only bad fare and worse attendance, dirt, discomfort and high prices. A few others again were of a superior class; but, of course, still higher charges had to be made for the better accommodation.

The oil and gas boomtowns of the present—in Wyoming, North Dakota, and Alberta, among other places—follow this model. Lots of money sloshes around boomtowns, but everyday life is shaped by scarcity, not abundance. The boom employees are mostly newcomers. They work long hours, earn high wages, drive up the cost of housing for the locals, drive out some locals, eat out, drink a lot, brawl, overload local services, and often get addicted or injured. In Wyoming in 2011 I met a disability counselor who told me about the young men who go into the coal and gas mining business and make more money than they've ever seen. Soon they go into debt on a trailer home, a fancy truck, and extravagant pleasures. Some then get permanently disabled on the job and watch their lives fall apart. A journalist who'd been reporting on the boom in North Dakota told me about ranches ruined by toxins and about a trailer park full of Native Americans who'd lived there for many decades and were evicted to make room for higher-paying miners with brand-new trailers. Like a virus, mining destroys its host and then moves on. There are ghost towns across the West full of dying businesses with the landscape around them ground into heaps leaching toxic residue.

There are ways in which Silicon Valley is nothing like this: it's clean, quiet work, and here to stay in one form or another. But there are ways in which technology is just another boom and the Bay Area is once again a boomtown, with transient populations, escalating housing costs, mass displacements, and the casual erasure of what was here before. I think of it as frontierism, with all the frontier's attitude and operational style, where people without a lot of attachments come and do things without a lot of concern for their impact, where money moves around pretty casually, and people are ground underfoot equally casually. Sometimes the Google Bus just seems like one face of Janus-headed capitalism; it contains the people too valuable even to use public transport or drive themselves. In the same spaces wander homeless people undeserving of private space or minimal comfort and security; right by the Google bus stop on Cesar Chavez Street, immigrant men from Latin America stand waiting for employers in the building trade to scoop them up or to be arrested and deported by the government. Both sides of the divide are bleak, and the middle way is hard to find.

February 2013

WE'RE BREAKING UP

Noncommunications in the Silicon Age

On or around June 1995, human character changed again. Or rather, it began to undergo a metamorphosis that is still not complete, but is profound—and troubling, not least because it is hardly noted. When I think about, say, 1995, or whenever the last moment was before most of us were on the Internet and had mobile phones, it seems like a hundred years ago. Letters came once a day, predictably, in the hands of the postal carrier. News came in three flavors—radio, television, print—and at appointed hours. Some of us even had a newspaper delivered every morning.

Those mail and newspaper deliveries punctuated the day like church bells. You read the paper over breakfast. If there were developments you heard about them on the evening news or in the next day's paper. You listened to the news when it was broadcast, since there was no other way to hear it. A great many people relied on the same sources of news, so when they discussed current events they did it under the overarching sky of the same general reality. Time passed in fairly large units, or at least not in milliseconds and constant updates. A few hours wasn't such a long time to go between moments of contact with your work, your people, or your trivia.

You opened the mail when you came home from work, or when it arrived if you worked from home. Some of the mail was important and personal, not just bills. It was exciting to get a letter: the paper and handwriting told you something, as well as the words. Going back a little further, movies were seen in movie theaters, and a whole gorgeous ritual went along with seeing them. The subsidiary pleasures—dressing up, standing in line with strangers and friends, the smell of popcorn, holding hands in the dark—still exist, but more and more often movies are seen on smaller and smaller and more private screens. It used to be the case that when you were at a movie, you were 100 percent there, in the velvety darkness watching lives unfold in flickering light (unless you were making out). But with televisions, DVD players, and the rest, you were never totally committed to what they showed; you were always cheating on them, chatting and wandering away, fast-forwarding and rewinding, even when commercials didn't shatter their continuity.

That bygone time had rhythm, and it had room for you to do one thing at a time; it had different parts; mornings included this, and evenings that, and a great many of us had these schedules in common. I would read the paper while listening to the radio, but I wouldn't check my email while updating my status while checking the news sites while talking on the phone. Phones were wired to the wall, or if they were cordless, they were still housebound. The sound quality was usually good. On them people had long, deep conversations of a sort almost unknown today, now that phones are used while driving, while shopping, while walking in front of cars against the light and into fountains. The general assumption was that when you were on the phone, that's all you were.

Letters morphed into emails, and for a long time emails had all the depth and complexity of letters. They were a beautiful new form that spliced together the intimacy of what you might write from the heart with the speed of telegraphs. Then emails deteriorated into something more like text messages. (The first text message was sent in 1992, but phones capable of texting spread later in the 1990s.) Text messages were bound by the limits of telegrams—the state-of-the-art technology of the 1840s—and were almost as awkward to punch out. Soon phone calls were made mostly on mobile phones, whose sound quality is mediocre and prone to failure altogether ("you're breaking up" or "we're breaking up" is the cry of our time) even when one or both speakers aren't multitasking. Communication began to dwindle into peremptory practical phrases and fragments, while the niceties of spelling, grammar, and punctuation were put aside, along with the more lyrical and profound possibilities. Communication between two people often turned into group chatter: you told all your Facebook friends or Twitter followers how you felt, and followed the popularity of your post or tweet. Your life had ratings.

Good things came about with the new technologies. Many people now have voices without censorship; many of us can get in touch with other ordinary citizens directly, through every new medium, from blogs to tweets to texts to posts on Facebook and Instagram. In 1989, Tiananmen Square was the fax revolution. Email helped organize the Seattle WTO shutdown in 1999; Facebook was instrumental in the Arab Spring's initial phase in 2011; Occupy Wall Street was originally a Twitter hashtag. WikiLeaks uploaded Bradley Manning's leaked data to a place where its subjects could read it, which played a role in the Arab Spring too. But the old, irreplaceable dance of democracy, which those digital media helped make happen, still took place between bodies in public. Indeed, the vitality of Occupy for its long season seemed in part to come from the rapture of the American young at the unfamiliar emotional and political power of coexisting in public together, body and soul.

I have reconnected via Facebook to old friends who might otherwise never have resurfaced, and followed grassroots politics and movements. And I've wasted countless hours on it that I could've spent going deeper, with a book, a film, a conversation, or even a walk or a task. Meanwhile the quality of my emails deteriorated; after many years of marvelous correspondences, it became hard to find anyone who still wrote anything resembling a letter. Everyone just dashed off notes about practical things, with maybe a little personal stuff in the mix, and you can't get epistolary with someone who won't receive it with enthusiasm, or at least I can't. A gratuitous clutter of bureaucratic and soliciting emails filled all our inboxes, and wading through that clutter consumed a great deal of everyone's time.

Previous technologies have expanded communication. But the last round may be contracting it. The eloquence of letters has turned into the unnuanced spareness of texts; the intimacy of phone conversations has turned into the missed signals of mobile phone chat. I think of that lost world, the way we lived before these new networking technologies, as having two poles: solitude and communion. The new chatter puts us somewhere in between, assuaging fears of being alone without risking real connection. It is a shallow between two deep zones, a safe spot between the dangers of contact with ourselves, with others.

I live in the heart of it, and it's normal to walk through a crowd—on a train, or a group of young people waiting to eat in a restaurant—in which everyone is staring at the tiny screens in their hands. It seems less likely that each of the kids waiting for the table for eight has an urgent matter at hand than that this is the habitual orientation of their consciousness. At times I feel as though I'm in a bad science fiction movie where everyone takes orders from tiny boxes that link them to alien overlords. Which is what corporations are anyway, and mobile phones decoupled from corporations are not exactly common.

Our lives are a constant swirl of information, of emails that can be checked on phones, and phones that are checked in theaters and bedrooms for texts, and news that streams in constantly. There is so much information that our ability to focus on any piece of it is interrupted by other information, so that we bathe in information but hardly absorb or analyze it. Data are interrupted by other data before we've thought about the first round, and contemplating three streams of data at once may be a way to think about none of them.

"When Carnegie Mellon researchers interrupted college students with text messages while they were taking a test," the *Boston Globe* recently reported, "the students had average test scores that were 20 percent lower than the scores of those who took the exam with their phones turned off. Another study found that students, when left to their own devices, are unable to focus on homework for more than two minutes without turning to Web surfing or email. Adults in the workforce can make it to about 11 minutes."

Nearly everyone I know feels that some quality of concentration they once possessed has been destroyed. Reading books has become hard; the mind keeps wanting to shift from whatever it is paying attention to to attend to something else. A restlessness has seized hold of many of us, a sense that we should be doing something else, no matter what we are doing, or doing at least two things at once, or going to check some other medium. It's an anxiety about keeping up, about not being left out or getting behind. (Maybe it was a landmark when Paris Hilton answered her mobile phone while having sex while being videotaped a decade ago.)

The older people I know are less affected because they don't partake so much of new media or because their habits of mind and time are entrenched. The really young swim like fish through the new media and hardly seem to know that life was ever different. But those of us in the middle feel a sense of loss. I think it is for a quality of time we no longer have, and that is hard to name and harder to imagine reclaiming. My time does not come in large, focused blocks, but in fragments and shards. The fault is my own, arguably, but it's yours too—it's the fault of everyone I know who rarely finds herself or himself with uninterrupted hours. We're shattered. We're breaking up.

It's hard, now, to be with someone else wholly, uninterruptedly, and it's hard to be truly alone. The fine art of doing nothing in particular, also known as thinking, or musing, or introspection, or simply moments of being, was part of what happened when you walked from here to there alone, or stared out the train window, or contemplated the road, but the new technologies have flooded those open spaces. Space for free thought is routinely regarded as a void and filled up with sounds and distractions.

I now feel under-equipped if I walk out of my apartment without my mobile phone, but I used to travel across the world with almost no contact with the people who loved me, and there was a dizzying freedom, a cool draught of solitude, in that. We were not so monitored, because no one read our letters the way they read our emails to sell us stuff, as Gmail does, or track our communications as the National Security Administration does. We are moving into a world of unaccountable and secretive corporations that manage all our communications and work hand in hand with governments to make us visible to them. Our privacy is being strip-mined and hoarded.

It will not be easy to go back, though I did see a poster recently (on Facebook) that made the case for buying books from independent bookstores in cash. And librarians fought a fierce battle in the Bush era when they refused to hand over our library records; but they are part of the old world. The new one has other priorities and didn't put up much fight to protect our information from the NSA (though squealed a little about it afterward; plus, post–Edward Snowden, Yahoo did win a lawsuit allowing it to declassify documents that prove it resisted the NSA's snooping, and two data encryption companies have since folded rather than be corrupted).

A short story that comes back to me over and over again is Kurt Vonnegut's "Harrison Bergeron," or one small bit of it. Since all men and women aren't exactly created equal, in this dystopian bit of science fiction, a future America makes them equal by force: ballerinas wear weights so they won't be more graceful than anyone else, and really smart people wear earpieces that produce bursts of noise every few minutes to interrupt their thought processes. They are "required by law to wear it at all times. It was tuned to a government transmitter. Every twenty seconds or so, the transmitter would send out some sharp noise to keep people like George from taking unfair advantage of their brains." For the smartest person in Vonnegut's story, the radio transmitter isn't enough: "Instead of a little ear radio for a mental handicap, he wore a tremendous pair of earphones, and spectacles with thick wavy lenses. The spectacles were intended to make him not only half blind, but to give him whanging headaches besides."

We have all signed up to wear those earpieces, a future form of new media that will chop our consciousnesses into small dice. Google has made real the interrupters that Vonnegut thought of as a fantasy evil for his dystopian 2081. Google thinks that glasses that interrupt you constantly would be awesome, at least for Google, and they are now in development. I tried on a pair that a skinny Asian guy was wearing in the line at the post office. (Curious that someone with state-of-the-art technology also needs postal services.) A tiny screen above my field of vision had clear white type on it. I could have asked it to do something, but I didn't need data at that juncture, and I'm not in the habit of talking to my glasses. Also, the glasses make any wearer look like, yes, a geek. Google may soon be trying to convince you that life without them is impossible.

A year or so ago I watched in horror a promotional video for these glasses that showed how your whole field of vision of the real world could become a screen on which reminder messages spring up. The video portrayed the lifestyle of a hip female Brooklynite whose Google glasses toss Hello Kitty–style pastel data bubbles at her from the moment she gets up. None of the information the glasses thrust into her field of vision is crucial. It's all optional, based on the assumptions that our lives require lots of management and that being managerial is our highest goal. Is it?

I forget practical stuff all the time, but I also forget to look at the distance and contemplate the essential mysteries of the universe and the one-ness of all things. A pair of glasses on which the temperature and chance of rain pops up or someone's trying to schedule me for a project or a drink is not going to help with reveries about justice, meaning, and the beautiful deep marine blue of nearly every dusk.

Furthermore, Google glasses probably aren't going to spring pastel-col-ored bubbles on you that say "It's May Day! Overthrow tyranny," let alone "Don't let corporations dictate your thoughts," or "It would be really mean-ingful to review the personal events of August 1997 in the light of what you know now." That between you and me stands a corporation every time we make contact—not just the post office or the phone company, but a titan that shares information with the NSA—is dismaying. But that's another subject: mine today is time.

I wonder sometimes if there will be a revolt against the quality of time the new technologies have brought us, as well as the corporations in charge of those technologies. Or perhaps there already has been, in a small, quiet way. The real point about the slow food movement was often missed. It wasn't food. It was about doing something from scratch, with pleasure, all the way through, in the old methodical way we used to do things. That didn't merely produce better food; it produced a better relationship to ma-terials, processes, and labor, notably your own, before the spoon reached your mouth. It produced pleasure in production as well as consumption. It made whole what is broken.

Some of the young have taken up gardening and knitting and a host of other things that involve working with their hands, making things from scratch, and often doing things the old way. It is a slow-everything movement in need of a manifesto that would explain what vinyl records and homemade bread have in common. We won't overthrow corporations by knitting—but understanding the pleasures of knitting or weeding or making pickles might articulate the value of that world outside electronic chatter and distraction, and inside a more stately sense of time. (Of course, for a lot of people, this impulse has been sublimated by cooking shows: watching the preparation of food that you will never taste by celebrities you will never meet, a fate that makes Tantalus's seem rich.)

There are also places where human contact and continuity of experience hasn't been so ruined. I visit New Orleans regularly, where music is often live and people dance to it, not just listen to it sitting down, and where people sit by preference out front and greet strangers with endearments. This old leisurely enjoyment of mingling with strangers in the street and public venues forms a dramatic contrast with the Bay Area, where contact with strangers is likely to be met (at least among the white middle class) with a puzzled and slightly pained expression that seems to say you've made a mistake. If you're even heard, since earphones—they still look to me like some sort of medical equipment, an IV drip for noise—are ubiquitous, so that on college campuses, say, finding someone who can lend you an ear isn't easy. The young are disappearing down the rabbit hole of total immersion in the networked world—and struggling to get out of it.

Getting out of it is about slowness and about finding alternatives to the alienation that accompanies a sweater knitted by a machine in a sweatshop in a country you know nothing about, or jam made by a giant corporation that has terrible environmental and labor practices and might be tied to the death of honeybees or the poisoning of farmworkers. It's an attempt to put the world back together again, in its materials but also its time and labor. It's both laughably small and heroically ambitious.

Perhaps the young will go further and establish rebel camps where they will lead the lives of 1957, if not 1857, when it comes to quality of time and technology. Perhaps. Right now we need to articulate these subtle things, this richer, more expansive quality of time and attention and connection, to hold onto it. Can we? The alternative is grim, with a grimness that would be hard to explain to someone who's distracted.

July 2013

PALE BUS, PALE RIDER

Silicon Valley Invades, Cont'd

The young woman at the blockade was worried about the banner the Oaklanders brought, she told me, because it might distract attention from evicted tenants' stories and the larger issues. But the words "FUCK OFF GOOGLE" in giant letters on a purple sheet held up in front of a blockaded Google bus gladdened the hearts of other San Franciscans. That morning—it was Tuesday, January 21, 2014—about fifty locals were also holding up a Facebook bus: a gleaming luxury coach transporting Facebook employees down the peninsula to Silicon Valley. A tall young black man held one corner of the banner; he was wearing a *Ulysses* T-shirt, as if analog itself had come to protest against digital. The Brass Liberation Orchestra played the Eurythmics's "Sweet Dreams" as the television cameras rolled.

The white buses took up most of the four lanes of Eighth Street at Market, and their passengers were barely visible behind the tinted windows, scowling or texting or looking at their laptops for the half-hour they were delayed by the blockade. GET OFF THE BUS! JOIN US, another banner said, and the official-looking signs from the December 9 blockade were put up at either end of the Facebook bus: WARNING: INCOME GAP AHEAD the one at the front said. STOP DISPLACEMENT NOW, read the one at the back. One protester shook a sign on a stick in front of the Google bus; a young Google employee decided to dance with it, as though we were all at the same party.

We weren't. One of the curious things about the crisis in San Francisco—precipitated by a huge influx of well-paid tech workers driving up housing costs and causing evictions, gentrification, and cultural change—is that they seem unable to understand why many locals don't love them.

They're convinced that they are members of the tribe. Their confusion may issue from Silicon Valley's own favorite stories about itself. These days in TED talks and tech-world conversation, commerce is described as art and as revolution and huge corporations are portrayed as agents of the counterculture.

That may actually have been the case, briefly, in the popular tech Genesis story according to which Apple emerged from a garage somewhere at the south end of the San Francisco Peninsula, not yet known as Silicon Valley. But Google set itself up with the help of a $4.5 million government subsidy, and Apple became a giant corporation that begat multimillion-dollar advertising campaigns and overseas sweatshops and the rest that you already know. Facebook, Google, eBay, and Yahoo (though not Apple) belong to the conservative anti-environmental political action committee ALEC (the American Legislative Exchange Council).

The story Silicon Valley less often tells about itself has to do with dollar signs and weapons systems. The industry came out of military contracting, and its alliance with the Pentagon has never ended. The valley's first major firm, Hewlett-Packard, was a military contractor. One of its cofounders, David Packard, was an undersecretary of defense in the Nixon administration; his signal contribution as a civil servant was a paper about overriding the laws preventing the imposition of martial law. Many defense contractors have flourished in Silicon Valley in the decades since: weapons contractors United Technologies and Lockheed Martin, as well as sundry makers of drone, satellite, and spying equipment and military robotics. Silicon Valley made technology for the military, and the military sponsored research that benefited Silicon Valley. The first supercomputer, made by New York's Remington Rand, was for nuclear weapons research at the Bay Area's Lawrence Livermore National Laboratory.

The Internet itself, people sometimes remember, was created by the military, and publicly funded research has done a lot to make the hardware, the software, and the vast private fortunes possible. Which you wouldn't know from the hyperlibertarian language of the tech world's kings. Even the mildest of them, Bill Gates, said in 1998: "There isn't an industry in America that is more creative, more alive and more competitive. And the amazing thing is that all this happened without any government involvement." The current lords talk of various kinds of secession, quite literally at the Seasteading Institute, an organization that's looking into building artificial islands outside all national laws and regulations. And taxes. Let someone else subsidize all that research.

The same morning the buses were stopped in downtown San Francisco, some hell-raisers went to the Berkeley home of a Google employee who, they say, works on robots for the military. (Google recently purchased eight robotics companies and is going in a lot of new directions, to put it mildly.) After ringing his doorbell, they unfurled a banner that read GOOGLE'S FUTURE STOPS HERE, and then blockaded the Google bus at one of its Berkeley stops.

So there's a disconnect in values and goals: Silicon Valley workers seem to want to inhabit the anti-war, social-justice, mutual-aid heart of San Francisco (and the Bay Area). To do so they often displace San Franciscans from their homes. One often hears objections: it isn't the tech workers coming here who are carrying out the evictions. But they are moving into homes from which people have been evicted. Ivory collectors in China aren't shooting elephants in Africa, but the elephants are being shot for them. Native sons and daughters also work in the industry, and many of the newcomers may be compassionate, progressive people, but I have seen few signs of resistance, refusal to participate, or even chagrin about their impact from within their ranks.

It may be that 2013 was the year San Francisco turned on Silicon Valley and may be the year the world did too. Edward Snowden's revelations began to flow in June: Silicon Valley was sharing our private data with the National Security Agency. Many statements were made about how reluctantly it was done, how outraged the executives were, but all the relevant companies—Yahoo, Google, Facebook—complied without telling us. These days it appears that the NSA is not their enemy so much as their rival; Facebook and Google are themselves apparently harvesting far more data from us than the U.S. government is. Last year, Facebook's chief security officer went to work for the NSA, and the *New York Times* said the move underscores the increasingly deep connections between Silicon

Valley and the agency and the degree to which they are now in the same business. Both hunt for ways to collect, analyze, and exploit large pools of data about millions of Americans. The difference is that the NSA does it for intelligence, and Silicon Valley does it to make money.

The corporations doing this are not the counterculture or the underground or bohemia and are only the avant-garde of an Orwellian future.

Last September, City of Refuge, a church serving people of color and queer people, left San Francisco—a city that has long considered itself a refuge—and moved to Oakland. "It became clear," its pastor said, "what the neighborhood was saying to us: This is not a haven for social services." The current boom is dislodging bookstores, bars, Latino businesses, black businesses, environmental and social-services groups, as well as longtime residents, many of them disabled and elderly. Mary Elizabeth Phillips, who arrived in San Francisco in 1937, will be ninety-eight when she is driven out of her home of more than forty years.

In many other places eviction means you go and find a comparable place to live; in San Francisco that's impossible for anyone who's been here a while and is paying less than the market rate. Money isn't the only issue: even people who can pay huge sums can't find anything to rent because the competition is so fierce. Jonathan Klein, a travel-agency owner in his sixties living with AIDS, jumped off the Golden Gate Bridge last year after being driven out of his home, with his business in the Castro facing eviction. "EVICTION = DEATH," a sign at the memorial said, echoing the old SILENCE = DEATH slogan of the AIDS-activist era.

When it comes to buying a home, your income needs to be nearly one and a half times higher in San Francisco than in the next most expensive city in the United States. What began as vague anxiety a couple of years ago has turned into fear, rage, and grief. It has also driven people to develop strategies aimed at changing the local and statewide laws that permit the evictions.

When a Google bus was surrounded on December 9, 2013, it made the news all over the English-speaking world. Though what the blockaders wanted wasn't so easily heard. They were attacked as people who don't like carpools, by people who don't get that the buses compete with public transport and that their passengers displace economically vulnerable San Franciscans. It's as though death came riding in on a pale horse and someone said: "What? You don't like horses?" Many of the displaced then become commuters, but they don't have luxury coaches pulling up in their neighborhoods to take them to their jobs and schools in San Francisco; they drive or patch together routes on public transport or sink into oblivion and exile. So the Google bus and the Apple bus don't reduce commuting's impact. They just transfer it to poorer people.

San Francisco was excoriated again and again by lovers of development and the free market for not being dense enough, on the grounds that if we just built and built and built, everyone would be happily housed. "Let San Francisco have the same housing density as Tokyo & Taipei, both earthquake zones, then watch rental costs crater," a tech worker tweeted. (His feed also features photographs of a toy mule, the mascot of the company he works for, and occasional outbursts aimed at Edward Snowden.) Another day he insisted with the blithe confidence Silicon Valley seems to beget (as well as the oversimplification Twitter more or less requires): "Higher minimum wage and looser, pro-development zoning laws, housing problem in San Francisco goes away. Simple as that." (Minimum wage would have to be more than $50 an hour for someone to be able to buy a house in San Francisco, or to ensure that a $3,200 a month rent accounted for no more than a third of their pre-tax income.)

San Francisco is already the second densest major metropolitan area in the United States, but this isn't mentioned much, nor is the fact that the densest, New York, is also unaffordable and becoming more so even in its outer boroughs, despite a building boom. Meanwhile San Francisco developers are building 48,000 more units of housing in the few cracks and interstices not already filled in, mostly upscale condominiums far out of most people's reach, and most of which won't be available in time to prevent the next round of evictions.

How do you diagnose what is wrong with San Francisco now? People bandy about the word *gentrification*, a term usually used for neighborhoods rather than whole cities. You could say that San Francisco, like New York and other U.S. metropolises, is suffering the reversal of postwar white flight: affluent people, many of them white, decided in the past few decades that cities were nice places to live after all and started to return, pushing poorer people, many of them non-white, to the margins.

You can also see the explosion as a variation on the new economic divide, in which the few have more and more, and the many have less and less: a return to nineteenth-century social arrangements. (It gets forgotten that the more generous arrangements of the twentieth century, in much of Europe and North America, were made in part to sedate insurrectionary fury from below.) It's the issue to which Occupy Wall Street drew our attention.

It is often said that this city was born with the Gold Rush and that the dot-com boom of the late 1990s bore a great deal of resemblance to this current boom: lots of young technology workers wanted to live here then as now. The dot-commers were forever celebrating the Internet as a way to never leave the house and never have random contact with strangers again and even order all their pet food online. But it turned out that many of them wanted exactly the opposite: a walkable, diverse urban life with lots of chances to mingle, though they mingled with their own kind or at least with other young, affluent people in the restaurants and bars and boutiques that sprang up to serve them. Then it all collapsed, and quite a few of the tigers of the free market moved back in with their parents, and for several years San Francisco was calm again.

You can think of these booms as half the history of the city: the other half is catastrophe, earthquake, fire, economic bust, deindustrialization, and the scourge of AIDS. And maybe you can think of them as the same thing: upheavals that have remade the city again and again. Though something was constant, the sense of the city as separate from the rest of the country, a sanctuary for nonconformists, exiles, war resisters, sex rebels, eccentrics, environmentalists, and experimentalists in the arts and sciences, food, agriculture, law, architecture, and social organization. San Francisco somehow remained hospitable to those on the margins throughout its many incarnations, until now.

But people talking about the crisis don't talk about urban theory or history. They talk about the Google bus: whether the Google bus should be regulated and pay for the use of public bus stops, and whether it's having a damaging effect on public transport. There were municipal transport studies on the Google bus, which is shorthand for all the major Silicon Valley tech shuttles that make it possible to commute forty miles down a congested freeway and back daily in comfort, even luxury, while counting the time as being at work. (The buses have Wi-Fi; the passengers have laptops.) In *New York Magazine* Kevin Roose pointed out that the Google bus was typical of the neoliberal tendency to create elite private solutions and let the public sphere go to hell. A Google bus song was released on YouTube (which belongs to Google), with mocking lyrics about its cushiness and the passengers' privilege.

A recent bus decoration competition called Bedazzle a Tech Bus seemed to suggest that artists could love tech and tech could love artists: the prize was $500. That's about enough to buy some aspirin or whiskey and pay for a van to take you and your goods to one of the blue-collar cities on the periphery of the Bay Area that are, like most of the United States, still struggling in the aftermath of the 2008 crisis. The artist Stephanie Syjuco began soliciting proposals from friends and acquaintances and swamping the competition with scathing mock-ups. One showed a bus bearing advertisements for the 1849 Gold Rush; in another, a bus was wrapped in Géricault's *Raft of the Medusa*; in a third, a photograph of a homeless encampment was pasted on one of the sleek white buses with tinted windows that transport the well-compensated employees to their tech campuses, as we now call these corporate workplaces. (There are also a lot of badly compensated employees in Silicon Valley, among them the bus drivers, who work for companies that contract their services to the tech giants; the security guards; the people who photograph the innumerable books Google is scanning, whose mostly brown and black hands are occasionally spotted in the images; and the janitors, the dishwashers, and others who keep the campus fun for the engineers.)

The winner of the competition submitted a Google Street View photograph of the neighborhood: not of a generic spot, but of the hallowed charity shop Community Thrift and the mural-covered Clarion Alley next to it. The murals are dedicated to the neighborhood and to radical politics, and have been painted by some of the city's best artists of the last twenty years. Against their express wishes, the competition would have their work

become the décor—or, as the organizers put it, "camouflage"—for a multinational corporation's shuttle bus. The winning artist withdrew her proposal out of respect for Clarion Alley's artists, and in the end, nobody won.

On the afternoon of January 21, the city's Municipal Transportation
Agency held a meeting to discuss putting in place a pilot program to study
the impact of the buses and limit them to two hundred bus stops in the city.
As the San Francisco writer Anisse Gross has pointed out, if you evade
your fare on a bus, you get fined $110; if you pull a car in at a bus stop, you
get fined $271; if you just pay your fare, it's $2 per person. But if you're the
Google bus, you will now pay $1 to use the public bus stop. This pissed off a
lot of people at the hearing. Not everyone, though. Google had dispatched
some of its employees to testify.

The corporation's memo to the passengers had been leaked the previous
day. The memo encouraged them to go to the hearing on company time
and told them what to say.

> If you do choose to speak in favor of the proposal, we thought you might
> appreciate some guidance on what to say. Feel free to add your own style and
> opinion:
>
> My shuttle empowers my colleagues and I to reduce our carbon emissions
> by removing cars from the road.
>
> If the shuttle program didn't exist, I would continue to live in San
> Francisco and drive to work on the peninsula.
>
> I am a shuttle rider, SF resident, and I volunteer at . . .

The idea of the memo was to make it seem that the luxury buses are
reducing, not increasing, Silicon Valley's impact on San Francisco. "It's not
a luxury," one Google worker said of the bus: "It's just a thing on wheels
that gets us to work." But a new study concludes that if the buses weren't
available, half the workers wouldn't drive their own cars from San Francisco to Silicon Valley; nearly a third wouldn't be willing to live here and
commute there at all.

There's a new job category in San Francisco, though it's probably a
low-paying one: private security guard for the Google bus.

February 2014

ON THE DIRTINESS OF LAUNDRY

AND THE STRENGTH OF SISTERS

Or, Mysteries of Henry David Thoreau, Unsolved

There is one writer in all literature whose laundry arrangements have been excoriated again and again, and it is not Virginia Woolf, who almost certainly never did her own washing, or James Baldwin, or the rest of the global pantheon. The laundry of the poets remains a closed topic, from the tubercular John Keats (blood-spotted handkerchiefs) to Pablo Neruda (lots of rumpled sheets). Only Henry David Thoreau has been tried in the popular imagination and found wanting for his cleaning arrangements, though the true nature of those arrangements is not so clear.

I got prodded into taking an interest in the laundry of the author of "Civil Disobedience" and "A Plea for Captain John Brown" in the course of an unwise exchange. Let me begin again by saying that I actually like using Facebook, on which this particular morning I had sent birthday wishes to my Cuban translator and disseminated a booklet about debt resistance. I signed up for Facebook in 2007 to try to keep track of what young Burmese exiles were doing in response to the uprising in that country, and so I use it with fewer blushes than a lot of my friends—and perhaps even my "friends," since Facebook has provided me with a few thousand souls in that incoherent category.

And really, this is an essay about categories, which I have found such leaky vessels all my life: everything you can say about a category of people—immigrant taxi drivers, say, or nuns—has its exceptions, and so the category obscures more than it explains, though it does let people tidy up the complicated world into something simpler. I knew a Franciscan nun who started the great era of civil-disobedience actions against nuclear weapons at the Nevada Test Site that were to reshape my life so profoundly and lead to the largest mass arrests in American history, but remind me someday to tell you about the crackhead nun on the lam who framed her sex partner as a rapist and car thief. A private eye I know exonerated him, as I intend to do with Thoreau, uncle, if not father, of civil disobedience, over the question of the laundry.

It's because I bridle at so many categories that I objected to an acquaintance's sweeping generalization on Facebook that Americans don't care about prisoners. Now, more than 2 million of us *are* prisoners in this country, and many millions more are the family members of those in prison or are in the category of poor nonwhite people most often imprisoned, and all these people probably aren't indifferent. In my mild response I mentioned a host of organizations like the Center for Constitutional Rights, which has done a great deal for the prisoners in Guantanamo. I could've mentioned my friend Scott, who was a pro-bono lawyer for the Angola Three for a decade or so, or my friend Melody, a criminal defense investigator who did quite a lot for people on death row. They are a minority, but they count.

Having ignored the warning signs of someone looking for people to condemn, I recklessly kept typing: "We were the nation of Thoreau and John Brown and the Concord Female Anti-Slavery Society when we were also the nation of slaveowners—and slaves." Which was a way of reiterating my sense that the opposite is also true of almost anything you can say about this vast messy empire of everybody from everywhere that pretends to be a coherent country, this place that is swamps and skyscrapers and mobile homes and Pueblo people in fourteenth-century villages on the Rio Grande. And 2.5 million prisoners. Truth for me has always come in tints and shades and spectrums and never in black and white, and America is a category so big as to be useless, unless you're talking about the government.

The poster replied: "And the nation of Thoreau's sister who came every week to take his dirty laundry." This was apparently supposed to mean that Thoreau was not a noble idealist but a man who let women do the dirty work, even though it had nothing to do with whether or not Thoreau or other Americans cared about prisoners, which is what we were supposed to be talking about. Or maybe it suggested that Thoreau's sister was imprisoned by gender roles and housework. It was also meant to imply that I worshipped false gods. I have heard other versions of this complaint about Thoreau. Quite a lot of people think that Thoreau was pretending to be a hermit in his cabin on Walden Pond while cheating by going home and visiting people and eating in town and otherwise being convivial and enjoying himself and benefiting from civilization. They think he is a hypocrite.

They mistake him for John Muir, who went alone deep into something that actually resembled the modern idea of wilderness (although it was, of course, indigenous homeland in which Muir alternately patronized and ignored the still-present Native Americans). Then, after his first, second, and several more summers in the Sierra, Muir married well and eventually lived in a grand three-story house in Martinez, California, and ran his father-in-law's big orchard business that paid for it all. Even John Muir is difficult to categorize, since he was gregarious enough to cofound the Sierra Club and complicated enough to labor as a lumberjack and sheepherder in the mountains he eventually wished to protect from logging and grazing. None of us is pure, and purity is a dreary pursuit best left to Puritans.

The tiny, well-built cabin at Walden was a laboratory for a prankish investigation of work, money, time, and space by our nation's or empire's trickster-in-chief, as well as a quiet place to write. During his two years there, Thoreau was never far from town, and he was not retreating from anything. He was advancing toward other things. The woods he roamed before, during, and after his time in the famous shack contained evidence of Indians, locals doing the various things people do in woods, including gathering wood and hunting, and escaped slaves on the long road north to Canada and freedom. He traveled with some of these slaves, guided them a little, and they guided him in other ways.

Slavery was very much on his mind during the time he lived at Walden Pond. His mother's and sisters' organization, the Concord Female Anti-Slavery Society, met at least once in his cabin (for a celebration of the anniversary of the liberation of slaves in the Indies, shortly after he himself spent a night as a prisoner). This is how not a recluse he was: there were meetings in that tiny cabin that engaged with the laws of the nation and the status of strangers far away, and he also went to jail during that time because he was fiercely opposed to the territorial war against Mexico and to slavery.

The threads of empathy and obligation and idealism spun out from those people and those meetings. The Concord abolitionists chose to care about people they had never met; they chose to pit themselves against the most horrific injustices and established laws of their society; and they did it at a time when they were a small minority and the end of slavery was hardly visible on the horizon.

And the laundry? I did a quick online search and found a long parade of people who pretended to care who did Thoreau's laundry as a way of not having to care about Thoreau. They thought of Thoreau as a balloon and the laundry was their pin. Andrew Boynton in *Forbes* magazine observed in 2007 that his mother did his laundry; a cheesy website noted that he "took his dirty laundry home to mom!"; in 1983, a ponderous gentleman named Joseph Moldenhauer got in early on the accusation that he "brought his mother his dirty laundry"; a blogger complained that "he had someone else do his laundry"; another writer referred offhandedly to the "women who did his laundry."

A writer on an environmental website recently complained, "While philosophizing about self-sufficiency in his solitary shack, he would drop off his laundry at his mother's place back in town"; even Garrison Keillor got involved in the laundry question—"He wrote elegantly about independence and forgot to thank his mom for doing his laundry"; there's even a collection of short stories called *Thoreau's Laundry*, as well as a website that sells a Thoreau laundry bag. Search engines having a genius for incoherent categories, I also learned that Thoreau, New Mexico, a pleasant little town on Interstate 40, has four Laundromats.

The standard allegation, the reader will note, is that Thoreau's mother, Cynthia Dunbar Thoreau, did his washing, not his sister, and no one suggests that she had to fetch it first. Besides which, he had two sisters, Sophia and Helen. The sneering follow-up message I got from the person who claimed that Thoreau was a man whose sister did his washing made me feel crummy for a day or so during an otherwise ebullient period of being around people that I love and who love me back. I composed various ripostes in my head.

Having grown up with parents who believed deeply in the importance of being right and the merit of facts, I usually have to calm down and back up to realize that there is no such thing as winning an argument in this kind of situation, only escalating. Facebook's verb "friend" is annoying, but its corollary, "unfriend," is occasionally useful.

I decided against unfriending and opted for simply avoiding the person into whose unfriendly fire I'd strayed. The thing to do was to seek out more convivial company. I had dinner the next night with my friend Thomas, whom I've known almost twenty years and at whose wedding I was best man. A half-Burmese Londoner, he's only been in this hemisphere about five years, and he told me that reading *Walden* recently helped reconcile him to American individualism by exhibiting it as something energetic and eccentric as well as assertive. We began to correspond about Thoreau, and that dialogue deepened what was already a great friendship. I know two actual Thoreau scholars—one whom I met in the 1990s in Reno, and another who sought me out via Facebook (before the incident in question) and with whom I'd corresponded a little. I turned to them for more informed opinions on the washing. I wasn't going to argue about it; but I did want to know the truth for my own satisfaction.

The first acquaintance, Professor Michael Branch at the University of Nevada, Reno, was tired of hearing about the laundry: "The problem with explaining how much work the guy did is that you end up defending the wrong cause. I've stepped into this bear trap before," wrote Branch. He listed some of the kinds of labor the shaggy Transcendentalist performed, including teaching, surveying, and running his family's pencil factory. But, he cautioned, "once you make this case, you've accidentally blessed the idea that paying attention to the world, studying botany, and writing a shitload of amazing prose isn't real work. Better to just say he never did a damned thing except write the century's best book and leave it at that. Lazy fucker."

Do we care who did the chores in any other creative household on earth? Did Dante ever take out the slops? Do we love housework that much? Or do we hate it that much? This fixation on the laundry is related to the larger question of whether artists should be good people as well as good artists, and probably the short answer is that everyone should be a good person, but a lot of artists were only good artists (and quite a lot more were only bad artists). Whether or not they were good people, the good artists gave us something. Pablo Picasso was sometimes not very nice to his lady friends, but he could paint. I was friends with the artist and filmmaker Bruce Conner for a quarter century, and his unreasonable insistence on perfection made his work brilliant and his company exacting and sometimes terrifying.

It wasn't as though if he hadn't made those seminal films and assemblages he would've been an uncomplicated good guy; it's not as though he was giving to art what he should have given to life; he was putting out what he had, and it was a huge and lasting gift on this impure earth, even if it came from an imperfect man. Thoreau was a moralist, a person who wrote about what we should do, how to walk, or how to fight the government about slavery; and a moralist holds himself up to a higher standard: does he, so to speak, walk his talk? Or so moralists are always tested, but their premises are right or not independent of whether or not they live up to them. Martin Luther King Jr. was right about racism and injustice whether or not he led a blameless life. Digging into his dirty laundry doesn't undo those realities, though the FBI tried to blackmail and undermine him that way.

The second scholar I wrote to was also a Michael, Michael Sims, who was working on a book about the young Thoreau, and he was well primed for the question. "Thoreau did visit the village almost every day, and see his parents, and do chores around the house for them," he wrote. He continued:

> While he was at Walden, they were in a house he helped build the year before he moved to the cabin—he and his father mainly—so he had considerable goodwill in the bank. During his entire adult life, he paid rent while at his parents' boarding house, and paid it faithfully, with records sometimes kept on the backs of poems or other writings. He worked in the garden, helped keep the house in good repair, provided foods from his own garden, and so on.
>
> People did drop by the cabin to bring him food sometimes, but people dropped by each other's houses with food all the time. It was the most common gift. He brought other people food, especially melons. (He was

legendary for his talent in raising a vast array of melons.) I don't know if
I have an actual record of the family doing his laundry, but I'll check as
I go through some of that over the next month. But I would bet they did
sometimes do his laundry. He was quite emotionally dependent upon his
family, especially his mother, but he also contributed constantly. When his
brother died young, Henry helped take up the slack in financial help. When
his father died, Henry became not only the man of the house but the major
force in the pencil business (which he had already almost revolutionized with
his analysis of better ways to make pencils). So I think what I'm trying to say
is that even at Walden he was very much a part of the family in every way.

After looking into the laundry accusations, I opened *Walden* again and
examined the section where he does his accounts, which, as the historian
Richard White points out, were a sort of parody of nineteenth-century pre-
occupations with efficiency and profitability, with the pettiness of keeping
score and the souls of bookkeepers. He mentions "washing and mending,
which for the most part were done out of the house, and their bills have not
yet been received." It's not clear if that's out of his own cabin or his mother's
house, during the Walden era, but it suggests that maybe his washing was
done by strangers in a commercial transaction, or that maybe he thought
that the question of who did the laundry was amusing and made an indeci-
pherable joke about a bill his family wasn't really going to send.

He was, after all, the man who warned us against enterprises that required new clothes, often wore shabby ones, and was certainly not very
concerned about having clean ones. He never married and did little to
make work for women and did quite a bit of dirty work himself, including
shoveling manure—of which he wrote, "Great thoughts hallow any labor.
To-day I earned seventy-five cents heaving manure out of a pen, and made
a good bargain of it." He worked quite hard, often for his sisters' benefit,
though he also played around with the idea of work, appointing himself
inspector of snowstorms and proposing that his employment could be
watching the seasons, which he did with such precision, describing what
bloomed when and which bird species arrived on what date in his corner
of Massachusetts, that his journals have been used to chart climate change

in the present. We call that work—which was also so clearly a pleasure for him—science.

Intermittently, throughout his adult life, he was also struggling with tuberculosis, the disease that killed his older sister, Helen, in 1849 and sometimes sapped his strength long before it killed him in 1862. At the time of his death, he was lying in bed downstairs in a parlor with his younger sister Sophia at his side. Though we talk so much about the twenty-six months he dwelt at Walden Pond, he spent most of the rest of the forty-five years of his life at home with his family, as an intimate and essential part of what appears to have been an exceptionally loving group.

Labor was divided up by gender in those days, but it's hard to argue that women always had the worst of it in an era when men did the heavy work on farms and often the dirtiest and most physically demanding work around the house (in those days of outhouses, chopping wood, shoveling ashes and coal, handling horses and livestock, butchering, pumping water, and other largely bygone chores). Everyone worked around the home, until they became so affluent no one worked beyond the symbolic femininity of needlework. In between those two poles was a plethora of families who had hired help with the housework. I don't think women were particularly subjugated by domestic work in the centuries before housewives in the modern sense existed, though gender roles themselves deprived them of agency, voice, and rights. Thoreau's sisters resisted and maybe overcame them without their brother's aid.

Thoreau's mother ran a boardinghouse, and yet another writer on Thoreau, Robert Sullivan, points out that, like a lot of nineteenth-century households, they had help, and that the Transcendentalists were uncomfortable with the hierarchy of servants and employers. (Emerson tried having the maid sit at the dinner table with the family, but the cook refused to do so.)

Perhaps Thoreau, his mother, and his sisters all had their washing done by the same servant, or servants, who Sullivan suggests were likely to be recent Irish immigrants. Ireland's Catholics, fleeing the potato famine and British brutality, had started to arrive in the 1840s, and a torrent of desperate Irish would pour into this country for several decades. In his journal entry for June 9, 1853, Thoreau expresses sympathy for an Irish maid named Mary who told him she quit her position on a dairy farm because she was supposed to do the washing for twenty-two people, including ten men with two pairs of dirty overalls apiece.

The project of liberation is never-ending, most urgent at its most literal but increasingly complex as it becomes metaphysical. Only free people can care about slaves or prisoners and do something about slavery and prisons, which is why the project of liberating yourself is not necessarily selfish (as long as you don't go down that endless solitary path marked After I'm Perfect I'll Do Something for Others, but stay on the boulevard marked My Freedom Is for Your Liberation Which I Must Also Attend to Now). On October 13, 2012, a few weeks after the unpleasant interchange about prisoners and laundry, I went to San Quentin State Prison to hear the prisoners read.

San Quentin was even more prisonlike than I'd imagined, with a patchwork of intimidating architectural styles: some crenellations like a medieval fortress, guard towers, sheer walls, razor-wire coils, warning signs, and entrance via steel gates that actually did slam shut with an echoing clang. We, the mostly female, mostly white audience for the reading, had been sent a long list of colors we were not allowed to wear: blue, of course, but so many other colors that finally only black and purple and pink and patterns seemed safe for sure, so we looked as though we were going to a funeral or a punk concert. The prisoners were wearing various shades of blue, work boots or running shoes, and some jewelry. One had a Santa beard, one had dreadlocks, and the Latino murderer had a sharp pompadour and thick mustache. Only one of them looked young.

They read in the Catholic chapel, which was cold, low slung, made of cinder blocks, with a pure white crucified Jesus on the wall and grillwork visible through the fake stained glass. A lot of the stories were moving; some were unsettling, particularly the ones in which old rages and convoluted senses of causality (as evidenced by the passive tense used to describe killing a friend) lived on and women seemed more like possessions than fellow human beings. The category of maximum-security prisoner did not describe the range of these men. I was most touched by Troy Williams's straightforward account of weeping when he told his daughter, via telephone, that his parole had been denied. He was fearful of being seen to cry in a tough place like prison, but someone reached out to him, and he found a little more humanity than he expected.

"What kind of a prison have I put my child in?" he asked himself, expanding the idea of prison to include the way she was tied to his fate and locked out of his life. My friend Moriah had brought me to the event; she had been the year before and was moved not just by what she heard but by the fact that the small cluster of strangers from outside was about the most significant audience these guys were going to get. She had heard about it because her daughter was in school with a girl who lived in the same household as Zoe Mullery, the creative writing teacher who had for six years or more come once a week to work with these men. One of the men wrote in his biography in the handout we all received, "I picked up a book and was able to depart the brutal confines of the penitentiary, as well as the margins of my depressed mind. Reading became an escape without my actually escaping."

Zoe later told me that she had once looked at the history of the word *free* and it might interest me. According to the *Oxford English Dictionary*, *free* has the same Indo-European root as the Sanskrit word *priya*, which means "beloved" or "dear." If you think of etymology as a family tree, the dictionary says that most descendants of that ancient ancestor describe affection, and only the Germanic and Celtic branches describe liberty. The scholars say that the word may hark back to an era when a household consisted of the free people who were members of the extended family and the unfree ones who were slaves and servants. Family members had more rights than slaves and servants, so even though "free" in the United States is often seen as meaning one who has no ties, it was once the other way around. Which is another way of saying that freedom has less to do with that Lynyrd Skynyrd "Freebird" sense of the word (in which we don't care about prisoners or anyone else) and more to do with the idea of agency.

It doesn't actually matter who did Thoreau's washing, though I remained curious to see if we knew who that might be. We don't. But we do know quite a lot about the Thoreau family's values. The second Thoreau scholar, Michael Sims, had sent me an excellent essay by Sandra Harbert

Petrulionus about the Concord Female Anti-Slavery Society that the writer's mother and sisters belonged to, along with Mrs. Emerson, and after the laundry issue was raised on Facebook, I read it again. "The influence they brought to bear on some of America's most noted antislavery speakers and writers had a pronounced and far-reaching impact," Petrolonious declares. "Thanks directly to eight women, six of whom lived in his home, Henry Thoreau had long been exposed to the most radical antislavery positions during his formative young-adult years."

The women seemed to find a kind of liberation for themselves in this movement for the liberation of others; they were able to act independently of husbands and fathers, to take public stands, to become political beings in a new way. The women's suffrage movement, the first feminist movement, grew directly out of the abolition movement: they went to liberate someone else and found that they too were not free. Thoreau's mother and sisters were more radical than he was initially; they even publicly supported the "disunion" position that would have had the North secede from the slave South long before the South actually seceded from the North. The Thoreau women were also participants in the Underground Railroad, and Henry David sometimes walked or drove the fugitives northward toward freedom. These Americans cared about prisoners enough to risk their own lives and liberty on their behalf.

A young abolitionist named Daniel Conway describes one such encounter on July 27, 1853, thus:

> In the morning I found the Thoreaus agitated by the arrival of a colored fugitive from Virginia, who had come to their door at daybreak. Thoreau took me to a room where his excellent sister, Sophia, was ministering to the fugitive. . . . I observed the tender and lowly devotion of Thoreau to the African. He now and then drew near to the trembling man, and with a cheerful voice bade him feel at home, and have no fear that any power should again wrong him. The whole day he mounted guard over the fugitive, for it was a slave-hunting time. But the guard had no weapon, and probably there was no such thing in the house. The next day the fugitive was got off to Canada, and I enjoyed my first walk with Thoreau.

In this vignette, brother and sister are collaborators in a project of liberation, and by this time, more than fifteen years after the founding of the Concord Female Anti-Slavery Society, Thoreau was wholeheartedly recruited to the cause. A year later Thoreau wrote, "I endeavor in vain to observe Nature—my thoughts involuntarily go plotting against the state—I trust that all just men will conspire." Many just women already had. And so in my reply to Sims, I said, "Reading that superb piece you sent a month or so ago deepened my sense that his abolitionist mother and sisters were political powerhouses in whose wake he swam. My position now is that the Thoreau women took in the filthy laundry of the whole nation, stained with slavery, and pressured Thoreau and Emerson to hang it out in public, as they obediently did."

This is the washing that really mattered in Concord in the 1840s, the washing that affected not only the prisoners of slavery, but the fate of a nation and the literature of the century. Thoreau's writing helped twentieth-century liberators—Gandhi and King the most famous among them—chart their courses; he helps us chart our own as well, while also helping us measure climate change and giving us the pleasures of his incomparable prose. His cabin at Walden was ten by fifteen feet, less than twice the size of a solitary-confinement cell at California's supermax Pelican Bay State Prison, though being confined to a space and retiring to it whenever you wish are far more different than night and day. In a sense Thoreau is still at work, and so are his sisters, or at least the fruit of Helen and Sophia Thoreau's work to end slavery is still with us, along with their brother's liberatory writings. Though there are other kinds of slavery still waiting to be ended, including much of what happens in our modern prison system.

Continuing my reply to Sims, I wrote,

> Thoreau's relationship to his sisters reminds me a little of mine to my brother, who is a great activist and a great carpenter and builder, a support and ally to me in every possible way, and someone for whom I often cook and sometimes assist in other practical ways. (Though of course in this version the sister is the socially inept writer person and the brother the more engaged activist who leads his sibling into the fray.)

My brother David actually built me a home at one point. In that home in which he sometimes stayed and often ate (and usually did the dishes after he ate), we held political meetings as well as family gatherings. In it, as before and since, I helped him with activist publications, because for almost all our adult life he has been a political organizer who seems to end up volunteering for publications. We've been through three books of his that way, and each of these projects for which I am an informal editor has drawn me deeper into political engagement.

David cares about prisoners and has worked on their behalf many times, most recently Bradley Manning. Sometimes I've joined him. He has often been arrested, spent time in jails from Georgia to Ontario, and is named after our grandfather, who was named after Thomas Davis, the Irish revolutionary and poet. He has provided astute critiques of my writing and ideas, and without him I might have been lost in the clouds, stuck in an ivory tower, or at least less often called into the streets. Though I am the writer, he taught me a word when we were building the home that was mine for a while. The word is *sister*, which is a verb in the construction industry, as in "to sister a beam." This means to set another plank alongside a beam and fasten the two together to create a stronger structure. It is the most fundamental image of the kind of relationship Thoreau had with his sisters and I with my brother: we reinforce each other.

It is what we are here to do, and to raise melons and build houses and write books and to free anyone who might possibly need freeing, including ourselves and the meanings of our lives in all their uncategorizable complexity. By this, I don't mean freedom only in that sense that many Americans sometimes intend it, the sense in which we are free from each other; I mean freed to be with each other and to strengthen each other, as only free people can.

2013

REVOLUTIONARY PLOTS

On Urban Gardening

The anti-war poet and soldier Siegfried Sassoon reports that toward the end of World War I, Winston Churchill told him that war is the normal occupation of man. Challenged, Churchill amended this to "war—and gardening." Are the two opposites? Some agriculture is a form of war, whether it's clear-cutting rainforest, stealing land from the poor, contaminating the vicinity, or exploiting farmworkers, and some of our modern pesticides are descended from chemical warfare breakthroughs for the First World War. But gardening represents a much wider spectrum of human activity than war, and if war is an act of the state, gardening is far, far more ancient than city-states (if not nearly so old as squabbling).

Can it be the antithesis of war, or a cure for social ills, or an act of healing the divisions of the world? When you tend your tomatoes, are you producing more than tomatoes? How much more? Is peace a crop, or justice? The American Friends Service Committee set up a series of garden plots to be tended by people who'd been on opposite sides of the Yugoslavian wars, but a lot of people hope to overcome the wars of our time more indirectly through their own gardening and farming. We are in an era when gardens are front and center for hopes and dreams of a better world or just a better neighborhood or the fertile space where the two become one.

There are farm advocates and food activists, progressive farmers and gardeners, and maybe most particular to this moment, there's a lot of urban agriculture. These city projects hope to overcome alienation from food, from labor, from embodiment, from land; the conflicts between production and consumption, between pleasure and work; the destructiveness of industrial agriculture; the growing problems of global food scarcity and seed loss. The list of ideals being planted and tended and sometimes harvested is endless, but the question is simple. What crops are you tending? What do you hope to grow? Hope? Community? Health? Pleasure? Justice? Gardens represent the idealism of this moment and its principal pitfall, I think. A garden can be, after all, either the ground you stand on to take on the world or how you retreat from it, and the difference is not always obvious.

HOUSING PROJECTS AND CHOKECHERRIES

So many of the projects that end up involving a whole community or school or generating a nonprofit begin with one person with dirty fingernails and big dreams. Antonio Roman-Alcalá, for example, was in his very early twenties when he and a cohort of idealistic young anarchists developed a dream of starting a collective with two bases. One would be urban, the other rural, he told me as we knelt on the slope of Alemany Farm, the three-acre, city-owned plot next to the Alemany housing projects in southern San Francisco, eating ground cherries (which come inside a husk like tomatillos and burst on your tongue like tangy plums). They had decided that the ideal life involved being both urban and rural, not one or the other. The two have often been opposed, their denizens casting each other in hostile stereotypes—the rural hicks and rubes, the corrupt and alienated city people. Of course the country and the city depend on each other like day and night; you might not want to depend on the carbohydrates grown in Manhattan or on the medical technology available in a farm county. And with peregrines and raccoons in major metropolises and the Internet in most American farmhouses, if not in migrant farmworker shacks, the distinctions might not be as stark as they once were.

So the anarchist kids had an integrated vision, and then, thanks to Antonio, they had a next step. His mother's house is right on the border of Alemany Farm, so it was an obvious site—at least to him—to experiment. As we moved on to graze on early mulberries, he told me that Alemany Farm had been run by SLUG, the San Francisco League of Urban Gardeners, until its leadership got embroiled in a corruption scandal and the whole organization that had done so many good things was shut down.

The farm was abandoned and padlocked, though the padlock kept out only people who traveled the official routes. Children never stopped playing on this lush hillside that slopes down to what had once been Islais Creek, flowing east into San Francisco Bay, and is now the branch of Interstate 280 that snakes west from the 101.

Antonio proposed that he and his cohorts try out some guerrilla gardening—unpermitted work on public or government land—to see how they liked farming and working collectively. Only a few of the group came along with him, and the group's visions were never realized. But then the farm itself became a project and a vision, and for several years Antonio served as co-manager with Jason Mark, the editor of *Earth Island Journal*, who showed up several months later.

By this time we were eating the sweet fleshy petals of pineapple guava flowers and admiring the first blooms of pomegranates that, he told me, don't do very well in foggy San Francisco. Guerrilla gardening would've been the easy route, but the farm became official, and what began as an anarchist project has evolved into, among other things, an exercise in cultivating, weeding, and wringing something fruitful out of a bureaucracy designed to protect the city from lawsuits and govern pleasure-ground parks, not to oversee a food-producing landscape run by volunteers. Any vision of a purely autonomous zone involving only Antonio's companions decayed early on, and from that compost grew a project to engage with practically everyone. There is still a fence around Alemany, and a padlock keeps people from actually driving in. It makes the place look closed from the road, but there's an open gate a few steps away and another gate between the housing project and the farm.

As we desultorily ate some superb strawberries planted here and there on the slope—grids are not one of Alemany Farm's strong suits—Antonio told me about their complex relationship with the housing project's denizens, who inhabit a city-run set of bunker-like buildings. The mission statement of Alemany Farm describes it as "a project of the Alemany Resident Management Corporation, a non-profit organization dedicated to improving conditions in the Alemany Community, a 165-unit public housing development beset by high unemployment and recurring violence. The

Alemany Resident Management Corporation believes that we can address the root causes of violence by providing youth with meaningful opportunities for advancement." In practice, this means an informal relationship, but a relationship nonetheless, involving occasional disagreements, open space for kids to play, as well as "You Pick It" free food on Wednesdays for residents who want to show up and glean. Co-manager Jason Mark tells me the immigrant Chinese residents have been the most enthusiastic harvesters, and the farm now grows Asian vegetables such as long beans as part of the relationship.

A thin brown-skinned young man with bright eyes and shaggy hair, Antonio looks a little like Pan, the god of picnics and panics, and a little like a mild young Che Guevara. The farm is hardly the kind of preened and styled model garden that sometimes gets produced by, say, the Slow Food Festival in front of San Francisco City Hall, or by the architecture firm Work at PS1 in Queens, New York, gardens that are inspiring works of art but hardly viable economic models. At Alemany, there are some native plants on the slopes, some mixed grasses, a scattering of willows and mature fruit trees like the mulberry, many more young trees, and ledges of plantings, along with a few beehives, a wetland pond full of cattails, and a windmill that never pumped anything but does say *farm* pretty well.

Down below in the flatlands there are actual rows of vegetables, rows of garlic with a polite sign to please not poach the plants before the garlic is mature, as well as a little amphitheater for the classes that come. They come in droves. More than fifty school field trips and other groups visit annually. Among the crops the farm produces is education in this second densest major metropolitan area in the United States. The schoolchildren get to do what we were doing—eat food right off the vine or stem or branch, see compost and think about systems from the hyperlocal one producing whatever they've just tasted to the big systems producing the food they more routinely see, and sometimes even do a little work. Alemany Farm's principal crop is connection, though they raise plenty of food too. About 5,000 pounds a year, estimates Jason Mark, but that's an informal estimate. While the farm may be funky, it is productive in a lot of ways that can't be put on a scale to weigh.

PRINCIPAL CROPS

The second green revolution is an attempt to undo the destructive aspects of the first one, to make an organic and intimate agriculture that feeds minds and hearts as well as bodies, that measures intangible qualities as well as quantity. By volume, it produces only a small percentage of this country's food, but of course, its logic isn't merely volume. The first green revolution may have increased yield in many cases, but it also increased alienation and toxicity, and it was efficient only if you ignored its fossil fuel dependency, carbon output, and other environmental impacts. It was an industrial revolution for agriculture, and what might be happening now is distinctly postindustrial, suspicious of the big and the corporate, interested in the old ways and the alternatives. This is more than a production project; it's a reconnection project, which is why it is also an urban one: if we should all be connected to food production, food production should happen everywhere—urban and rural and in every topsoil-laden crevice and traffic island in between.

Today, major urban agriculture projects are firmly rooted in Burlington, Philadelphia, Detroit, Milwaukee, Chicago, Oakland, Los Angeles, San Francisco, and dozens of other American cities. Sales of vegetable seeds have skyrocketed across the country. Backyard chickens have become a new norm, and schoolyard gardens have sprung up across the nation and beyond since Alice Waters began Berkeley's Edible Schoolyard Project almost two decades ago. Organic farms and farmers' markets have proliferated, and for the first time in many decades the number of farmers is going up instead of down. Though those things can be counted, the transformation of awareness that both produces and is produced by all these things is incalculable.

We think more about food, know more about food, care more about food than we did twenty or thirty years ago. Food has become both an upscale fetish (those menus that overinform you about what farm your heirloom ham or parsnips came from) and a poor people's radical agenda, a transformation of the most intimate everyday practices that cuts across class—though it has yet to include all of us. In 1969, the Black Panthers ran breakfast programs to feed hungry inner-city children, and those children—or rather the children and grandchildren of those children—are still hungry, and the inner city is still a food desert: a place where access to decent food, or even to food, is not a given. But farming has come to the 'hood. And everywhere else.

Food is now a means by which a lot of people think about economics, scale, justice, pleasure, embodiment, work, health, the future. Gardens can be the territory for staking out the possibility of a better and different way of living, working, eating, and relating to the world, though by *gardens* we nowadays mostly mean food-producing gardens, gardens that verge on farms, or small farms that verge on gardens. Projects like Fritz Haeg's Edible Estates anti-lawn campaign and Michelle Obama's breaking ground for an organic vegetable garden on the White House lawn a couple of years ago make it clear a movement is under way. You can tell that it matters, because the Obama organic garden prompted the executive director of the Mid America CropLife Association to write to its members, "The thought of it being organic made Janet Braun, CropLife Ambassador Coordinator and I shudder. As a result, we sent a letter encouraging them to consider using crop protection products."

The rise of chickens, bees, and other agrarian phenomena in the city means that cities are now trying to craft ordinances to govern all aspects of food production, from backyard chickens and goats to the slaughter of animals raised for food. In Minneapolis plastic hoop houses—greenhouse-like incubators for vegetables—have come up for consideration, though some think of them as an eyesore, while others consider them useful occupants of vacant lots. Part of what is at stake is redefining the urban environment: do we want to see food produced? There are beautiful gardens; there's also compost, manure, and other less decorative aspects, including butchery for those who've gone for animal husbandry as well as vegetable production.

UP FROM THE SEVENTIES

The back-to-the-land movement of the 1970s generated a lot of scary stories about drugged-out communards eating roadkill and going on food stamps and generally failing at alternatives. But the era produced quieter successes, notably the seeds of the food revolution that are still with us—the rise of organic producers, markets, and consumers and the beginning of a new kind of attention to food. Some of it is still going: San Francisco Zen Center acquired the 115 mostly wild acres of Green Gulch Farm in 1972, and it's still an exemplary several-acre organic farm seventeen miles from the city. Those rows of lettuces and beets and chard supply a lot of the produce for its three Buddhist centers and the Greens Restaurant (itself the first gourmet vegetarian restaurant of note, a key part of the food revolution, and the place where cookbook author Deborah Madison got her start). Some of the excess is sold at farmers' markets. What might have been innovative about Zen Center then is that it established centers in urban, rural, and wilderness settings, seeing the three as complementary rather than contradictory.

Nowadays, though a surprising number of young idealists take on the grueling work of running an organic farm in the country, there is no longer such a strong sense of separation, and urban agriculture is what might be newest about this new green revolution. (Maybe farmers' markets helped bridge the divide.) Urban means that it stays small, for the most part, and that it engages with what cities have, both good and bad. That means, among other things, hunger, health issues, race, poverty, and alienation, as well as diverse cultures, lively engagements, and cross-pollinations. Places like the once and possibly future South Central Farm in Los Angeles—at fourteen acres, once the largest of the urban farms—flourish from the skill and energy of immigrants with agrarian backgrounds.

In my region, the San Francisco Bay Area, the new models have proliferated. In 1992 Catherine Sneed and now-retired Sheriff Mike Hennessey started to take prisoners from the San Francisco County Jail outside to work the arable land there. A huge success, both in providing a calm and positive experience for inmates often suffering from trauma and addiction, and in training them for jobs outside, the Garden Project continues twenty years later. I have been to the big greenhouses, which are something any university or model farm would be proud of. The superb produce grown by inmate labor goes to senior centers, needy families, and others in the community. And Berkeley's Edible Schoolyard Project, founded in 1995 to give kids a hands-on relationship to raising and eating good food, is still going, and has inspired countless spinoffs and emulations around the globe.

In 2001 a young woman who'd grown up in the Bay Area's agrarian Sonoma County decided that the abundance of vacant lots and the dearth of decent food sources in impoverished, isolated West Oakland had a clear solution. Willow Rosenthal started City Slicker Farms there, a thriving project that is in some ways the opposite of Alemany Farm. The latter started with land and figured out how to work with people. The former started with people. Though they farm several leftover and abandoned parcels of land in the neighborhood, their most impressive achievement is setting up locals to become backyard gardeners. They provide soil testing and the skills and materials to get started, share labor at the outset, and maintain relationships with the backyard gardeners. In theory, the small nonprofit could vanish tomorrow and the food would keep growing.

The public patches of land are where interns and volunteers work, where neighbors come by to chat and check out the chickens or the beets, and some of the land has even been set up to create hangout places. The public sites produced more than 9,000 pounds of food in 2011, but as Executive Director Barbara Finnin pointed out to me, the backyards produced more than 23,000 pounds. It's not feeding the community—they estimate they're producing 4 percent of the food—but it's modeling the ways such a project could scale up to become a major source of food and a transformation of place.

City Slicker's staff estimates that it would take seventy-seven acres—3 percent of West Oakland—to grow 40 percent of the fruits and vegetables consumed in West Oakland. They're nowhere near that now, but maybe you can see there from here. I asked Joseph Davis, City Slicker's farm manager, how he feels about the big goals and big ideas. He was pulling up fava beans they'd planted as a cover crop in a triangular lot, which was also more or less a grand traffic island, and directing an intern on how to plant lettuce seeds. He gestured with a gloved hand and said, "That's like the sky." It's far away, not the terrain he works directly, but omnipresent, he seemed to mean, and he kept on pulling and planting.

Finnin took me onward to see a neighbor's big chicken paddock and then the corner lot where City Slicker's own chickens reside. It was once a ground crops farmlet, but the kind neighbor who let them pipe in her water was foreclosed upon, and without a good water source they've shifted to a less water-intensive orchard and hen run. Several people, mostly older men, all African American, were sitting on benches that had been built as part of the farm, and they greeted Barbara and me warmly, and she greeted some of them back by name. These odd fragments, corners of leftover and neglected land, are part of what City Slickers Farms has, but the organization also has big dreams and realistic possibilities.

The food is great, the community relations seem to be thriving, and yet the project faces the same problem so many people in the neighborhood do: money. They have to raise it, there's never enough, and there's no self-sufficiency in sight for the staff of seven and the public farms, whose food is sold at farm stands on a sliding scale from free to full price. Since they're farming community and skills and hope as much as lettuce, there's no way to put a price on what they produce.

Some projects have been ephemeral, such as Futurefarmers' San Francisco Victory Gardens project, which supports "the transition of backyard, front yard, window boxes, rooftops, and unused land into food production areas." But the revival of the memory of World War II's extensive agrarian achievement alone—Futurefarmers' website points out that by 1943, 20 million victory gardens were producing 8 million tons of food—matters. Then there are the small and fly-by-night projects, like the San Francisco Guerrilla Grafters, who graft fruit-bearing branches onto the ornamental pears, plums, and cherries on city streets. This is just a sampling of the plethora of community and school gardens and other manifestations of the new urban agriculture in one region.

The achievements of the 1970s food revolution are still present in many ways, including a hugely increased array of produce and such supermarket items as tofu, granola, and organic anything and everything, multiplied by the rise of cage-free eggs and organic milk in the 1990s and the migration of integrated pest-management techniques from organic to other farms. San Francisco destroyed its old downtown produce district (the key site in the great noir movie *Thieves' Highway*) to make room for high-rise office and residence towers—but kept its big farmers' market (founded in 1943) on Alemany Boulevard, a short walk from Alemany Farm. Since the 1980s, farmers' markets have proliferated here, as elsewhere, and there are now two other large ones in San Francisco and dozens of smaller ones.

You might say that the Bay Area has so many of these things because it's the Bay Area, and it's true that the area is exceptionally affluent, good at innovation, and obsessed with food, but that very affluence makes access to land in and near urban areas difficult. Places like Philadelphia and, most famously, Detroit have the opposite situation: a fairly dire economy but lots of available land to cultivate. In 2006, when I went to look at Detroit's post-ruin landscape of agriculture and weedy nature, I was amazed that the city even then had forty square miles of abandoned open space—places where the concrete or asphalt was mostly gone, along with the buildings. That hole was being filled in a little with community gardens, small farms, and abundant volunteer plants in the empty quarters. The place was in some profound sense post-urban. It had the space to do what West Oakland's farmers dream of: grow a lot of its own food.

Detroit without money and jobs looks like the future that may well eventually arrive for the rest of us, and its experiments in urban agriculture were not the pleasure gardens, elegant laboratories, or educational centers that many urban gardens are now, but attempts to figure out how to survive. Much of the gardening that is now often educational or idealistic may soon come to meet practical needs in the United States, and given the rising levels of hunger in this country, it's necessary now. In Detroit, a significant number of people get meaningful amounts of their annual diet from gardens. Clearly there is room to increase this informal do-it-yourself food supply. And as our economy continues to produce unemployed young people, nonwage economies and nonwage productivity will become important new arenas for growth.

The victory gardens model suggests how prolific backyard and urban gardeners can be and how, scaled up, they can become major contributors to feeding a country and to food security. A recent study by Sharanbir Grewal and Parwinder Grewal of Ohio State University envisioned what it would look like for Cleveland—another Rust Belt city with lots of potential green space and lots of hungry people—to feed itself. In the most modest scenario, using 80 percent of every vacant lot generated 22 to 48 percent of the city's fruits and vegetables, along with 25 percent of its poultry and eggs and 100 percent of its honey. The most ambitious proposal also included 62 percent of every commercial and industrial roof and 9 percent of every occupied residential lot: it could provide up to 100 percent of the city's fresh produce, along with 94 percent of its poultry and eggs (and 100 percent of its honey again). It would keep up to $115 million in food dollars in the city, a huge boon to a depressed region. It would also improve health, both through diet and through exercise.

Clearly what might work in Detroit or Cleveland or Oakland is not so viable in superheated Phoenix or subarctic Anchorage. And then climate change can upset these enterprises as much as it can any agriculture: last year the Intervale Community Farm in Burlington, Vermont, at 120 acres the biggest urban agriculture project in the country, was devastated by torrential rain that washed out soil as well as plants. Spring deluges interfered with planting; Hurricane Irene did in many of the fall crops. The organization's newsletter emphasizes that the summer season still produced a bounty of tomatoes, melons, and salad greens.

In an increasingly uncertain time, what is certain is that agriculture has invaded cities the way that cities have been invading agriculture for the past many millennia, that the reasons for this are as manifold as the results, and that the peculiar postwar affluence is over for most of us, and everything is going to become a little more precarious and a little less abundant. Given these circumstances, urban agriculture has a big future. Or several big futures, depending on the soil and the needs. Another lesson from the victory gardens is that with seeds and sweat equity, a lot can happen quickly: if the need to grow food arises, as it did during the Second World War, the gardens will come.

ATTACKS AND RETREATS

You can argue that vegetable seeds are the seeds of the new revolution. But the garden is an uneasy entity for our time, a way both to address the biggest questions and to duck them. "Some gardens are described as retreats, when they are really attacks," famously said the gardener, artist, and provocateur Ian Hamilton Finlay. A garden as a retreat means a refuge, a place to withdraw from the world. A garden as an attack means an intervention in the world, a political statement, a way in which the small space of the garden can participate in the larger space that is society, politics, and ideas. Every garden negotiates its own relationship between retreat and attack, and in so doing illuminates—or maybe we should say *engages*—the political questions of our time.

At its worst, the new agrarianism is a way to duck the obligation to change the world, a failure to engage with what is worst as well as best. In the ambiguously cynical end of Voltaire's novel *Candide*, he concludes, "Il faut cultiver notre jardin" (we must cultivate our garden), which suggests that the garden can be a small piece of the world we can manage and order after giving up on the larger world. Certainly neoliberalism has been about destroying the public, privatizing the common, and taking care of yourself.

But you can't have a revolution where everyone just abandons the existing system—it'll just be left to the opportunists and the uncritical. Tending your own garden does not, for example, confront the problem of Monsanto. The corporation that developed genetically modified organisms as a way to promote its pesticides and is trying to control seed stock worldwide is a scourge. Planting heirloom seeds is great, but someone has to try to stop Monsanto, and that involves political organizing, sticking your neck out, and confrontation. It involves leaving your garden. Which farmers have done—some years back, the wheat farmers of North Dakota defeated Monsanto's plans to introduce GMO wheat worldwide. But they didn't do it by planting heirloom organic wheat or talking to schoolkids about what constitutes beautiful bread or by baking. They did it by organizing, by collective power, and by political engagement. The biggest problem of our time requires big cooperative international transformations that cannot be reached one rutabaga patch at a time.

The fact that gardens have become the revolution of the young is good news and bad news. Baby boomers of the Sixties revolutionary variety had their hectoring bombastic arrogant self-righteous flaws, but they were fearless about engagement. The young I often meet today have so distanced themselves from the flaws of the baby boomers that they've gone too far in the opposite direction of mildness, modesty, disengagement, and nonconfrontation. (At a recent conference on the Occupy movement, two youngish people in the audience suggested that the slogan "We are the 99%" might hurt the feelings of the 1%; they wanted a polite revolution that wasn't exactly against anything and offended no one, which is a nice way to be totally ineffectual.) The garden suits them perfectly because it is a realm of quiet idealism—but that too readily slides over into disengagement or the belief that your activism can stop with the demonstration of your own purity and lack of culpability.

Feeding the hungry is noble work, but figuring out the causes of that hunger and confronting them and transforming them directly needs to be done too. And while urban agriculture seems like a flexible, local way to adapt to the hungry, chaotic world that climate change is bringing, we all need to address the root causes directly. Maybe there's something in the fact that the word *radical* comes from the Latin for "root"; the revolutionary gardener will get at the root causes of our situation, not just cultivate the surface.

Churchill cast gardening and war as opposites because he saw gardening as a retreat into a peaceful private realm. Our age demands engagement. Gardens like Alemany Farm and City Slicker Farms produce it as one of their crops, while other gardens and food fetishism generally can be a retreat into privilege, safety, and pleasure away from the world and its problems. But gardening and all its subsidiary tasks are sturdy metaphors. You can imagine the whole world as a garden, in which case you might want to weed out corporations, compost old divides, and plant hope, subversion, and fierce commitments among the heirloom tomatoes and the chard. The main questions will always be: What are your principal crops? And who do they feed?

2012

THE VISIBILITY WARS

I: WAR

Almost twenty years ago, a group of Nevadans took me with them into the center of their state, across hundreds of miles of rough, remote, little-known country. In all that distance we saw a few small settlements and occasionally a grove of cottonwoods marking a ranch house at one side or another of the long north–south sagebrush valleys. We had begun at the Nevada Test Site, an expanse the size of Rhode Island where for forty years most of the nation's nuclear bombs were "tested." More than a thousand bombs were detonated at the site in those years. There was no physical difference between a nuclear test and a deployment of a bomb in war except the site chosen; and so you can argue that a long quiet war was waged against the land and people of the deep desert, one that resulted in considerable contamination (and the suppression or dismissal of that fact before it was forgotten).

We skirted Nellis Air Force Base, a military site the size of Belgium or Connecticut, which contained the Nevada Test Site, and ended up at another site that had once been a Pony Express station and then become a one-time nuclear test site. The actual crater from the explosion of that atomic bomb was not far from where we camped that night. Fallon Naval Air Station, another vast base, was not far to the north, and Hawthorne was to the northwest, the premier ammunition storage site in the nation, full of earthen berms loaded with explosives. Along the way, the Nevadans explained what we were seeing, and not seeing, and a new world opened to me, or rather the world I had been living in all along began to look very different. A large portion of Nevada was given over to the military, and civilian mapmakers often left these sites off their maps, producing instead the blank spots of which radical geographer and artist Trevor Paglen writes (in his book *Blank Spots on the Map: The Dark Geography of the Pentagon's Secret World*). Other spots were blank because they were still nominally public lands or land illegally withdrawn from the public.

I traveled again in the area around Fallon Naval Air Station in the late 1990s with a local activist. We were in a beautiful green oasis, Dixie Valley, still home to a lot of migratory birds, though its human population had been driven out by naval aircraft testing sonic booms there, shattering windows, stampeding livestock, and generally making the area uninhabitable. The people of Dixie Valley fought back before their ranches and homes were condemned by eminent domain. Only ruins remained, and some contaminated tanks had been hauled in to use for target practice. My friend who'd fought alongside the former residents of the valley told me how her political career began in that same landscape: a military plane flew so low, for fun apparently, that it forced her car off the road. She had two small children in the car. "And that," she told me with fierce satisfaction, "was when the Pentagon made its first mistake." She fought well for many years, founding an organization that defended the rural victims of militarism.

That day in Dixie Valley, we were buzzed by a warplane that seemingly appeared from nowhere, as though it had ripped open the sky, and then roared low over us with a sound so loud and visceral the term *sound* hardly describes how it invaded my body and the air around. It then vanished again, as though into a hole in the sky, moving astonishingly fast out of the range of the visible in the blue, blue desert sky. By then I had come to understand that in some sense the United States was perpetually at war—and that war was a pervasive process, a mind-set—in a lot of places at home and abroad, and in some sense every place on earth up into the outer atmosphere and to some extent outer space. So pervasive that it is largely unseen, even beyond the vast realm of military secrecy that Paglen documents so powerfully.

Carl von Clausewitz, in his famous book *On War*, defined it thus: "War therefore is an act of violence to compel our opponent to fulfill our will. Violence arms itself with the inventions of Art and Science in order to contend against violence." That is, it contends against others' violence, not against violence itself, the latter being a task at which violence is helpless. Asked what war is, most people would answer that it was a type of activity. A peculiar kind in which human beings as proxy for nation-states try to kill each other, the theory being the side that inflicts overwhelming or unbearable damage wins. Of course modern warfare involves huge quantities of civilian casualties, and the killing is done by increasingly remote means.

Spears, catapults, arrows; then guns, cannons, and bombs; and in the twentieth century, airplanes and then missiles; and in the twenty-first century, unmanned drones make the site of the killers increasingly removed from the site of the killed. Intercontinental ballistic missiles completed the transformation from, say, Gettysburg, where men killed each other at close range with screams and gore around them, to a system in which technicians in control rooms could wipe out civilians en masse on other continents. Drones in Afghanistan are now operated by men at a base near Las Vegas engaged in an activity that must be hard for them to differentiate from a video game, so removed is the violence when armed with these inventions of art and science. If the killer is in an air-conditioned room in Indian Springs, Nevada, and the killed are in a village in Afghanistan, the question of where the battlefield is arises and with it the possibility that battlefields are now anywhere, or everywhere. The drones seem to have a propensity for wiping out wedding parties in Iraq and Afghanistan. It's a photographic problem in part; the poor image quality results in poor judgment about what is a band of armed men and what is a family celebration.

We still tend to think of war as an activity, and an activity confined to a place, to the battlefield. The idea of the battlefield is still sometimes relevant, especially if you're willing to recognize whole regions—much of Iraq, the Congo, and so forth—as battlefields of sorts, more violent and dangerous than elsewhere. Perhaps it would be better to regard war as akin to wildfire or contagious disease that may flare up anywhere in the affected region, though human beings and their weapons are in this case the pathogens or sparks. The kind of violent acts Clausewitz discusses are enabled by other acts committed far from the site of battle. Research, development, and mass manufacture of the technologies of killing and the supporting equipment have become the very core of pork-barrel funding spread around the country so that almost every federal representative has a stake in continuing them. All this has an afterlife as well, as contaminated places and equipment, or shrapnel, or live ordnance in land that has returned to other uses, and as veterans, with all the damage, physical and psychological, veterans are prone to. There is a landscape of war, and it includes munitions factories, mines, ships, barracks, bases, recruiting centers, and afterward veterans' hospitals. When the United States declared its war on terror, signs of it were intentionally planted everywhere, in the form of men with guns whose camouflage uniforms did the opposite of making them blend in to Penn Station or the Golden Gate Bridge. They were signs of what we had become.

To say that battlefields are everywhere is to say that war is a miasma, a condition in which nations live, notably ours, which has several hundred bases around the world, in sixty-three countries, on every continent but Antarctica, and spends nearly as much on its military as all other nations put together. This condition—of pervasive war on a global scale—is invisible to most Americans, as is the imperial oddness of the premise that the United States may and must intervene globally. Reversing the situation to ask whether Korea or Kuwait should have military bases in the United States, or to imagine Cuba running an outlaw gulag in Florida, makes the uniqueness of the situation clear. An online article by geographer Jules Dufour, president of the United Nations Association of Canada, put it thus: "The surface of the earth is structured as a wide battlefield." He added, "The U.S. tends to view the Earth surface as a vast territory to conquer, occupy and exploit. The fact that the U.S. Military splits the World up into geographic command units vividly illustrates this underlying geopolitical reality." That is, shortly after 9/11 the Bush administration divided the world into USNORTHCOM, USAFRICOM, and so forth. Nothing was left out. And everything was under one command or another. It is all battlefield now, at least in concept and designation, every place on earth overseen by one military command or another, with implicit permission to act there, and potential for violence anywhere. The militarization of outer space is another arena few recognize. Paglen tells me that the next arena for a U.S. military command is virtual space, though whether WEBCOM or FIBERCOM, or whatever it is to be called, will be a new branch of the military or a new department or departments in existing branches remains to be determined. In that territory, the battles, the exposures, and the secrecies will be purely about information, which has always been part of war's arsenal, never more than now.

War is a series of landscapes, from the manufacturing, testing, training, and storage sites to the battlefields and hospitals—and cemeteries. Cemeteries for the official casualties of war, as well as those who died of contamination from some of its products, or from the violence it generates outside its official battlefields, or of the deformed financial landscape of a war economy. If there is a warscape, there is also a war economy, and it's worth noting that when the economy collapsed in 2008, all sorts of cuts were proposed and many made to the federal budget, but despite the fact that the military was half that budget, a serious cutback was never broached in the mainstream. In 2009, Congressman Barney Frank remarked in the wake of that crisis and the widespread claims that we could not afford universal health care, "It is particularly inexplicable that so many self-styled moderates ignore the extraordinary increase in military spending. After all, George W. Bush himself has acknowledged its importance. As the December 20 *Wall Street Journal* notes, 'The president remains adamant his budget troubles were the result of a ramp-up in defense spending.'" People who were aghast at the idea of a $700 billion bailout hardly noted that the sum was only slightly larger than the annual military budget; universal health care was made to sound unaffordable by describing it as a trillion-dollar program, though that was the cost over a decade, with substantial benefits, and no one was saying that by such measures, a $6 or $7 trillion military budget was a burden, let alone an outrage.

There are other kinds of absence: the absence of funding for a host of other concerns, all of them constructive in opposition to war's destructiveness, but our country has remained on a war footing since the Second World War began, ducking the "peace dividend" that was supposed to appear after the dissolution of the Soviet Union. Essentially Americans are told that they cannot have health care, or decent education, or a well-cared-for infrastructure and environment because defense comes first and takes all. If war is an act of violence to compel others to do our will, you can speculate on how the American people have been essentially subjugated by the war economy to keep paying for it, the way that Germany paid reparations after its defeats, the way that subject nations and colonies pay tribute to their masters. In this sense, we civilians are a conquered colony of an imperial war mission; this is the other war, the war within our society, the one we have so far largely lost, though the battle is ongoing. If it were visible the outcome could be different. And secrecy and invisibility are at the heart of modern warfare. William James imagined a war against war; if it is being fought today, it is fought in part by making the invisible visible. War is a stain that has sunk so deeply into the fabric of our society that it is now its ordinary coloring; we now live in war as a fish lives in water. Ours is a society of war, and a society at war with itself. This is so pervasive and so accepted that it is invisible. And its invisibility is a shield seldom ruptured. But it is ruptured here.

II: VISIBILITY

There are many kinds of invisibility. There is the invisibility of what is so taken for granted that few see it, the custom of the country, the water in which the fish swim. Thus to perceive that the United States is an empire on a permanent wartime basis is to be alien to, or become alienated from, the mainstream. There is the invisibility of what is literally out of sight on remote military bases and in weapons laboratories—and kept out of public scrutiny. There is the less geographical invisibility that is the secretive workings of the military and the related work of the Central Intelligence Agency—and here the word *intelligence* means covert information in a military context, as in "we have intelligence on the secret weapons labs." That is, you can see the Pentagon, the massive building near the nation's capitol, but you may not see much of what the Pentagon, the military, does. The unseen is itself a vast realm, the black budget of the Pentagon and the "black sites" Paglan documents. Most people don't make much effort to know about this realm, and the knowledge that emerges is quickly forgotten or dismissed. "We are a peaceful nation" is a popular thing to say in the United States. Those who might say this have been denied the intelligence to know what is done in their name and to decide democratically whether it should be done. Or they have ducked it. The blank spots on the map that Paglan writes about have their corollary in the blank spots in the mind and in public dialogue. We do not debate developing new systems of killing, the militarization of space, the cost of our military budget; and most of us know little or nothing about the programs in question. Then there is the invisibility of what is literally hard or impossible to see. This includes planes, space, shuttles, satellites, and drones above the earth, as well as forces—radioactive, biological, chemical—that are not visible to the naked eye.

Photography has made visible each kind of invisibility described here. A project like *The Americans* by émigré artist Robert Frank portrays the country in ways that it might not see itself, or wish to; artists are, at their best, honorary aliens seeing the familiar through strange eyes and the unseen in plain view. What is literally out of sight has been depicted many ways—Richard Misrach's photographs of remote and off-limits military sites in the 1980s and 1990s (including the Enola Gay hangar in Utah and the Bravo 20 Bombing Range in Nevada) did so spectacularly. Systems are hard to photograph, but consequences are not, and wartime atrocity photographs are one means by which the workings of the military have been made visible. Finally, warfare itself has become increasingly technological, full of extra-human perception, with its infrared night-vision goggles, its sonar and radar, its spy satellites and encoded data. At least some of this can be made visible—notably the satellites Paglan has captured in his series "The Other Night Sky." To see and to make visible is itself often a protracted process of education, research, investigation, and often trespassing and law breaking, a counter-spying on the intelligence complex.

Invisibility is in military terms a shield, and to breach secrecy is to make vulnerable as well as visible. Invisibility grants advantage over enemies unable to predict your actions or counterattack; it protects exclusive knowledge and technology; and it sets its actions and modes of operating out of reach of criticism and dissent. Invisibility and secrecy have been more than a strategy or a mode of operation for the military and the CIA for the past six decades; they have been its essence. Daniel Ellsberg titled his memoir about making public the Pentagon Papers—the documents revealing presidential duplicity and disregard for democratic process and human life in the war on Vietnam—*Secrets*. He expected to spend the rest of his life in prison for revealing them. The revelation of secrets is sometimes considered treason—Ethel and Julius Rosenberg were executed in 1953 for sharing atomic-weapons secrets—and sometimes does provide practical aid to the enemy. Often disclosure instead provides disturbing truths to the civilians the military is supposed to serve. Perhaps the most common disclosure is that the military violates our most fundamental values in the course of what is usually claimed to be defending those values. Civilians who oppose the military are often seen as traitors. The United States as a nation is officially a democracy, but as an empire it is no such thing. Since the 1950s, government agencies have routinely spied upon, harassed, attacked, and imprisoned domestic dissenters and antiwar activists. Far worse sometimes awaits dissidents abroad. When such action becomes visible, legislators sometimes denounce and rein it in, but these are temporary fixes. Democracy depends on public participation, which itself depends on visibility. Invisibility is thereby undemocratic.

There is another kind of invisibility with another status: that of unseen crimes, suffering, and death. If invisibility protects perpetrators, visibility protects victims, so much so that much humanitarian and antiwar effort has focused on witness and visibility. A group called Witness for Peace took Americans to Central America during the bloody civil wars there to stand with civilians and prevent, or at least witness, the crimes against them to make the violent accountable. Photographic theory of the 1980s often proposed that the camera was indeed like a gun, that to photograph was to shoot or otherwise violate the subject. Susan Sontag took this stance when she suggested in her classic *On Photography* that we will become overexposed to horror and thereby inured to it. There is considerable, but far from comprehensive, truth to this position. Sontag herself modified it in *Regarding the Pain of Others,* in which she critiqued Virginia Woolf's reflections, in *Three Guineas,* on pictures of war atrocities. She is still suspicious of our looking: "Perhaps the only people with the right to look at images of suffering of this extreme order are those who could do something to alleviate it—say the surgeons at the military hospital where the photograph was taken—or those who could learn from it. The rest of us are voyeurs, whether or not we mean to be." But we too, when it is our money and our military, could try to alleviate suffering, if not that of the depicted sufferer, at least by preventing future such inflictions; we could withdraw the money or the machinery of violence. And we could learn from it existential lessons about compassion and practical lessons about our tax dollars at work. It is for this reason that militaries and the regimes they serve desire secrecy and invisibility.

There is more to Sontag's argument. Such photographs could be used and have been used, she reflects, to denounce war altogether, but they could also be used to advocate for supporting one side against the other. That is, to argue that war itself is not criminal, but the enemy is: you can just as readily say that this atrocity is the evidence of the barbarism of your opponents as the barbarism of war, and almost every nation makes visible the enemy's inhumanities and hides its own. Photographs are manipulable and they can be used to these ends. Still, Sontag advocates for making visible. She argues against the positions that "the appetite for such images is a vulgar or low appetite," that we are all inured to what we see on television, the position that derides "the efforts of those who have borne witness in war zones as 'war tourism.'" In the end she mourns a lack of imagination and empathy that pictures may not amend.

Sontag's subject is pictures. Pictures may serve or fail to serve justice and humanity. There is another subject, namely the lack of pictures. The war in Iraq was fought at home as an exemplary war of propaganda, and the best counter-weapons were photographs. A nondescript spy-satellite photograph of an installation in Iraq was used in the United States and Britain to buttress claims that the country had "weapons of mass destruction," a term that entered the media then and that seemed to carry an ominous weight that would have been dispelled by pointing out that nearly every country owns such weapons. At key moments, more iconic images were made visible as propaganda: President Bush on the flight deck of an aircraft carrier in front of a "Mission Accomplished" banner a few months into the war that had years more to run; an incident in which the occupying army in Baghdad pulled down an enormous statue of Saddam Hussein; the capture of a shaggy, feral-looking Hussein in a pit near Tikrit, Iraq. Far more images were suppressed, for to see the war was to see its monstrosity, the death, pain, bodily destruction, waste, and mess at its heart, the horror that is denied by all the hero-welcoming rites of the culture. (Native American cultures, a friend tells me, often instead treat the returning soldier as someone who needs to be ritually cleansed, acknowledging the dirtiness of war.) This is true of most wars, perhaps more true of modern ones with their preponderance of civilian casualties. The U.S. press obligingly avoided horrific and even difficult images that were widely seen elsewhere in the world, creating a parallel universe in which those maimed children, those bloody streets, and body fragments did not exist.

In one landmark incident during the week of the second inauguration of G. W. Bush, American soldiers killed a father and mother at a checkpoint, leaving their five children instantly orphaned as well as bloodied inside the family car. The sequence of images captured by photographer Chris Hondros was widely seen in Europe, and a U.S. general in Qatar reportedly demanded the television station Al Jazeera stop showing them, but few Americans saw them. Photographs of the coffins of dead soldiers were not permitted throughout the war, though Russ Kick of the website *The Memory Hole* obtained several through Freedom of Information Act requests and released them in April of 2004. When news anchor Ted Koppel commemorated the dead by showing their faces and reciting their names, he too was denounced as unpatriotic; patriotism consisted of voluntarily renouncing intelligence of all kinds, even unclassified intelligence. Most dramatically of all, photographs taken by the torturers themselves of torture at Abu Ghraib Prison near Baghdad launched one of the biggest scandals of the war when they were leaked to the media and journalists such as Seymour Hersh made something of them—one of the few proud moments in a fairly shameful era for the news. Photojournalists were making compelling and even revelatory pictures, but the media were mediating | *307* between them and the pacified public.

At the start of the war on Iraq, then–Secretary of Defense Donald

Rumsfeld famously proposed, "There are known knowns. These are things we know that we know. There are known unknowns. That is to say, there are things that we know we don't know. But there are also unknown unknowns. There are things we don't know we don't know." It was a weirdly interesting statement from an ordinarily thoughtless man. The philosopher Slavoj Žižek added a fourth category for him: "the 'unknown knowns,' things we don't know that we know, which is precisely the Freudian unconscious, the 'knowledge which doesn't know itself,'" as [psychoanalyst Jacques] Lacan used to say." You could translate that into visual terms. There are the things we know we see. There are the things we know we do not see. Then there are the things we do not know we do not see. And finally, there are the things in plain sight we choose not to see, or repress. Walter Benjamin referred to photography as the "optical unconscious," and that's one way to describe this fourth category.

Photography and visibility have a tangled history. The 1838 picture by Louis-Jacques-Mandé Daguerre often hailed as the first photograph depicts in sharp detail a Parisian boulevard on which a lone figure is visible, or rather his legs are, because he stood still while his shoes were shined. The shoe shiner is a blur at his feet, and his upper body and head are also dissolved into the atmosphere that is time itself. The rest of the people are invisible, because they were in motion and the exposure was slow. The photograph is usually described as failing to show the people who were on the boulevard. It could also described as a different way of seeing—the image saw through the people present to perceive all the hard still surfaces, a little reminiscent of the neutron bomb that would annihilate people but leave structures and infrastructure intact. The first photograph is a bomb of vision, showing us the world as we do not see it, and it is handily emblematic that it scraped human beings from the view. Photography has ever since represented various kinds of visibility and invisibility. The blue-sensitive films of the wet-plate era turned blue and cloudy skies into milk-white expanses, unless you exposed separately for the sky and the ground—as many did, and some, such as Eadweard Muybridge, added clouds from other negatives; photography was also manipulated from the start. The slowness of vision was another way the camera saw differently than the eye—water became filmy white stuff, and anything in motion blurred—until Muybridge's 1870s breakthroughs that turned photography into a medium faster than the human eye could see, and another world of the real motion of horses' legs, women's gestures, water's splashes and spills opened up.

The snapshot was originally a term for guns—for pulling up your gun suddenly to take a shot—and cameras were only thought of in terms of guns when they became light and fast. Shooting was never more than a metaphor. Paglen points out, though, that Muybridge's sequential motion studies led to Harold Edgerton's stroboscopic photographs of super-fast motion, which led both to his photography of the first atomic explosion and to his work on triggers for such bombs. Knowledge is power, and visual knowledge is one variety of it, but information rarely otherwise crosses over into action in such an extraordinary way. X-rays provided a look inside the human body, and telescopic and microscopic photography allowed us not only to see into scales and distances otherwise off-limits to the human eye but also record those images permanently. Infrared film provided another version of the world, and in recent decades a whole range of technologies, from CAT scans to probes inserted into the body, have appeared. Satellites show what a human eye might see if the human body were capable of sustaining itself in endless whirling orbit around the earth, but show it with a degree of detail at distance the human eye does not have. For a long time, the "photographic world" chose to deal largely with art photography, but in recent years the whole panoply of mechanical image-making technologies have come under scrutiny, the imagistic regime under which we now live.

Photographs are mute. The drab satellite image of Iraq that was used to insist the place was making forbidden weapons was almost meaningless without the language that contextualized and explained it, truthfully or not. The incomprehensible is another kind of invisibility. Where most of us see nothing or see meaningless signs, doctors see symptoms, or trainers and fellow athletes see aptitude, or detectives see tiny signs giving away insincerity and anxiety, or carpenters see types of wood, technique, and structural soundness. Much military activity also requires educated eyes to see. The bright, moving dots in the night sky that are surveillance satellites, the planes at regional airports that are torture transports, the offices that are fronts for dubious activities, the buildings in which secret operations are carried out take effort to see at all—and yet another kind of effort to recognize, to see with knowledge of what one is seeing, with knowledge that is not strictly visible. They are perhaps another kind of unknown knowns, invisible visibles. A minority dedicates themselves to learning to see this way. We could call what they do seeing in the dark.

2010

REVOLUTION OF THE SNAILS

Encounters with the Zapatistas

I grew up listening to vinyl records, dense spirals of information that we played at 33⅓ revolutions per minute. The original use of the word *revolution* was in the sense of something coming round or turning round, the revolution of the heavenly bodies, for example. It's interesting to think that just as the word *radical* comes from the Latin word for "roots" and means going to the root of a problem, so revolution originally means to rotate, to return, or to cycle, something those who live according to the agricultural cycles of the year know well.

Only in 1450, says my old *Oxford Etymological Dictionary*, does it come to mean "an instance of a great change in affairs or in some particular thing." The year 1450: forty-two years before Columbus sailed on his first voyage to the not-so-new world, not long after Johannes Gutenberg invented moveable type in Europe, where time itself was coming to seem less cyclical and more linear—as in the second definition of this new sense of revolution in my dictionary, "a complete overthrow of the established government in any country or state by those who were previously subject to it."

We live in revolutionary times, but the revolution we are living through is a slow turning around from one set of beliefs and practices toward another, a turn so slow that most people fail to observe our society revolving—or rebelling. The true revolutionary needs to be as patient as a snail.

The revolution is not some sudden change that has yet to come, but the very transformative and questioning atmosphere in which all of us have lived for the past half century, since perhaps the Montgomery Bus Boycott in 1955 or the publication of Rachel Carson's attack on the corporate-industrial-chemical complex, *Silent Spring*, in 1962; certainly since the amazing events of 1989, when the peoples of Eastern Europe nonviolently liberated themselves from their Soviet-totalitarian governments; or since the people of South Africa undermined the white apartheid regime of that country and cleared the way for Nelson Mandela to get out of jail; or since 1992, when the Native peoples of the Americas upended the celebration of the five hundredth anniversary of Columbus's arrival in this hemisphere with a radical rewriting of history and an assertion that they are still here; or even since 1994, when this radical rewriting wrote a new chapter in southern Mexico called *Zapatismo*.

Five years ago, the Zapatista revolution took as one of its principal symbols the snail and its spiral shell. Their revolution spirals outward and backward, away from some of the colossal mistakes of capitalism's savage alienation, industrialism's regimentation, and toward old ways and small things; it also spirals inward via new words and new thoughts. The astonishing force of the Zapatistas has come from their being deeply rooted in the ancient past. "We teach our children our language to keep alive our grandmothers," said one Zapatista woman. And so that force also comes from the half-born other world in which, as they say, many worlds are possible. They travel both ways on their spiral.

REVOLUTIONARY LANDSCAPES

At the end of 2007, I arrived on their territory for a remarkable meeting between the Zapatista women and the world, the third of their *encuentros* since the 1994 launch of their revolution. Somehow, among the miracles of Zapatista words and ideas I read at a distance, I lost sight of what a revolution might look like, *must* look like, on the ground—until late last year when I arrived on that pale, dusty ground after a long ride in a van on winding, deeply rutted dirt roads through the forested highlands and agricultural clearings of Chiapas, Mexico. The five hours of travel from the big town of San Cristobal de las Casas through that intricate landscape took us past countless small cornfields on slopes, wooden houses, thatched pigsties and henhouses, gaunt horses, a town or two, more forest, and then more forest, even a waterfall.

Everything was green except the dry cornstalks, a lush green in which December flowers grew. There were tree-sized versions of what looked like

the common, roadside, yellow black-eyed Susans of the American West
and a palm-sized, lavender-pink flower on equally tall, airily branching
stalks whose breathtaking beauty seemed to come from equal parts vitality,
vulnerability, and bravura—a little like the women I listened to for the
next few days.

The van stopped at the junction that led to the center of the community
of La Garrucha. There, we checked in with men with bandannas covering
the lower halves of their faces, who sent us on to a field of tents further
uphill. The big sign behind them read, "You are in Territory of Zapatistas
in Rebellion. Here the People Govern and the Government Obeys." Next
to it, another sign addressed the political prisoners from last year's remarkable uprising in Oaxaca in which, for four months, the inhabitants held the
city and airwaves and kept the government out. It concluded, "You are not
alone. You are with us. EZLN."

As you may know, EZLN stands for Ejército Zapatista de Liberación
Nacional (Zapatista Army for National Liberation), a name akin to those
from many earlier Latin American uprisings. The Zapatistas—mostly
Mayan indigenous rebels from remote, rural communities of Chiapas,
Mexico's southernmost and poorest state—had made careful preparations
for a decade before their uprising on January 1, 1994.

They began like conventional rebels, arming themselves and seizing six
towns. They chose that first day of January because it was the date that
the North American Free Trade Agreement went into effect, which meant
utter devastation for small farmers in Mexico; but they had also been inspired by the five hundredth anniversary, fourteen months before, of Columbus's arrival in the Americas and the way Native groups had reframed
that half-millennium as one of endurance and injustice for the indigenous
peoples of this hemisphere.

Their rebellion was also meant to take the world at least a step beyond
the false dichotomy between capitalism and the official state socialism of
the Soviet Union, which had collapsed a few years before. It was to be
the first realization of what needed to come next: a rebellion, above all, | 313
against capitalism and neoliberalism. Fourteen years later, it is a qualified
success: many landless *campesino* families in Zapatista-controlled Chiapas

now have land; many who were subjugated now govern themselves; many who were crushed now have a sense of agency and power. Five areas in Chiapas have since that revolution existed outside the reach of the Mexican government under their own radically different rules.

Beyond that, the Zapatistas have given the world a model—and, perhaps even more important, a language—with which to reimagine revolution, community, hope, and possibility. Even if, in the near future, they were to be definitively defeated on their own territory, their dreams, powerful as they have been, are not likely to die. And there *are* clouds on the horizon: the government of President Felipe Calderón may turn what has, for the last fourteen years, been a low-intensity conflict in Chiapas into a full-fledged war of extermination. A war on dreams, on hope, on rights, and on the old goals of Emiliano Zapata, the hero of the Mexican Revolution a century before: *tierra y libertad*, land and liberty.

The Zapatistas emerged from the jungle in 1994, armed with words as well as guns. Their initial proclamation, the First Declaration of the Lacandon Jungle, rang with familiar, outmoded-sounding revolutionary rhetoric, but shortly after the uprising took the world by storm, the Zapatistas' tone shifted. They have been largely nonviolent ever since, except in self-defense, though they are ringed by the Mexican army and local paramilitaries (and maintain their own disciplined army, a long line of whose masked troops patrolled La Garrucha at night, armed with sticks). What shifted most was their language, which metamorphosed into something unprecedented—a revolutionary poetry full of brilliant analysis as well as of metaphor, imagery, and humor, the fruit of extraordinary imaginations.

Some of their current stickers and T-shirts—the Zapatistas generate more cool paraphernalia than any rock band—speak of "el fuego y la palabra," the fire and the word. Many of those words came from the inspired pen of their military commander, the nonindigenous Subcomandante Marcos, but that pen reflected the culture of a people whose memory is long and environment is rich—if not in money and ease, then in animals, images, traditions, and ideas.

Take, for example, the word *caracol*, which literally means "snail" or "spiral shell." In August 2003, the Zapatistas renamed their five autonomous communities *caracoles*. The snail then became an important image. I noticed everywhere embroideries, T-shirts, and murals showing that land snail with the spiraling shell. Often the snail wore a black ski mask. The term *caracol* has the vivid vitality, the groundedness, that often escapes metaphors as they become part of our disembodied language.

When they reorganized as *caracoles*, the Zapatistas reached back to Mayan myth to explain what the symbol meant to them. Or Subcomandante Marcos did, attributing the story as he does with many stories to "Old Antonio," who may be a fiction, a composite, or a real source of the indigenous lore of the region:

> The wise ones of olden times say that the hearts of men and women are in the shape of a *caracol*, and that those who have good in their hearts and thoughts walk from one place to the other, awakening gods and men for them to check that the world remains right. They say that they say that they said that the caracol represents entering into the heart, that this is what the very first ones called knowledge. They say that they say that they said that the caracol also represents exiting from the heart to walk the world. . . . The *caracoles* will be like doors to enter into the communities and for the communities to come out; like windows to see us inside and also for us to see outside; like loudspeakers in order to send far and wide our word and also to hear the words from the one who is far away.

The *caracoles* are clusters of villages, but described as spirals, they reach out to encompass the whole world and begin from within the heart. And so I arrived in the center of one caracol, a little further up the road from those defiant signs, in the broad, unpaved plaza around which the public buildings of the village of La Garrucha are clustered, including a substantial two-story, half-built clinic. Walking across that clearing were Zapatista women in embroidered blouses or broad collars and aprons stitched of rows of ribbon that looked like inverted rainbows—and those ever-present ski masks in which all Zapatistas have appeared publicly since their first moment out of the jungles in 1994. (Or almost all: a few wear bandannas instead.)

That first glimpse was breathtaking. Seeing and hearing those women for the three days that followed, living briefly on rebel territory, watching people brave enough to defy an army and the world's reigning ideology, imaginative enough to invent (or reclaim) a viable alternative was one of the great passages of my life. The Zapatistas had been to me a beautiful idea, an inspiration, a new language, a new kind of revolution. When they spoke at this Third Encounter of the Zapatista Peoples with the People of the World, they became a specific group of people grappling with practical problems. I thought of Martin Luther King Jr. when he said he had been to the mountaintop. I have been to the forest.

THE WORDS OF THE THIRD ENCOUNTER

The *encuentro* was held in a big shed-like auditorium with a corrugated tin roof and crossbeams so long they could only have been hewn from local trees—they would never have made it around the bends in the local roads. The wooden walls were hung with banners and painted with murals. (One, of an armed Zapatista woman, said, "cellulite sí, anorexia, no.") An unfinished mural showed a monumental ear of corn whose top half merged into the Zapatista ski mask, the eyes peering out of the kernels. Among the embroideries local artisans offered were depictions of cornstalks with Zapatista faces where the ears would be. All of this—snails and corn-become-Zapatistas alike—portrayed the rebels as natural, pervasive, and fruitful.

Three or four times a day, a man on a high, roofed-over stage outside the hall would play a jaunty snippet of a tune on an organ and perhaps 250 of the colorfully dressed Zapatista women in balaclavas or bandannas would walk single file into the auditorium and seat themselves onstage on rows of backless benches. The women who had come from around the world to listen would gather on the remaining benches, and men would cluster around the back of the hall. Then, one *caracol* at a time, they would deliver short statements and take written questions. Over the course of four days, all five *caracoles* delivered reflections on practical and ideological aspects of their situation. Pithy and direct, they dealt with difficult (sometimes obnoxious) questions with deftness. They spoke of the challenge of living a revolution that meant autonomy from the Mexican government but also of learning how to govern themselves and determine for themselves what liberty and justice mean.

The Zapatista rebellion has been feminist from its inception: many of the *comandantes* are women—this *encuentro* was dedicated to the memory of deceased Comandante Ramona, whose image was everywhere—and the liberation of the women of the Zapatista regions has been a core part of the struggle. The testimonies addressed what this meant—liberation from forced marriages, illiteracy, domestic violence, and other forms of subjugation. The women read aloud, some of them nervous, their voices strained—and this reading and writing was itself testimony to the spread both of literacy and of Spanish as part of the revolution. The first language of many Zapatistas is an indigenous one, and so they spoke their Spanish with formal, declarative clarity. They often began with a formal address to the audience that spiraled outward: "Hermanos y hermanas, compañeras y compañeros de la selva, pueblos del Mexico, pueblos del mundo, sociedad civil . . ." (Brothers and sisters, companions of the rainforest, people of Mexico, people of the world, civil society . . .) And then they would speak of what revolution had meant for them.

"We had no rights," one of them said about the era before the rebellion. Another added, "The saddest part is that we couldn't understand our own difficulties, why we were being abused. No one had told us about our rights."

"The struggle is not just for ourselves, it's for everyone," said a third. Another spoke to us directly: "We invite you to organize as women of the world in order to get rid of neoliberalism, which has hurt all of us."

They spoke of how their lives had improved since 1994. On New Year's Eve, one of the masked women declared:

> Who we think is responsible [for the oppressions] is the capitalist system, but now we no longer fear. They humiliated us for too long, but as Zapatistas no one will mistreat us. Even if our husbands still mistreat us, we know we are human beings. Now, women aren't as mistreated by husbands and fathers. Now, some husbands support and help us and don't make all the decisions— not in all households, but *poco a poco*. We invite all women to defend our rights and combat machismo.

They spoke of the practical work of remaking the world and setting the future free, of implementing new possibilities for education, health care, and community organization, of the everyday workings of a new society. Some of them carried their babies—and their lives—onstage and, in one poignant moment, a little girl dashed across that stage to kiss and hug her masked mother. Sometimes the young daughters wore masks too.

A Zapatista named Maribel spoke of how the rebellion started, of the secrecy in which they met and organized before the uprising:

> We learned to advance while still hiding until January 1. This is when the seed grew, when we brought ourselves into the light. On January 1, 1994, we brought our dreams and hopes throughout Mexico and the world—and we will continue to care for this seed. This seed of ours we are giving for our children. We hope you all will struggle even though it is in a different form. The struggle [is] for everybody.

The Zapatistas have not won an easy or secure future, but what they have achieved is dignity, a word that cropped up constantly during the *encuentro*, as in all their earlier statements. And they have created hope. Hope (*esperanza*) was another inescapable word in Zapatista territory. There was *la tienda de esperanza*, the unpainted wooden store of hope, that sold tangerines and avocados. A few mornings, I had *café con leche* and sweet rice cooked with milk and cinnamon at a *comedor* whose hand-lettered sign read: "Canteen of autonomous communities in rebellion . . . dreams of hope." The Zapatista minibus was crowned with the slogan "The collective [which also means bus in Spanish] makes hope."

After midnight, at the very dawn of the New Year, when men were invited to speak again, one mounted the platform from which the New Year's dance music was blasting to say that he and the other men had listened and learned a lot.

This revolution is neither perfect nor complete—mutterings about its various shortcomings weren't hard to hear from elsewhere in Mexico or the internationals at the *encuentro* (who asked many testing questions about these *campesinas*' positions on, say, transgendered identity and abortion)— but it is an astonishing and fruitful beginning.

THE SPEED OF SNAILS AND DREAMS

Many of their hopes have been realized. The testimony of the women dealt with this in specific terms: gains in land, rights, dignity, liberty, autonomy, literacy, and a good local government that obeys the people rather than a bad one that tramples them. Under siege, they have created community with each other and reached out to the world.

Emerging from the jungles and from impoverishment, they were one of the first clear voices against corporate globalization—the neoliberal agenda that looked, in the 1990s, as though it might succeed in taking over the world. That was, of course, before the surprise shutdown of the World Trade Organization in Seattle in 1999 and other innovative, successful global acts of resistance against that agenda and its impact. The Zapatistas articulated just how audacious indigenous rebellion against invisibility, powerlessness, and marginalization could be—and this was before other indigenous movements from Bolivia to northern Canada took a share of real power in the Americas. Their image of "a world in which many worlds are possible" came to describe the emergence of broad coalitions spanning great differences, of alliances between hunter-gatherers, small-scale farmers, factory workers, human rights activists, and environmentalists in France, India, Korea, Mexico, Bolivia, Kenya, and elsewhere.

Their vision represented the antithesis of the homogenous world envisioned both by the proponents of "globalism" and by the modernist revolutions of the twentieth century. They have gone a long way toward reinventing the language of politics. They have been a beacon for everyone who wants to make a world that is more inventive, more democratic, more decentralized, more grassroots, more playful. Now, they face a threat from the Mexican government that could savage the *caracoles* of resistance, crush the rights and dignity that the women of the *encuentro* embodied even as they spoke of them—and shed much blood.

During the 1980s, when our government was sponsoring the dirty wars in Central America, two U.S. groups in particular countered those politics of repression, torture, and death. One was the Pledge of Resistance, which gathered the signatures of hundreds of thousands who promised to respond with civil disobedience if the United States invaded Sandinista-run

Nicaragua or otherwise deepened its involvement with the dictatorships and death squads of Central America. Another was Witness for Peace, which placed *gringos* as observers and unarmed protectors in communities throughout Central America.

While killing or disappearing *campesinos* could be carried out with ease in countries like El Salvador and Guatemala, doing the same to U.S. citizens, or in front of them, was a riskier proposition. The Yankee witnesses used the privilege of their color and citizenship as a shield for others and then testified to what they saw. We have come to a moment when we need to strengthen the solidarity so many activists around the world have felt for the Zapatistas, strengthen it into something that can protect the sources of "the fire and the word"—the fire that has warmed so many who have a rebel heart, the word that has taught us to imagine the world anew.

The United States and Mexico both have eagles as their emblems, predators which attack from above. The Zapatistas have chosen a snail in a spiral shell, a small creature, easy to overlook. It speaks of modesty, humility, closeness to the earth, and of the recognition that a revolution may start like lightning but is realized slowly, patiently, steadily. The old idea of revolution was that we would trade one government for another and somehow this new government would set us free and change everything. More and more of us now understand that change is a discipline lived every day, as those women standing before us testified; that revolution only secures the territory in which life can change. Launching a revolution is not easy, as the decade of planning before the 1994 Zapatista uprising demonstrated, and living one is hard too, a faith and discipline that must not falter until the threats and old habits are gone—if then. True revolution is slow.

There's a wonderful passage in Robert Richardson's biography of Thoreau in which he speaks of the Europe-wide revolution of 1848 and says of the New England milieu and its proliferating cooperative communities at that time, "Most of the founders were more interested in building models, which would be emulated because they succeeded, than in the destruction of the existing order. Still American utopian socialism had much in common with the spirit of 1848."

This says very directly that you can reach out and change the state and its institutions, which we recognize as revolution, or you can make your own institutions beyond the reach of the state, which is also revolutionary. This creating—rather than simply rebelling—has been much of the nature of revolution in our time, as people reinvent family, gender, food systems, work, housing, education, economics, medicine and doctor-patient relations, the imagination of the environment, and the language to talk about it, not to speak of more and more of everyday life. The fantasy of a revolution is that it will make everything different, and regime revolutions generally make a difference, sometimes a significantly positive one, but the making of radical differences in everyday life is a more protracted, incremental process. It's where leaders are irrelevant and every life matters.

Give the Zapatistas time—the slow, unfolding time of the spiral and the journey of the snail—to keep making their world, the one that illuminates what else our lives and societies could be. Our revolution must be as different as our temperate-zone, post-industrial society is to their subtropical agrarianism, but it is also guided by the slow forces of dignity, imagination, and hope, as well as the playfulness they display in their imagery and language. The testimony in the auditorium ended late on December 31. At midnight, amid dancing, the revolution turned fourteen. May it long continue to spiral inward and outward.

2008

ACKNOWLEDGMENTS

I hope that this book is, for the readers, an adventure. For its writer, it's a travel journal, a list of experiments, a bouquet of theories and practices, and a few proposals about how things could be. Rereading its almost thirty pieces filled me with gratitude for the friends and companions on encounters around the world and for the editors I worked with on the resultant essays. People from four publications stand out: Tom Engelhardt, Nick Turse, and Andy Kroll of Tomdispatch.com, the little website with the huge global reach, where nearly a quarter of the pieces here originated; Luke Mitchell at *Harper's*; Jennifer Sahn at *Orion*; and the editorial department at the *London Review of Books*. A significant percentage of the book first appeared in these four venues, though Richard Kim at *The Nation*, Yuka Igarashi at *Granta*, Jon Christensen at *Boom*, and many others at the *Guardian*, the *Financial Times*, and elsewhere facilitated the birth of other pieces. Lisa Gabrielle Mark, then of the Los Angeles Museum of Contemporary Art, invited me to explore 1970s California, a fascinating, unsettling experience. Ann McDonald at Artspace Books commissioned what became "Inside Out," one of the essays that was particularly a pleasure to write.

Tyrone Martinnson invited me to Svalbard in 2011, one of the most enchanting passages of my life. In 2006, my magnificent friend Sam Green and I hatched a plan to go to Detroit that resulted in "Detroit Arcadia." Trevor Paglen's amazing work and warm friendship were the occasion for "The Visibility Wars," and Bob Fulkerson and Grace Bukowski were the friends who'd taken me deep into Nevada in every sense beforehand. Many friends in San Francisco, Oakland, and New York, notably Sunaura Taylor, David Solnit, Marko Muir, Rupa Marya, Mona Caron, Adriana

Camarena, and David Graeber joined me in the Occupy movement in 2011, which lit up several essays here. Astra Taylor was a great friend and traveling companion at both Occupy Wall Street and the BP blowout in the Gulf of Mexico. Marina Sitrin was a wonderful friend and a companion at the Zapatista *encuentro*, and her own brilliant work on civil society, popular power, and social change are a major influence on my political ideas. In New Orleans Rebecca Snedeker and A. C. Thompson were indispensable friends and collaborators. The people who came together as civil society and rewrote history again and again are at the heart of many of these pieces, and in my heart as well, and to them I owe another kind of thanks. Thanks as well to Barbara Ras for taking on this book, and to Sarah Nawrocki and BookMatters for seeing it through.

The essays in this book were previously published in the following publications and are reprinted here with thanks (and, in some cases, minor revisions).

"The Visibility Wars" was in Aperture's book of Trevor Paglan's visual investigations of surveillance and military infrastructure, *Invisible.*

"Inside Out" was the text for an Artspace book also featuring the paintings of Stefan Kurten.

"Concrete in Paradise" accompanied Alex Fradkin's photographs of the Marin Headlands in *Boom* magazine.

"Journey to the Center" was the text for a book documenting Elín Hansdóttir's magnificent labyrinth *Path*, published by Crymogea.

Harper's originally published "Detroit Arcadia" and "Notes from Nowhere: Iceland's Polite Dystopia."

The *London Review of Books* is where "Dry Lands," "Oil and Water: The BP Spill in the Gulf," "The Great Tōhoku Earthquake and Tsunami," and the trilogy on Silicon Valley, "The Google Bus: Silicon Valley Invades," "We're Breaking Up: Noncommunications in the Silicon Age," and "Pale Bus, Pale Rider" originally appeared.

"Rattlesnake in Mailbox" was originally published in the 2011 exhibition catalogue *Under the Big Black Sun: California Art 1974–1981* by the Museum of Contemporary Art, Los Angeles, and DelMonico Books • Prestel. Reprinted by permission of the publishers.

The two New Orleans pieces, "Reconstructing the Story of the Storm" and "We Won't Bow Down," were first published in *The Nation*.

Orion was the original venue for "Cyclopedia of an Arctic Expedition," "One Nation under Elvis," "Winged Mercury and the Golden Calf," the essay on Thoreau's laundry, and "Revolutionary Plots: On Urban Gardening."

Tomdispatch.com was the place of origin for these seven essays: "The Butterfly and the Boiling Point," "In Haiti, Words Can Kill," "Icebergs and Shadows," "The Volcano Erupts: Iceland in Upheaval," "Letter to a Dead Man on the Occupation of Hope," "Apologies to Mexico," and "Revolution of the Snails: Encounters with the Zapatistas."

INDEX

Dederich, Chuck (cult leader), 40–41
democracy, 23, 24, 36, 47, 72, 160–162,
 164, 165, 167–171, 173, 176, 214, 218,
 220, 222, 243, 258, 305, 319
Democracy Now!, 235
Detroit, Michigan, 2, 68–83, 87–88, 153,
 289, 294, 295
Diablo Canyon Power Plant, 45
Diamond, Jared, 166
Dōgen Zenji (priest, monk, writer), 201
domestic violence, 116, 149, 317
Douglas, Mary, 110
Dowley, Jennifer, 49, 51
dreams, 11, 19, 153, 300, 304
drones, 52, 224, 265, 300, 304
drugs, 224–230
Dubček, Alexander, 22

Eagles (band), 33
Earth First!, 66, 67, 89
Egypt, Egyptian revolution, 22–30, 57,
 194, 213, 215
Eight Mile Road, 69
Eliade, Mircea (scholar), 155, 156
Eliot, T. S., 61
Ellsberg, Daniel, 305
empathy, 139, 140, 275, 306
Encalade, Byron (head, Louisiana Oys-
 terman Association), 123
Evans, Derrick, 120
Exxon Mobile Corporation, 58, 118
EZLN: see Zapatistas

Facebook, 23, 25, 26, 30, 111, 179, 218, 249,
 257, 258, 260, 264, 265, 266, 272, 273,
 276, 282
farms, farmers, farmworkers, farming,
 30, 37, 47, 61–62, 67, 68, 75, 81, 89,
 90–93, 102, 170, 185, 241, 250, 279, 280,
 285–297, 313
feminism, feminists, 35–36, 43, 45, 47,
 134, 207, 244, 282, 317

Finlay, Ian Hamilton, 295
Fleetwood Mac (band), 47
food (see also farms, gardens), 19, 23,
 43–44
Ford automobiles, manufacturing, 73–75,
 78, 79
Fort Pontchartrain, 68, 69
Fortune magazine, 177
Frankenstein (novel), 8
French Revolution, 23, 30, 58, 220
Fukushima, Japan, nuclear catastrophe
 in, 183, 186–191, 193, 195
Fushimi Inari-taisha, Kyoto (shrine),
 197–202
Futurefarmers, 293

gays, lesbians, queers, rights and politics,
 35–36, 44, 45, 47, 140, 174, 267
Gallant, Mavis, 30
Gandhi, Mohandas, 25, 283
gardens (see also farms), 8, 80–82, 94,
 143, 191, 200, 262, 277–278, 285–297
Gates, Bill (mogul), 265
Gibson-Graham, J. K. (economists),
 134–135
Giffords, Gabrielle, 26–27
glaciers, 7, 8, 10, 13, 21, 68
Glen Canyon Dam, 61, 63, 65, 66
gold, 95–108
Gold Rush, in California, 46, 60, 96–107,
 249, 253–254, 269, 270
Golden Gate National Recreation Area:
 see Marin Headlands
Google Corporation, Google bus,
 248–255, 261, 264–271
Google glasses, 261–262
Gorbachev, Mikhail, 194
graves, 8
Great Salt Lake, 107
Grímsson, Ólafur Ragnar (president),
 159–162, 164, 168, 171, 174
Gross, Anisse, 271

San Francisco writer REBECCA SOLNIT is the author of sixteen books about art, landscape, public and collective life, ecology, politics, hope, meandering, reverie, and memory. They include *The Faraway Nearby; Men Explain Things to Me; Infinite City: A San Francisco Atlas; A Paradise Built in Hell: The Extraordinary Communities That Arise in Disaster; Storming the Gates of Paradise; A Field Guide to Getting Lost; Hope in the Dark: Untold Histories, Wild Possibilities; Wanderlust: A History of Walking; As Eve Said to the Serpent: On Landscape, Gender, and Art;* and *River of Shadows: Eadweard Muybridge and the Technological Wild West,* for which she received a Guggenheim fellowship, the National Book Critics Circle Award in criticism, and the Lannan Literary Award. She has worked on climate change, Native American land rights, and antinuclear, human rights, and antiwar issues as an activist and journalist. A contributing editor to *Harper's* and a frequent contributor to the political site Tomdispatch.com, Solnit has made her living as an independent writer since 1988.